FORGOTTEN NEWS

The Crime of the Century
and Other Lost Stories

Jack Finney

A FIRESIDE BOOK
Published by Simon & Schuster, Inc.
NEW YORK

I thank Harvey Susser for his fine work in the copy photography needed for reproducing the illustrations for this book.

And I thank Elaine Chubb for a job of copy editing so complete, imaginative, and far beyond routine requirement that it has sharply and creatively improved this book. Her work even makes it appear—and I'm grateful—that I can spell and write grammatically.

J.F.

First Fireside Edition, 1985

Published by Simon & Schuster, Inc.
Simon & Schuster Building
Rockefeller Center
1230 Avenue of the Americas
New York, New York 10020

Reprinted by arrangement with Doubleday & Company, Inc.

FIRESIDE and colophon are registered trademarks
of Simon & Schuster, Inc.

Manufactured in the United States of America

10 9 8 7 6 5 4 3 2 1 **Pbk.**

Library of Congress Cataloging in Publication Data

Finney, Jack.
   Forgotten news.

   "A Fireside book."
   Reprint. Originally published: Garden City, N.Y. :
Doubleday, 1983.
   1. New York (N.Y.)—History—1865-1898—Addresses,
essays, lectures.   2. New York (N.Y.)—History—
1775-1865—Addresses, essays, lectures.   3. History,
Modern—19th century—Addresses, essays, lectures.
I. Title.
[F128.47.F49   1985]   974.7'103   85-2043
ISBN 0-671-50645-5 Pbk.

For Don Goodwin

What Is This Book?

Some several years ago I was thinking of writing a novel—which I did, eventually, calling it *Time and Again*—whose central character would somehow be able to do what I've always wanted to do: visit the nineteenth century. Physically, literally, go back in time to a New York of the last century, and walk around seeing the sights. But I wanted him to see a lot more than what all of us know he'd see: more than gaslights and horsecars. I wanted him to see everything I wished I could; as clearly and with the greatest actuality I could manage.

So I began something I called "research," though really too much fun to entitle me to describe it as soberly as that. I spent a winter, that is, exploring nineteenth-century newspapers, on microfilm. Picked a decade arbitrarily, limiting myself to the 1880s. Got up each day, had breakfast, and spent the rest of the day till mid-afternoon, head in the viewer, reading everything that seemed directly useful, straying into plenty that wasn't. Day after day I read the New York *Times,* following the excitements of another time. And the *Tribune.* And *Frank Leslie's Illustrated* (weekly) *Newspaper,* looking at the pictures (and, with *Leslie's,* ranging well beyond and before the eighties). Made notes from the *Times* on what the produce market was selling, so I'd know something of what people were eating. Read the ads to see something of what they were buying and wearing. Stuck pins in a big wall map of an earlier New York to determine for myself where the people in the crime news lived, and where the rich people lived, and had their fun. Read what they were seeing in the theaters, and attended the opening—through a fine lavish description in the *Times*—of a glittering new Wallack theater, equipped with a lobby fountain that sprayed perfume. That winter I didn't envy anyone, and, looking friends in the eye, I told them I was working, too.

Easily the best part of all this was *Leslie's;* which, as you may know, was a kind of nineteenth-century *Life* magazine stuffed with splendid trifles, and bounteously illustrated: if you couldn't show it, it wasn't news, seemed to be Frank Leslie's policy, and some of his old woodcuts are magnificent. I expect it's a lost art. The best of them have a hard-edged bright clarity that excites the eye, especially those done by his best artists directly from photographs. Every time I turned a page it was with a small thrill of anticipation: What next?

A look at the Pope's new private railroad car, maybe; its

entire exterior hand-carved by crazed Italians, the miter on its roof tall as a smokestack.

Or Horace Greeley's watch and chain. Or a

splendid view of the New York City morgue in the days when women wore hoopskirts.

Or a glimpse of discipline as practiced in the United States Navy . . . or

at justice as dispensed by New York cops before they had to worry about abstractions like civil liberties.

And a fine double-page spread illustrating a gang battle in the streets of Manhattan, which continued for three days one summer,

and which featured street barricades; the positioning of a large cannon to command an entire city block, although it was never fired; and the almost complete absence of the police, until the gangs got tired out and things quieted down.

Below at the left are the gang leaders:

silk hat heads "The Bowery Boys," the other "The Dead Rabbits."

Leslie's gave me this glimpse of the mysterious parade of the "Belva Lockwood Marching Club," all men identically dressed in women's costume.

And of ways that New Yorkers used to have fun: in summer, like this

in Central Park; in the winter, like this in upper Manhattan; and in

Albany like this, with joker in pith helmet, carrying fan. Where else

but *Leslie's* for the annual "Ball of the Lunatics" on Blackwell's Island?

Page after page of stuff like that; hundreds and hundreds of that kind of picture. And I was working!

A fine winter, and when it was over, and I had to quit working and go to work, I missed *Leslie's*. And when the novel whose preliminaries had led me to *Leslie's* was written; and when some more years had passed; the addict's hunger had not gone away. I still wanted more *Leslie's,* and there *were* more: thirty-odd years of them yet that I'd never seen. So finally I did what I'd wanted to do ever since my first fix. Arranged with the state library to send me half a dozen bound volumes at a time, beginning with the first issue, in 1856. The real thing this time, not microfilm but tall gilt-stamped old books, covers loose, spines sprung. But the pages inside strong and white, the ink as powerfully black, as in the days when *Leslie's* hung from the eaves of vanished New York newsstands. They generally used good material in the century before the world went bad.

Every page—I turned through them all—of every issue of *Leslie's* right up to nearly the end of that hustling century, when muddy photographs replaced bright woodcuts. And the artists who'd made them, along with beer gardens, vaudeville, sleighing on Fifth Avenue, and plenty of other things better than television, joined the Great Auk. As I turned *Leslie's* pages I made notes on, and later Xeroxed the illustrations for, hundreds of forgotten marvels and glimpses of lost times. Some kind of book was what I had in mind. But vaguely, not sure what kind. I was waiting to see.

Pretty soon I thought it might be a thick book packed with as many as a hundred or more of the kind of thing I was saving, every one illustrated by a woodcut, and amplified, not just a book of old reprints. I'd redo every one of them; nineteenth-century newspaper prose can be deadly. And expand them; make them more complete and informative and interesting in whatever ways ingenuity might suggest. Thus, I mailed a Xerox of a *Leslie's* story, very brief but hugely illustrated, describing and picturing what seemed to be a helicopter flying across the low Manhattan cityscape of 1876, to an aircraft designer, Joseph Lippert, Jr. And, both our tongues in cheek a little bit, he replied solemnly that yes indeed, this machine, as illustrated and described, really could have flown across New York a long century ago. And he supplied a drawing showing how similar were the workings of the old machine and today's helicopters. (This particular item was published on the New York *Times* Op-Ed page, with Lippert's drawing included, and brought me some startled mail, and a couple of excited phone calls: one from *Life,* the other from *Reader's Digest.* But I felt obliged to tell them what Mr. Lippert and I had neglected to mention: that while the 1876 machine undoubtedly did fly, as reported in *Leslie's,* it was probably only a spring-wound model.)

I dealt with the White House on other items, the Smithsonian, Greenwood Cemetery, and I wrote to the Vatican about the Pope's railroad car. I wanted photographs of that, especially of the interior. They told me where to get them: from a Roman museum. To which I wrote, first having my letter translated into Italian. And wrote them again . . . and again . . . and again, never receiving a reply, so that the Pope's car never got into the book.

A kind of light, entertaining bedside volume, I thought, to open at random and find something briefly intriguing for eye and mind. Most items no longer than a page, some only half a page. Others might run two or three pages, a few might go half a dozen, and maybe one or two—such as the killing of Dr. Harvey Burdell and the sinking of the steamship *Central America,* both serious stories with interesting ramifications— might run as long as ten, twelve, or fourteen pages.

One day it occurred to me that probably I should check what other publications of the day had reported about some of my stories; and maybe learn a little bit more I could use. So I went over to the Berkeley campus and its Newspaper Room to check the New York *Times* coverage on the death of Harvey Burdell. And I mean it truly when I say that what I found appalled me.

Because the Harvey Burdell story turned out to be, not what the few pages of summary in *Leslie's* had suggested, but instead what may very well be one of the biggest single stories the *Times* has ever covered. I don't know that, and perhaps it is not the case, but there cannot have been many longer-running stories in the *Times*'s history. I sat there in Berkeley numbly turning past endless columns of fine newsprint on this story, running day after day after day, and wondering what I was supposed to do now.

For a while I thought, urged on by my wife, of finding a job some- where away from home and typewriter; outdoors, maybe, working with my hands. Instead I decided to buy the microfilmed *Times* for 1857, and give one month to reading into that mass of material as far as I could in the time. And then decide whether it yielded up enough more of interest to be worth continuing. I ended up, over far longer than a month, by reading every word of that long coverage; and with over a hundred single-spaced pages of typed notes. And facing a story, one story alone, not of a dozen pages but one which itself could not be told in much less than book length. It was as though I'd come upon a scattering of small stones, and in trying to dig one out had uncovered a kind of Pompeii.

For in the murder of Harvey Burdell I found a forgotten or semifor- gotten story of the past so strange and complex, so sensational and end- lessly surprising, that it astonishes me yet. It turned out, at least for me, rich in event and character: peopled with as strange a lot, as malevolent, eccentric, and amusing, as any I could ever hope to come across. Reading column after column of directly quoted testimony—hearing, in the old type, these long-ago people speaking, arguing, lying, and shouting in their own words—made them real. And from *Leslie's* I had many of their actual portraits, drawn from photographs; and some of the very places they talked about, drawn from life. And came much, much closer now, than in the research I'd done for a novel, to moving back into a lost past.

In the story of the sinking of the *Central America* I found one more such story: the long detailed account, most of it in its people's own words, of a story alive with human behavior and the kind of powerful personality peculiar, it seems to me, to the nineteenth century. And my book became, not a hundred light amusing tidbits, but two long—at times almost melodramatic, and sometimes chilling—very serious stories.

Not quite entirely, though. I couldn't leave out all the others, though maybe I should have: the book is really the two long stories. But I included a few of the others anyway. Between the two principal stories as a kind of breathing spell. And a few more at the end. Their purpose, I've told myself and now tell you, is to be a kind of setting for the two main stories. To give you a heightened sense of the remarkable century in which they occurred. This may even be true. It was a wonderful varied time, the last century; and if this book can help you visit it with anything like as much pleasure as it's held for me, then it was worth the three years I never dreamed it would take me. It was worth it anyway.

Jack Finney

FORGOTTEN
NEWS

1

This is the house I hoped to find still standing at number 31 Bond Street, New York City, when I walked out of the Algonquin Hotel one morning in June a couple of years ago: an unlikely yet not quite impossible hope. I took a bus downtown, camera hung from my neck, a tourist, and found Bond Street where my map said it would be: below Eighth Street between Broadway and the Bowery. From the bus stop I walked back along a fairly busy Broadway, then turned off it, to the right, onto this little two-block-long street: Bond Street today.

Once this was "a fashionable and reputable part of town," said the New York *Tribune* of 1857, although the *Times* thought Bond "simply genteel." But today it looked about as I'd expected; there are a lot of obscure lower Manhattan streets like it. Most of its remaining worn-out old houses have been converted long ago into small-business premises, their upper windows blank and dusty, although people still live in some of them.

Not surprisingly, my number 31 was gone. On its site stood a newer 31; it's there at the right: the one with the fire escape and the arched windows. I didn't go in, though if my 31 had been there still, it would have taken police to have kept me out of it.

Just as unsurprisingly, since lower Manhattan is filled with relics of earlier New Yorks, even though the old 31 was gone there were still a few houses left that, for well over a century, had survived to the present from this moment of a long-ago February day in 1857 when crowds stood along

a tree-lined Bond Street staring up at number 31 in awe and excitement at what had just happened inside it.

I think the drawing is accurate. It was made by a *Leslie's Illustrated Newspaper* artist, who then signed it under the tree at lower right; and presently I'll explain why I think it meticulously represents the way Bond Street looked when Copcutt stood with his pad or notebook where I followed with my camera, standing where he stood, a hundred and twenty years later.

You can see from his drawing that several groups of houses on Bond Street then were identical; people called them "pattern" houses. Now look carefully at 31, the house with the crowd on its stoop: notice that like the other beside it, the two dormer windows have angled roofs . . . the lintels over the windows are straight . . . there's an ornamental arch over the doorway . . . a keystone at its top, stone insets along its sides. . . .

Now look at the house at left, number 26 Bond Street, still here today.

 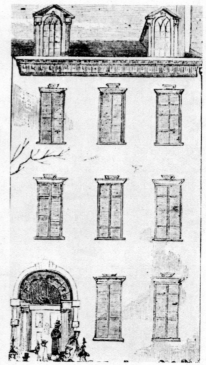

Mentally remove the fire escape and added-on storefront, then compare it with the drawing I've repeated beside it of the long-vanished 31 for which I came down here looking; and there number 26 Bond Street still stands, as it stood near midnight, Friday, January 30, 1857, when "Murder!" sounded in the darkness and the night air stank of burning wool and leather.

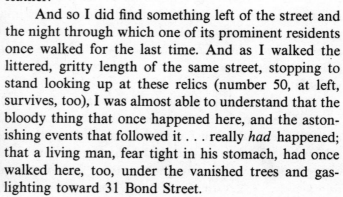

And so I did find something left of the street and the night through which one of its prominent residents once walked for the last time. And as I walked the littered, gritty length of the same street, stopping to stand looking up at these relics (number 50, at left, survives, too), I was almost able to understand that the bloody thing that once happened here, and the astonishing events that followed it . . . really *had* happened; that a living man, fear tight in his stomach, had once walked here, too, under the vanished trees and gaslighting toward 31 Bond Street.

6

This is the man; it is how he really looked: this and other portraits that

follow are precise woodcut renditions of actual photographs from professional studios of the day: Meade, Bacon, Fredrick's, and others.

He is Dr. Harvey Burdell, well-known dentist and physician, of 31 Bond Street—which he owned and in which he conducted a dental practice, becoming rich in consequence, then as now.

On Sunday afternoon, January 25, 1857, he arrived at Bacon studios and spoke to a friend, Mrs. Ann Benjamin, a photographer there. People who knew Harvey Burdell said he talked very rapidly and with a "sort of twang to his voice," said a cousin, "a sort of barking." What he almost surely told Mrs. Benjamin in this odd voice—for by now he was saying it to most everyone—was how frightened he was for his life. And that he wanted his portrait made, right now.

There he sits facing the big wooden camera, Mrs. Benjamin hunched under the black cloth. He is motionless, quite possibly holding his breath, the back of his head held steady by a clamplike device. As he waits for his image to etch the plate for this final portrait of his life he is terrified: this is known. And I think he *looks* frightened, that it shows in his eyes.

If that is so—if that's fear staring out at us across a century—

7

this is the woman who put it there: Emma Augusta Cunningham, thirty-

six, widow of a Brooklyn distiller; as formidable in fact as she is in appearance: no fear in those eyes.

They're gray, her hair dark brown, complexion dark, but it isn't easy to see in this portrait—another careful woodcut copy, of an ambrotype— what Harvey Burdell saw in Emma Cunningham when first they met. ". . . we understand she was formerly very prepossessing," a newspaper reporter said, "[but] she is not at the present moment an extra-ordinarily attractive woman." Still: cover her antique dress with one hand, obscure the old hairstyle with the other, then picture her smiling, and possibly you'll see something of the attractiveness Dr. Burdell saw. Or it might have been this: the same reporter said Mrs. Cunningham was "very well preserved, her bust showing considerable fullness," and Burdell liked women, at least in bed: maybe that explains what this portrait doesn't.

But do you agree that a determination can be seen in her eyes, a hardness of purpose? Possibly not, maybe I'm straining, but apparently it could be seen in the living face, because a *Leslie's* reporter wrote: ". . . her lips and mouth generally display remarkable determination." This observation didn't follow after the fact, either: the world didn't yet know the unbelievable—I mean literally unbelievable—extent of this re-markable woman's single-mindedness. One time Harvey Burdell told a cousin, Mary Wilson, as she recalled it, that Emma Cunningham was " 'a very dangerous woman. She is always planning, and she told me she had never been thwarted in her life; that whatever plans she attempts she generally carried out.' " This turned out to be true; and Mrs. Cunningham almost literally scared Harvey Burdell to death.

Burdell said they met at "a watering place" in 1854: Saratoga Springs, I expect, because he went there a lot. He thought she was "pleas-ant, ladylike in her appearance and conduct," he told another of his many cousins, and for a time all was circumspect: he'd stay at Congress Hall, while she went to a boardinghouse—and school—run by Dr. Luther F. Beecher, cousin to Henry Ward Beecher.

There has been some ridiculous fiction written about people traveling back in time to earlier days, but absurd though such books are, I wish they were true. Because my wife and I are mild fanatics about the Saratoga Springs of the last century, and when the Time Machine is invented we're going to nineteenth-century Paris and New York City, including a visit to Bond Street; and to Saratoga Springs, a gorgeous place then. Meanwhile we've made our pilgrimage to today's Saratoga to see what's left. Of course the magnificent old hotels are gone, one of them replaced—a requirement of the twentieth century—by a most ordinary shopping center, with as-phalt parking lot, where women once strolled under parasols.

But Congress Hall Park is still marvelously there, many things to be seen in old photos like this, incredibly still there like this.

So again I was able to follow Harvey Burdell's steps, this time as he walked the paths of Congress Hall Park with Emma Cunningham. As they strolled—I picture them arm in arm—I believe she was thinking about marriage, because she would presently show in a variety of startling ways that she did desperately want to marry Harvey Burdell. Out of greed, maybe, for it seemed to be common knowledge that he was rich. Or possibly simply as a haven for her widowed self and five children. Or even from love or affection, no one can say otherwise, and he seemed to be attractive to women. I wonder also if for his own purposes Harvey Burdell didn't at least hint at marriage as they wandered that park and lovely town.

If he did, it's almost impossible to think he meant it, for some of his acquaintances told a *Tribune* reporter that "he was a confirmed bachelor. He was frequently in the habit of denouncing the sex in the most bitter terms; it was a favorite maxim of his . . . that no man who owned real estate ought to marry." The *Trib* man reported also that Burdell was a "man of large frame, full habit [which I take to mean good physique], very strong, fond of wine and women, and a frequent visitor at houses of pleasure."

So we have a rich, forty-five-year-old, man-of-the-world bachelor who, whatever he did or didn't hint or promise, seems dead set against marriage . . . walking the shady paths of Congress Hall Park with a smiling, attentive woman almost ferociously determined that he will marry her. The stage is set though there is no script; what now began happening to Harvey Burdell was improvised all the way, generally badly. Whoever was first responsible for thoughts of marriage, Dr. Burdell never dreamed where the pleasant paths of Congress Hall Park were leading him.

Back in New York, Mrs. Cunningham pushed the friendship; came to 31 Bond to have the Doctor fix her teeth; brought teenage daughter Augusta to have her teeth fixed. And presently Harvey Burdell was calling regularly at the house Mrs. Cunningham rented on Twenty-fourth Street between Eighth and Ninth. Living with her were two small sons, Willie (or Willy) and George, nine and ten; another teenage daughter, Helen; and two servants. Augusta was away, I don't know why. So Emma Cunningham had six people to feed; wages to pay; a boarding-school bill for Georgiana, her youngest daughter; and possibly she had to send money to Augusta. A man and his wife rented rooms in the house.

All this, incidentally, from the New York *Times* and *Tribune,* but I'll stop naming sources now unless there seems a reason to do it, because nearly everything in this account, and every direct quotation, is from one of those two papers or *Harper's Weekly* and *Leslie's Illustrated Newspaper.* When it isn't, I'll say so.

To me the reported facts of Mrs. Cunningham's life just now suggest that her money could have been running low. She'd received five thousand dollars' insurance at her husband's death, but that was several years ago. Anyway, she gave up the Twenty-fourth Street house, boarded at a Dr. Willington's, then, presently, told Dr. Burdell she had to find other quarters. Meanwhile, she'd need a place to stay temporarily.

That was easy. Burdell leased 31 Bond to a Mrs. Margaret Jones, who ran it as a boarding and lodging house, the Doctor continuing to live and conduct his practice there. Could Mrs. Jones accommodate a friend and her family for a few days? Certainly: Mrs. Jones's livelihood was renting out rooms, and she had several available.

So Emma Cunningham moved into Harvey Burdell's house, taking three attic rooms: for the boys, herself, and Helen. This arrangement of leasing a portion of one's house to a landlady sounds strange now but doesn't seem to have been then. It made sense: Burdell was rich but frugal, even stingy according to his servants, complaining of wasted coal and gas; and the arrangement was convenient and profitable. He collected several hundred dollars' annual rent; retained two large rooms on the second floor, a bedroom and his dental office; had a bathroom, which other rooms did not; and a dental laboratory, the use of which he also rented out: to other dentists of the neighborhood, Bond Street being a street of dentists and doctors. His bed was made daily, linen changed, clothes washed, rooms cleaned. And now, after only a day or so, Mrs. Cunningham said she was so happy here at 31 Bond that she didn't want to leave at all.

This was fine with landlady Jones, and so in addition to all the other benefits, Dr. Burdell had Emma Cunningham living snugly here in his own house. He must have thought he had it made.

I think some understanding is due Mrs. Cunningham. Even today it would be tough for a widow in her mid-thirties with five children on her hands. How was it in 1856? Infinitely tougher, I would suppose, and snaring this well-to-do man she'd met at Saratoga Springs may have seemed her last hope of any bearable future. And he'd promised to marry her, she always said. Installing herself under his roof meanwhile could have seemed the way to make sure he did.

It wasn't. She was under Burdell's roof, but right up under it: in the attic. While among the half-dozen other lodgers and boarders—and living right down on the Doctor's own floor, in the only other bedroom there —was his young cousin, a good-looking twenty-three-year-old separated from her husband and about to be divorced, to resume her name of Demis Hubbard. Mrs. Cunningham came to suspect the nature of the cousins' relationship, and saw Demis as a threat.

11

So she got herself pregnant, if that's the way to put it. Became pregnant, anyway, I don't know when. There's a lot we won't know of the queer developments of the next few months: it's as though we're seldom allowed inside 31 Bond but must stand waiting outside on the walk. Now and then a window is suddenly raised just long enough to overhear a sentence or two, a few angry words or a fragment of servants' gossip, before it is slammed shut again. Or the front door opens momentarily, and we see a departure or entrance or catch a glimpse of what's happening inside.

These holes and gaps could be filled: with imagined scenes, dialogue invented. But you can do that yourself, so I'll give you fact only and occasionally some surmise. Fact to the extent that I've been able to mine it from what has come down to us; if you read that Mrs. Cunningham's eyes are gray it's because a contemporary said so, and if I say it snowed it's because it did. And the surmise either labeled as such or obviously such. And supported; no idle speculation.

So not until Thanksgiving Day does the white-painted front door of number 31 open for us; and Dr. Burdell walks down the steps, turns east toward the Bowery, and Brooklyn, on an errand of some sort.

Inside the house, we learn from the newly hired cook, Emma Cunningham presently became ill. Helen Cunningham seems to have been out, and if the boys were home they were too young to help. The new cook was Hannah Conlon, described as "a genuine-looking Irish girl, of the most intense kind." Resting in her attic room, she heard Emma Cunningham call out from hers: " 'Oh, Doctor [or 'Oh, daughter!'], where are you!' "

The new girl said nothing. Silence for a time. Then it got dark, when things get worse, and Emma Cunningham appeared at Hannah Conlon's door. " 'My God, are you going to let me die here!' " she cried out, as Hannah recalled it: her face was smeared with blood, her nose bleeding, Hannah said. She had fallen against the stove, Mrs. Cunningham told her, and cut herself. Hannah got a basin of water, Mrs. Cunningham washed herself, but by now Hannah seems to have understood what was really the matter. "I ran for a doctor," she said.

We're hearing very close to Hannah Conlon's actual words, I think, because both the *Times*'s and *Tribune*'s accounts jibe about as closely as we could expect of two reporters listening to Hannah Conlon as she described that day, getting her words down as accurately as they could.

But their editors had different notions of what was fit for their readers' eyes. "I ran for a doctor," Hannah tells us in the *Tribune*, "and when I came back, [the chambermaid] and myself perceived that she had mis-

12

carried. She said the child belonged to the Doctor." I don't quite believe "perceived that she had miscarried"; and in the *Times* Hannah says, which sounds a little more like it to me, "I ran for a doctor, and when I returned the other girl and myself saw that a fetus was in the chamber. She said that the child belonged to the doctor." Dr. Burdell came home, and—a physician, too—he took over from the doctor Hannah had called in.

So Emma Cunningham had failed, if that pregnancy was planned. But she often failed, usually failed: she simply never gave up. It took a month before she could even come downstairs for meals, Hannah said; but once she was up and around again, she and Harvey Burdell resumed going out together; were seen, for example, at Niblo's Garden, a theater. And since he didn't board with Mrs. Jones, taking his meals at a hotel, Emma Cunningham sometimes invited Dr. Burdell here for dinner. Had him there for dinner that Christmas.

But things weren't really the same, I suspect. I wonder if now, after the miscarriage, Harvey Burdell might have considered himself no longer bound, if he had, in fact, promised marriage. Because—another glimpse inside 31—Mrs. Cunningham now began complaining to landlady Jones that the conversation of some of the Doctor's patients "was not refined and ladylike; she said she thought they came here to laugh and to joke instead of for professional services." Some people said that among his patients Dr. Burdell had more than his share of young prostitutes; maybe Emma Cunningham heard more giggling behind the closed doors of his office than is customary in filling teeth.

But she never quit, and now she said she no longer liked her attic room, and arranged—which must mean she'd made a friend of her—to share Demis Hubbard's room down on the Doctor's floor. Enabling her, of course, to keep an eye on comings and goings there.

People who persevere often get a break. Mrs. Jones now decided not to renew her lease when it expired in the spring, on May 1, so Emma told Harvey she'd like to take over as landlady. That was okay with him, she signed a year's lease, and thus, from temporary resident up in the attic . . . then permanent resident down on the Doctor's own floor . . . Mrs. Cunningham now took over the entire house.

Jones left, and: "The Doctor fixed up the house very nicely, and got new carpets," a friend said. He also took Mrs. Cunningham's note for the annual rental; began taking his meals at the new landlady's table; and they continued going out together, the Broadway Theatre being one at which they were seen.

But Demis was still there. And the Doctor had another female

13

cousin, Lucy Ann Williams; how young or good-looking I don't know, but a widow, and she and Dr. Burdell visited each other often. And then a third threat appeared on the front stoop. The Doctor had just hired the latest of a succession of boys he employed to answer the door for patients, run errands, lay fires, and so on. He was Samuel Ashton, fourteen or fifteen, who had to work, he said, because his father was "out West." The doorbell rang, young Sam answered it, and opened the door on what must have been a startling sight: a handsomely figured woman with a green head—eyes lost behind green-tinted spectacles, features blurred by a green veil. She'd come to see Dr. Burdell, and Sam led the mysterious lady upstairs, where Harvey Burdell took her into his office, and locked the door.

Mrs. Cunningham knew or learned who this visitor was: Sophronia Stevens, wife of Cyrenius Stevens, given names which I think belong in the same league as Demis. And whenever she came to 31 thereafter, which was often, Mrs. Cunningham set Sam to eavesdropping at the closed door of the Doctor's office, and reporting to her. He didn't hear much, but Mrs. Cunningham added Sophronia to the names on her hit list.

And one by one took care of them all. Each in a characteristically nutty way. For along with a determination so unwavering that it would soon astonish the city, the country, and most of Europe, Mrs. Cunningham demonstrated an equally persistent capacity for bungling. She is surely one of the classic screw-ups of all time, and one of the luckiest.

Lucy Ann Williams was first. One day, visiting 31 Bond, she was taken aside by Emma, who told her some disturbing news. They all knew a member of Congress from New Jersey, a Senator Vail; I don't know how. The Senator—actually a representative, says the Biographical Directory of the U. S. Congress, but they seemed to call him "Senator"—had received an anonymous letter, Emma told Lucy Ann, which said Mrs. Williams was not a lady of good character. Naturally Mrs. Williams went home, and wrote the Senator asking about this letter. He replied that it was true he'd received an anonymous letter saying bad things about her, but the odd thing was that he had never shown it to Mrs. Cunningham or told her what it said.

It didn't take Lucy Ann long to puzzle that out, and back she came to 31 Bond to accuse Mrs. Cunningham of writing the letter herself. Who denied it, there was a big blowup, and Burdell calmed things down: said he believed Emma Cunningham because she couldn't have known some of the things mentioned in the letter (which suggests, doesn't it, that they were factual?). He said he suspected one of his relatives had sent it.

Now, this goofy letter could hardly have fooled anyone, assuming,

14

as I certainly do, that Mrs. Cunningham sent it. Yet it worked: Mrs. Williams "dropped Mrs. Cunningham's acquaintance," she said, and kept away from 31 Bond Street.

Demis got it over the Fourth of July. The Fourth came on Friday, Demis went to the country for the long weekend, and when she came back, her former roommate and present landlady simply wouldn't let her into the house. Standing on the stoop arguing, Demis finally had to turn away, walk back down the stairs, and go look for another place to live.

But these awkward victories seem to have come at a price. When eighteen-year-old Augusta, oldest of the three daughters, returned to New York to join her family at 31 Bond, Dr. Burdell and her mother were no longer getting along well; quarreling often, Augusta said. She didn't say what about, but it is a fact that Harvey Burdell said he didn't like the summary ousting of Demis; and it seems impossible that he didn't understand who had written the poison-pen letter about Lucy Ann.

The front door of 31 Bond opens again for us, and Mrs. Cunningham comes down the steps. Women wore hoopskirts then, or puffed out their skirts with layers of starched petticoats, so we can almost see her. Which way she turned I don't know, but quite possibly toward Broadway: lawyers often had offices on this main street of the town. Now—persuasion having failed to make her Mrs. Harvey Burdell—Mrs. Cunningham turned to the law.

In the office of an attorney named B. C. Thayer, who would eventually do far more legal work for this client than either now imagined, she instructed him in what she wanted. He was to prepare the papers for a breach of promise suit, for which she had some spicy material.

Thayer listened, then turned over the actual drawing of the affidavit to another lawyer, Levi Chatfield. This affidavit was later lost, but Chatfield remembered what it said. Emma Cunningham swore that "a contract of marriage," he said, "existed between her and Dr. Burdell sometime in 1855, in the summer or fall, to be performed about the first of June [1856]." What's more, "soon after the contract between them, Dr. Burdell stated to her that he had some property in real estate in New Jersey . . . my recollection is Elizabethtown. . . . That he invited her to go down and see it with him. She went . . . they were engaged in looking at the premises, as I recollect, until after the train left Elizabethtown . . . by design on his part, making it necessary for them to remain overnight. . . . They stopped at the hotel, he came into her room, and . . . after much resistance she finally yielded to his persuasions."

Breach of promise suits were taken seriously, and she had the Thanksgiving Day miscarriage to back up her story, but again she bun-

15

gled. Someone suggested to her that a complaint of seduction by a thirty-five-year-old woman with nearly grown children might not be impressive. So she brought her affidavit back to Chatfield, "and that part of it was stricken out, so as to leave the matter on the face of the paper as being a forcible thing altogether." She added that Harvey Burdell insisted on examining her as a physician, and that he produced the abortion—not what Hannah Conlon would testify later.

The suit seems to have been an ace in the hole, however, affidavit all signed, a summons on Dr. Burdell, dated September 16, prepared but unserved; she may still have had some lingering hope of marrying Dr. Burdell through persuasion. But now it looks as though possibly he began pressing her for money she couldn't pay. Because only four days later, on September 20, around seven in the evening, the front door of 31 Bond flew open, and Harvey Burdell ran down the steps and over to Broadway—it was this Broadway, the view here photographed in 1859—to call the cops.

When he returned with some cops he'd found there, Dr. Burdell told them that while he'd been napping, Mrs. Cunningham had sneaked in, taken the key to his safe from "his pantaloons pocket," one cop quoted him, unlocked the safe, and stolen back her own note for the annual rent of the house.

In the house, the cop said, Mrs. Cunningham came rushing out of the parlor "in a tremendous rage," telling him not to believe the Doctor, that he had ruined her family and her, and—one of the first threats of violence we know of—that she'd have his "heart's blood, or something to that effect." Another cop arrived, and to him Emma Cunningham said "she was [Burdell's] wife by every tie that could be," and struck Burdell in the chest. "The Doctor replied," said the cop, "that she had been seen with men in a house of assignation, she then stated that he

16

had upstairs instruments for producing abortion, he retorted that if he had them there, she had used them." Then as now in domestic disputes, the cops passed the buck, advising them to settle this between themselves, and got out.

People who knew Harvey Burdell said that while he was quick to excited anger, it seldom lasted long; and he continued taking his meals at Mrs. Cunningham's table. What happened about the note I don't know.

Mrs. Cunningham was tougher. Demis Hubbard showed up again, asking to be allowed back, and Mrs. Cunningham turned her down. As for Sophronia Stevens, one night Emma Cunningham sent a message to Sophronia's husband saying Dr. Burdell wanted to see him right away, right now. Stevens didn't believe it. He knew Burdell well, and there was no conceivable reason for such a message. Besides, he was sixty-seven, and wasn't going anywhere at night; he was afraid of garroters.

These were street robbers who grabbed pedestrians around the neck from behind, holding them half-strangled and helpless—sometimes killing them in the process—while a confederate or confederates robbed them. Our name for them, of course, is muggers; and most people were afraid of them. George Templeton Strong, in his famous diary of his life in New York, says, in 1857: "An epidemic of crime this winter. 'Garroting' stories abound. . . . A man was attacked the other afternoon at his own shop door in the Third Avenue. . . . Most of my friends are investing in revolvers and carry them about at night, and if I expected to have a great deal of late street-walking off Broadway, I think I should make the like provision. . . ."

Stevens did go to number 31 the next morning, was brought into the back parlor, by Tom Callahan, I expect—the Doctor's newest boy-of-all-work—and "I had only just taken my seat," Stevens said, "when a lady came in, took a seat near me, and called me by name. She said she had sent for me, not Dr. Burdell." Emma Cunningham then told Stevens that his wife was carrying on with Dr. Burdell, and also accused Mrs. Stevens of "filching money from me, and making use of Dr. Burdell to deposit it in some bank for her. I told her I would think of the matter, and see her again," but he didn't. "I thought it was all out of whole cloth, and considered she had great nerve. I thought she wanted to make a tool of me by working up my feelings against Dr. Burdell. I thought her motive was to ruin Dr. Burdell's character and get possession of his money."

So he didn't go back, and: "On the Saturday following a gentleman called and wanted to see me. He said his business was from Mrs. Cunningham; he said she had sent him to ask me to come up and see her. He said he was her counsel. He had got her, he said, out of some pretty serious

17

scrapes. I took a chair, and sat down beside him, and asked him if he knew what her business was with me. He said he did not know particularly. I asked him if he knew nothing about it. He represented that she was a wonderful, persevering, smart woman, and always accomplished all she undertook. He said she had money, and plenty of men around her who never failed her." This inexplicable nonsense, just as Stevens recalled it, is typical of the weirdness that so often tinged things Emma Cunningham had a hand in. "He said [his name] was Van Dolan," Stevens continued, "that he was a lawyer, and that his office was at Number 118 Chambers Street." But when he'd left, Stevens couldn't find any "Van Dolan" listed in the city directory as "lawyer," and when he "went down to Chambers Street next day," he "could not find such a name, or any such office; it appeared to be stores."

So Stevens didn't go see Mrs. Cunningham. "I did not know but what some scheme or plot might have been laid for me," he said. "Such curious things take place in this city, that I am a little cautious."

A few days later when he went to Harvey Burdell and told him all this, the Doctor replied that nothing had gone on between him and Sophronia; he had only removed a small tumor or obstruction from her eye. Since Cyrenius knew this was why she'd gone to Dr. Burdell—accounting, I expect, for the tinted glasses and veil—he believed him; believed him anyway, as an old friend. So while Sophronia Stevens, like Demis Hubbard and Lucy Ann Williams, quit coming to 31 Bond, Emma Cunningham had actually messed up once more.

And the Doctor at last quit her table, taking his meals here at the LaFarge House. I can't date this photograph, but I doubt that it's as early as 1856. Still, change in the last century came more slowly than now, and possibly Harvey Burdell could have recognized this as the tree-lined Broadway and the hotel, in the old New York of low buildings, to which he now walked three times every day for

"breakfast, dinner, and supper," the proprietor said. The LaFarge advertised its location as on Broadway "directly opposite Bond Street," so I believe the cross street in the middle distance is Bond, and Burdell's house, therefore, around its corner to the left, a short walk away.

I think Harvey Burdell deserves some sympathy. He was always alone. Never, said the proprietor of the LaFarge, did he see anyone eating with Dr. Burdell. A friend, Alvah Blaisdell, when also asked whether anyone ever ate with the Doctor, said, "I don't think he had anybody . . . he was not the kind of man [to invite a friend to dinner]; he was too close. . . ." So I see Harvey Burdell now, walking out of his house and over to the LaFarge each day to eat his silent meals, as a lonely man, afraid of marriage to Emma Cunningham or anyone else because afraid for his money; and beginning to be afraid of the strange, persistent woman he'd met at Saratoga Springs, who now had a lease on his house.

Afraid with reason: on October 10 Mrs. Cunningham returned to her lawyer, told him to go ahead and serve the Doctor with the already prepared summons charging rape, abortion, and breach of promise; and to draw up another to go along with it, charging slander in having accused her of stealing his note. On the day she so instructed her attorney, Harvey Burdell sat in his rooms and wrote:

"Cousin Demis: I received your letter two days since. You say you are ready to come to New York whenever I say the word. Mrs. Cunningham is about to take some steps to injure me, *I think.* Hold yourself in readiness to come to this city at a moment's warning. Perhaps I may go out after you, but if things go on quietly you had probably better stay where you are.

". . . Mrs. C. has slandered you and Lucy of the worst kind. . . .

"If I do not go to Sackett's Harbor in a few days I will send you some money. I am, in great haste,

"Yours, &c., Harvey Burdell."

A few days later he wrote: "Cousin Demis: . . . The trouble I expected with Mrs. Cunningham may not take place . . ." but he was wrong. On this same day a deputy sheriff, Hugh Ciombie, arrived at 31 Bond, served Emma Cunningham's double summons, and arrested the Doctor. "Emma Augusta Cunningham vs. Harvey Burdell, Action for Breach of Promise, Order of Arrest and $6000 bond," the first was headed, and the second summons, for slander, called for another $6,000 to be posted. When he saw what the papers were, Burdell became "very excited," said Crombie, "and said the suits were to extract money from him. He distinctly repudiated [this is the deputy speaking: everyone seemed more literate then] the idea of making a promise to marry. He said she did steal the note from him. . . ."

He settled the suits, though. And in a strange way. A friend signed a bail bond for him within an hour or so; and a week later Dr. Burdell signed an agreement with Emma Cunningham so peculiar I can't believe a lawyer drew it up. I wonder if they didn't work it out between them, and if he didn't outtalk her, because it read: "In consideration of settling the two suits now pending between Mrs. E. A. Cunningham and myself, I agree as follows:

"First, I agree to extend to Mrs. E. A. Cunningham and family my friendship through life;

"Second, I agree never to do or act in any manner to the disadvantage of Mrs. E. A. Cunningham;

"Third, in case I remain and occupy the house No. 31 Bond Street I now do, I will rent to Mrs. Cunningham the suites of rooms she now occupies 3rd floor, attic and basement at the rate of $800 a year."

Those first two provisions are so curious, and unlawyerlike in language, that I wonder—read them again; see what you think—if they may not be Emma Cunningham's almost pathetic attempt to define and make binding her idea of a husband's obligations, in the absence of marriage itself. And, third, to hang on to the home she had found. To me the document suggests compromise. If Emma Cunningham and her lawyer really did try to get money from him, this tightfisted man simply wouldn't give it; and if she'd hoped the threat of suits might force him to marry her, that didn't work either. But the threat worried him. Crombie said: "He was afraid [the suits] would injure his business reputation if published. The matter seemed to trouble him greatly." For whatever reason, he signed the agreement. Maybe he thought its strange provisions would be unenforceable.

He was furious, though. When he and Emma Cunningham's lawyer, Thayer, showed up at the sheriff's office to notify him that a settlement had been reached and the suits withdrawn: "His tongue was going all the time," Crombie said, "to the effect that they had tried to extort money from him; that he would not marry any woman; and that he had taken her to houses of assignation, and paid her as he had done with other women."

That last sounds doubtful, to say the least. A Bond Street friend of his, Dr. W. R. Roberts, said, "When the Doctor was angry with a person, no matter whether he was relative, friend, or foe, he would say anything to injure them; he would be very friendly afterwards. . . ." And a legal adviser of Burdell's, F. S. Sanxay (F. S. Sanxay: long gone, absolutely forgotten, until you and I momentarily evoke him again) said, "When the Doctor was angry at a person he was the most vituperative man I ever knew, and he did not hesitate to denounce in the most unmeasured terms any person whom he might imagine had injured him. He was quick-tempered and violent. I have known him to speak in terms of praise for an individual, then denounce him, in a few days afterward, most bitterly, and then praise him again. He was very extravagant when praising or denouncing anyone; I never heard such bitter language used by anybody as he used toward his brother William and his near relatives." If this explains what Harvey Burdell said about Emma Cunningham to Deputy Crombie, then I think he comes off as a weak man: blustering, fearful, but with a weak man's stubbornness. Crombie was asked later, "Do you believe he ever thought of marrying her?" and he replied, "Marry her! Why, he'd sooner have committed suicide first."

When she read over her signed document, Emma Cunningham seems to have thought she'd detected a loophole in the provision by which the Doctor said he'd continue to rent her the rooms she and her family occupied. Maybe there *was* a loophole intended, because the first dozen words read: "*In case I remain and occupy the house* No. 31 Bond Street . . ." But in case he did *not* remain at 31 Bond, it does sound as though he might then be free of this obligation. For whatever reasons, Emma Cunningham took a pen, and simply crossed out the offending words.

But I don't see how this document could have seemed much of a victory for her; it says nothing, in actual fact, and it would be hard to think she didn't see that. If so, she'd failed and knew it: failed to marry Harvey Burdell by persuasion, and now through force, if that was the point of the threatened suits. Doesn't it seem that there's nothing else to try? It didn't to Emma Cunningham. She now devised an extraordinary plan to become Mrs. Harvey Burdell. And the second act, wild and strange, began—with the arrival at 31 Bond Street of a new and sinister figure.

21

2

This is the man: he said he came to 31 Bond in response to an ad saying he "could obtain room and board there." But I searched the New York *Herald* through many days preceding his arrival there—most such ads appeared in the *Herald,* they had virtually a monopoly on them; searched other papers, too, and found no such ad. I found quite a few for Bond Street rentals: at number 6 . . . number 27 . . . 47; but none for number 31, and I don't think I could have missed one. It might have been a blind ad; there were a few such. But I wonder if, in fact, Emma Cunningham never ran any such ad at all.

For Dr. Burdell came to suspect that these two already knew each other; suspected, in fact, that this was the mysterious "Van Dolan" who'd come to the Stevenses' house on his strange errand for Mrs. Cunningham. And Sophronia Stevens said the Doctor was right.

As so many people were doing in those early days of photography, this new arrival had had his portrait taken: by Meade Brothers. From that photo a *Harper's Weekly* artist drew the picture on the previous page. And from the same photo a *Leslie's Newspaper* artist drew this, which I include

to show how carefully these woodcut artists worked from photographs: two different men, working independently, yet see how closely this resembles the cut from *Harper's*. Just behind these old cuts, if you can manage to look through them, lies the actual camera image of the living man who walked up the stone steps of 31 Bond, and pulled the bell. More than one person who knew him described his eyes as peculiar, a shade too close, and I think that can be seen in both these portraits.

He stands waiting on the stoop: five feet six inches tall and of powerful frame, said someone who'd studied his appearance closely. "His complexion is tawny or bilious, hair light brown, soft and curly. The top of his head is bald. . . . He is pitted with the small-pox, and wears a heavy beard and mustache. . . . His eyes are light blue, and his nose has the Hebrew curve."

The front door was opened by the Doctor's work-boy, and Mrs. Cunningham summoned. She would then, I expect, have shown the caller through the house, opening the doors of available rooms; and now we get our first direct look inside 31 Bond Street.

This is the room he selected: on the third floor right next to the suite

into which Mrs. Cunningham had moved from Demis's old room. The door there on the left, in fact, leads directly into Mrs. Cunningham's bedroom.

John J. Eckel was the new lodger's name; said to have been a butcher, now a dealer in animal hides and fats; and he moved in with twenty-one caged canaries, a few of which H. W. Copcutt shows in his drawing of Eckel's room.

The bookcase beside the window in Eckel's bedroom opened up into a desk like this, and it also turned into a bed at night. John Eckel bought

this useful piece soon after moving in, at the Crystal Palace, which stood in Bryant Park just behind the site of today's main Public Library. It was made of rosewood, a maid who admired it said.

Eckel was thirty-five, at least ten years younger than Harvey Burdell, and when he wanted to make the effort to appear so, he was sometimes described as handsome; except for the eyes. There were people who knew Eckel who said that he occasionally enjoyed disguising himself; and sometimes he dyed his graying whiskers black, and sometimes wore a toupee. When he did, he looked like this, and I wonder if for Emma Cunningham he may not have been

a welcome change from the increasingly morose and difficult owner of the house.

With the arrival of this man the cast at 31 Bond Street is almost complete, and the things that now began to happen concerning Dr. Burdell turned sinister.

Burdell felt it immediately. Eckel moved into 31 in mid-October, and in the same month Harvey Burdell ran into an acquaintance in the Crystal Palace. The two stood chatting. The man, "in the patent-carriage business," was exhibiting there, the Doctor politely said he'd like to ride in one of the carriages; and then, according to this mere acquaintance, "He said there was some damned cut-throat fellow about the house, and he did not like him."

When John Eckel had been at 31 Bond about two weeks, living with his twenty-one canaries directly beside Mrs. Cunningham's bedroom, something extraordinary happened; on October 28. Something downright weird, in fact, remarkable even by Mrs. Cunningham's standards. That afternoon, Dr. Samuel Parmly, a fifty-year-old dentist who lived across the street from number 31 Bond, glanced out his window and noticed a man dressing in the third-floor front room, he said, of number 31. This was Eckel's room. Leaving his house some minutes later, Parmly again glanced up at 31, from his own front stoop, and saw the same man, but "his appearance was changed, and the change gave me the impression that he was connected with the theatre, and was dressing himself for the stage." What especially struck Dr. Parmly, he said, was the man's greatly altered appearance about the head and face, "as if he had been transformed."

Somewhat later, between six and seven o'clock, getting dark, the doorbell of 573 Broadway rang; this was the home of Mrs. Sallenbach, a corset-maker, and her daughter, Emily. They didn't have a retail store but conducted the business on the second floor, living on the floor above. I don't know what the street floor was; a store, possibly, because the Metropolitan Hotel was directly across the street. Emily ran downstairs to answer the bell; her mother seems not to have been home. She opened the street door—I see it as between two storefronts—and recognized a customer standing there, Mrs. Cunningham. Her daughter Augusta stood with her, and Mrs. Cunningham explained that they'd come to wait upstairs at the Sallenbachs', for a gentleman.

If this sounds odd, it didn't seem to appear so to Emily, who was seventeen. Mrs. Cunningham, she explained, "was a very friendly lady and often came to our house on business, and I didn't take anything bad by it." Emily took the two ladies upstairs to their "back parlor" on the third floor. It was nearly dark: "she had to light the gas as soon as she came in."

Mrs. Cunningham sat down, with Augusta, and suggested that Emily "go and do my home business," Emily said, "or whatever had to be done." But if this was a hint, Emily didn't realize it; she thought it would be rude to leave, she said, and declined. There was a piano in the room, and Mrs. Cunningham then asked Emily to play something for them. Which she did: "I sung a piece for her . . . a ballad."

For twenty minutes, she thought, Emily played as the two Cunningham women sat there under the flame of the gas jet listening: smiling, I suppose, perhaps nodding politely in time to the beat; you can imagine them softly applauding between pieces. And down on the street, if the heavy iron-wheeled traffic of wagons, carriages, and the little horse-drawn white-painted buses had slackened enough by now, pedestrians of that long-ago Broadway may have heard the sound of that piano and the young voice singing a ballad.

I'd like to have been there, standing down on that Broadway sidewalk, near 573, hearing that piano. If only it were possible to spend even a few minutes at some selected place and moment of the lost past, there are a great many I'd want to visit. But for me this may be the one above all. I'd stand at the curb out of the way, unnoticed in the dark between the dim street lamps. I'd glance out often at that strange Broadway and the clattering traffic, smudged lanterns swinging under the rear axles; I'd look over at the yellow-lighted windows and entrance of the vanished Metropolitan Hotel on the other side; but I'd watch the approaching pedestrians through every moment, their faces moving into and out of the wavering light of the street lamps.

A bearded face is what I'm waiting for, but there are a lot of them passing. I watch them all, then suddenly one of them turns aside toward 573 and *I see his face.* I finally know who the man coming to join Emma and Augusta *really is.* . . . And when I knew that, I would know the entire answer to all the mysterious events that followed.

But when I try to imagine that moment I *don't* see the face. He turns out of the pedestrian flow too fast for me, and is standing there at 573, hand on the bellpull, his back to me, before I can glimpse his features. I can't grab him and swing him around, can't do that here where I don't belong at all. The door opens, I see Emily Sallenbach's young face, politely inquiring; see the man's hat removed in equal politeness, see the back of his head in the dim light from the curb. Then he steps in, never turning, the door closing, and I hurry over, and from behind the door hear their steps receding up the long staircase.

Emily brought the bearded man upstairs, and when they entered the back parlor Augusta was sitting at the piano, her mother standing beside her. "Good evening, Sir, how do you do," Mrs. Cunningham said, as

Emily recalled it, and the man replied similarly.

But Augusta didn't stand up and yield her place at the piano; she asked Emily "to get her a glass of water; when I came back with it they were all three talking together intimately, but I did not know what they said." Emily back in the room, Mrs. Cunningham and the new visitor sitting on the sofa looking at "some papers which were about the size of foolscap," Emily said, Augusta began to play the piano. "She seemed as if she wanted to occupy my attention," said Emily, who now stood politely beside Augusta.

Augusta played not ballads but polkas, and rather more loudly than Emily had done, and Emily couldn't hear much of what was going on behind her on the sofa. But she thought Mrs. Cunningham and the man extremely absorbed in Mrs. Cunningham's papers, and her young interested ears were able to pick out Mrs. Cunningham's voice saying she had come from her lawyers. And she heard her ask the man "if they were prepared to go, and she said to him, 'All things are right now.' " For ten minutes, the piano keys plunking under Augusta's fingers, the two on the sofa sat murmuring. Then Emily's visitors left.

The man, Emma Cunningham later insisted, was Harvey Burdell, and Augusta said so, too: they were all on their way to a minister's house where her mother and Dr. Burdell were to be married. Why the stop at the Sallenbachs'? Well, because after leaving 31 Bond, her mother and Dr. Burdell discovered that they'd both forgotten gloves. So Mrs. Cunningham suggested that she and Augusta would wait at the Sallenbachs' corset shop while Dr. Burdell bought new gloves for them; he would meet them there.

But Emily Sallenbach remembered no gloves; she remembered papers, and murmuring whispered talk. She hadn't been introduced to the bearded man, nor had he told her his name when she let him in. But some three months later Emily was in the house at 31 Bond Street; she saw John Eckel there and "I recognized him as the person who came to our house. . . . His whiskers were a good deal darker when he was at [our] house," she said, but she knew him just the same by his "very peculiar eyes."

If you think I'm going to tell you what that visit to the Sallenbachs' was all about, I'll have to fail you. For if Augusta told the truth, why stop at the Sallenbachs'? Why not all go to the glove store, buy the gloves, and on to the minister's? On the other hand, if the man was John Eckel about to impersonate Harvey Burdell in a fake marriage to Emma Cunningham, we can ask the same question: Why stop at the Sallenbachs'? And risk being identified later by Emily?

I can't see a connection between that strange visit and a fake marriage or a real one either. Number 573 Broadway is a short walk from 31 Bond: if the man was Eckel, why not meet at home where, locked in Emma

28

Cunningham's bedroom, the canaries trilling in Eckel's adjoining room, they could confer as secretly as they liked, no piano fortissimo needed?

If this were fiction I'd have to omit that inexplicable scene at the Sallenbachs'; or at least push it around a little to make it fit in if I liked it, as I certainly do. But these are real people. They lived in New York City in 1856, and the visit to the Sallenbachs' happened. So I give you the scene—Emma Cunningham and the bearded mystery man sitting at her corset-maker's murmuring legalities as daughter Augusta hammered out polkas—as simply pure Emma Cunningham. Maybe you'll spot something I've missed.

They left, the three of them; walked out onto gaslighted Broadway, and then west across town to 623 Greenwich Street, the house of the only actual person I've ever heard of named Uriah: the Reverend Uriah Marvine. He recognized the bearded man as the man who'd been there the day before to arrange the wedding. After he'd left, Marvine had told his wife he thought the man was in disguise because "I could see daylight between his face and his whiskers." His name, he had told Marvine, was Harvey Burdell.

Now tonight here he was again with his bride-to-be and her daughter as witness. Watching silently and secretly from an unlighted adjoining room stood a servant, Sarah M'Manilen, or McManahan, and her helper, this privilege apparently one of the rewards of working at the minister's house. As the Reverend Marvine read the ceremonial words, he eyed the stranger but this time under the gaslight could detect no space between whiskers and face. Perhaps he'd been mistaken about a false beard: no one ever said John Eckel's own beard had been shaved off around this time. A false beard over his own, of another color? Or not Eckel at all? I don't know.

But Marvine did think, and the spying servant girls said much the same, that the man's "conduct was singular during the ceremony; he stood behind the woman and appeared indifferent. The woman seemed to have more interest in the case."

Marvine pronounced them man and wife, and the man handed the Reverend a ten-dollar bill, which sounds pretty substantial for the time. The couple asked that the marriage not be published in the newspapers, and Marvine agreed; people did sometimes make this request. They wanted a marriage certificate, though, and Marvine said he'd have it ready next day.

Next day the man showed up for it, and again Marvine thought he "acted strangely. He held his head down, and did not speak with a clear bell-like voice." He looked at the certificate, and said it was all right, "and left with it." But the certificate wasn't all right: the man who said he was Harvey Burdell did not seem to notice that Marvine had misspelled his name *Berdell*.

29

At home Emma Cunningham, as she continued to be called, put her certificate away and told no one she was married now; not the servants, and not even daughter Helen. And only a day or so after the secret ceremony in Uriah Marvine's living room, Dr. Burdell arrived at Saratoga Springs for a short stay. The clerk who registered him had known him for years, so it was Harvey Burdell for sure this time. But he came alone: if Harvey Burdell was a new bridegroom, he did not bring a bride along. And sitting up in his room he wrote:

"Cousin Demis: . . . all trouble is at an end, I think. [Mrs. Cunningham] *is a designing, scheming, and artful woman. All her designs were to get me to marry her;* but the *old hag* has failed and *damned her soul to hell.* I would sooner marry an old toad than to marry such a thing as she is. Sam Weller says, 'beware of the vidders,' and I think he was right.

". . . Dinner is now ready and I must close with wishing you all well and happy.

"In haste, yours &c.,
Harvey Burdell."

What next with Emma Cunningham? Well, on November 4, a few days after the wedding, she took in another new lodger. He doesn't figure much in what followed, using 31 Bond merely as a place to sleep, but odd though this seems, the new lodger was no less than the Honorable Daniel Ullman, a prominent New York lawyer, and once a candidate for governor of New York who'd come close to being elected.

A week or so later Mrs. Cunningham brought in this lively nineteen-year-old banjo-playing kid, the son of a respectable Presbyterian clergyman. The Cunninghams knew him and his family, and he'd been coming around most evenings to call on the Cunningham girls. Now Emma Cunningham invited him to move in; at no charge. Why a non-paying guest? With three unmarried daughters on her hands, Mrs. Cunningham may have seen him simply as a prospective son-in-law, and it's true that he was soon spending a lot of time with fifteen-year-old Helen. But the name George Vail Snodgrass was also

"pretty well known about the saloons of the Fifteenth Ward," a reporter later said, and many people came to believe that Emma Cunningham brought him into the house as an ally in what her plans demanded next.

To Dr. Burdell things seemed quiet, the agreement of last month signed and apparently accepted; on November 13, about the time Snodgrass moved in, Burdell wrote, "Cousin Demis . . . There is no trouble now between me and Mrs. Cunningham. I think Mrs. C. will not make any more disturbance, and that she will be quiet and leave No. 31 Bond-street as soon as she can with a good grace.

"If you would like to come to this City, I have no objections, but it would not be proper to come to No. 31 Bond-street, as long *as the old 'she devil' stays here*—that is to live here. . . . *I shall certainly get rid of Mrs. Cunningham by Spring, and I may get rid of her now very soon, and when this monstrous b——h of Hell* leaves I would like to have you come at once to New-York. I assure you, as soon as I can get her out of my house, I shall, and may the old devil take her to himself in the infernal regions.

"I will send you some more money in a short time. . . ."

But he himself seemed closer to being out of 31 than his landlady. He was there now only to treat patients daytimes; took all his meals at the LaFarge; and he often spent his evenings out, too, coming home to go straight up to his rooms, to sleep alone behind locked doors just as though he weren't married at all.

While, without him, it was a pretty congenial group that sat down, now, around his dining room table, and at the kitchen table mornings: Emma Cunningham, I assume, at the table's head; the two girls, the two small boys, and the new men in the house—John Eckel, who enjoyed disguising himself, and the fun-loving, banjo-plinking, nineteen-year-old frequenter of saloons.

After dinner, the conviviality often continued. "Mrs. Cunningham and her daughters would ask for the pleasure of our company," George Snodgrass said, and they'd all climb the stairs to their landlady's suite. "We were all in the habit," said Snodgrass, "of going to her big sitting room." There, the gas jets lighted, they'd converse, and George would sometimes bring in his banjo and sing. He particularly liked what many people of the time thought in low taste: Negro minstrel music. Since we know Augusta was musical, it seems possible that sometimes she sang, too, and you can imagine them all joining in at times.

Occasionally they sat as late as eleven. Dr. Burdell often came home much earlier than that, having found nothing much else to do, I suppose. So it is easy to imagine him, too—though I don't know that this happened —sitting alone in his office or bedroom or lying on his bed, listening to

31

them singing upstairs.

Snodgrass and the girls began to suspect that John Eckel was spending the nights with his new landlady; and so did a new chambermaid, Mary Donaho, a gossipy, inquisitive "little Irish woman, about 40, but neither fat nor fair." She said, ". . . when I went into Eckel's room I did not think that he slept there. . . . It seemed as if somebody ran in there, and threw the pillows about. . . . It was a handsome bedstead; it could be closed up like a bookcase." But Mrs. Cunningham's "large double bed," Mary Donaho thought, "looked as though two persons had slept in it."

". . . I think Mrs. C. opened one of your letters," Harvey Burdell wrote to cousin Demis, November 19; and chambermaid Mary Donaho overheard an angry quarrel between the Doctor and Emma Cunningham, which seemed to be about Demis. " 'He wants to bring a woman of bad character here,' " Mrs. Cunningham told Mary later, " 'and I don't want her to associate with my daughters.' "

Mary seemed to have a nose for the action: later that same morning, after the Doctor had left the house, she was sweeping the stairs between the first and second floors, and watched Emma Cunningham appear with a key and unlock the Doctor's office door. Later Mary found occasion to come walking in, and found Augusta and her mother going through the Doctor's papers. "It was a very frequent thing," said Mary, "for Mrs. Cunningham to say that the Doctor was a very wicked bad man. . . ." Then something more menacing began to appear in Mrs. Cunningham's remarks. " 'It was time he was out of the world,' " Mary said she heard her say of the Doctor, " 'for he was not fit to live in it,' or something like that. . . ." And a Dr. Wilson, walking into the house and up the front stairs to use Dr. Burdell's laboratory, also overheard Emma Cunningham threaten the Doctor. Wilson's first name, incidentally, was Erastus: one of the extinct first names—Uriah, Levi, Hector, Cyrenius, Sophronia, Alvah, Silas, Phoebe, Cephas, Demis—of so many of the people in the Doctor's life.

One day in December, Dr. Burdell called Mary Donaho, and had her help him switch the furniture between his bedroom and office. This put his bedroom at the front of the house directly under Mrs. Cunningham's bedroom on the floor above. Mrs. Cunningham told Mary she thought the move was made in order that the Doctor might hear "every noise and foot" up in her room, and it does sound like it.

Why the spying, the *listening* to each other? Does it seem like simple jealousy? Jealousy of Harvey Burdell would hardly be consistent with Emma Cunningham's behavior with John Eckel these days, but of course she doesn't have to be consistent; she didn't know we'd be trying to puzzle out her behavior a hundred and twenty-odd years later. Is it possible that

Dr. Burdell and Emma Cunningham actually shared some sort of genuine feeling at the beginning? However less creditable some of their motives might have been? That maybe it wasn't all plot and counterplot but, however fierce her determination and will to survive, at least some of their bitterness toward each other now may have sprung from a disappointment this middle-aged pair felt at their own destruction of better feelings?

There's a gap for the entire rest of December. I wish someone—George Snodgrass, one of the girls, or Hannah or Mary—had spoken about Christmas Day, though. Were greetings and gifts exchanged in that house? Were there toys for Willie and George? Did the mail bring Christmas cards, which were enormously popular then? And if we stood outside on our walk watching for clues, would we see a tree in the window? With lighted candles at night? All we know is that George Snodgrass said Dr. Burdell was at home on Christmas Day, which surprised me. Personally, I'd have headed for Demis's.

Something seems to have happened in January, and I'd walk a long mile uphill to find out what it was that made Dr. Burdell suspect that John Eckel wasn't really just a man who happened to come here for lodging, but someone Emma Cunningham had previously known. Burdell, in fact, now became afraid that they intended to kill him, and to his friend Alvah Blaisdell he said something I find chilling: ". . . naming Mrs. Cunningham, her daughter, Mr. Eckel and Mr. Snodgrass . . . he said they had been in the habit after he had gone in his room evenings, of opening his door quietly, and when he turned round to look at them, they would pull it to, and would go out and go away, and he was very much afraid. . . ."

He went to see the Stevenses, telling them, said Cyrenius, that he had "worked hard and got a good deal of money, and, said he, I am actually afraid to stay in my own house." A man was living there now, he told them, who "appeared to be a kind of beau to Mrs. Cunningham"; and, said Sophronia Stevens, Dr. Burdell "wished us to come there and see if we could identify him as the man who came to see us, calling himself Van Dolan."

But the Stevenses had had enough of going to 31 Bond. " 'Why don't you get the people out of your house?' " Cyrenius asked Burdell. "He said he could not, because he had let it till the first of May to Mrs. Cunningham. 'Then,' says I, 'why don't you leave the house? You are a man of means; I would not stay if I feared for my life.' He said he was very cautious, and thought he would stay till May, and get the house clear. He was very urgent to have me and my wife come up . . . but I didn't feel disposed to go, and I never went."

Scared though he was, Harvey Burdell stayed on at 31 Bond, and in an atmosphere now heavy with rancor, mockery, and increasing threat, the last week of his life began.

Another violent quarrel between him and Emma: Burdell asked her to sign a paper promising for sure that she'd leave the house on May first. But she wouldn't do it, Augusta joining the battle and actually tearing the Doctor's hair, he said. He then ran through the house, said Mary Donaho, yelling, " 'My God what am I to do with these people, they will at last have my life!' " Over to Broadway again and back with a cop, and Burdell stood out on the sidewalk with him telling the cop his troubles until finally Helen Cunningham called, said Mary Donaho, " 'Oh, Doctor, for God's sake come in and go upstairs, and I will get my mother to give you those papers.' " That brought him in, and Mary heard no more.

He got his paper (apparently there was only one), and next day brought it to Brooklyn to show cousin Demis; but before taking the ferry over, Harvey Burdell did something else first. This is when he went to Bacon's studio where his friend Mrs. Benjamin worked, and had her take this final portrait of his life.

At Demis's he showed her his pathetic paper signed by Emma Cunningham; both she and Harvey Burdell seemed to place extraordinary faith in the power of signed promises. "She gave it to him Saturday night, he [told me] he wanted to keep it and show it to some other friends, and then he wished me to keep it for him, he was so afraid she would take it again."

At about the time Harvey Burdell sat there with Demis, Mrs. Cunningham did something odd: she'd also done it the night before. In the still-early middle of the evening she went down to the kitchen, and to their puzzlement ordered Mary and Hannah upstairs to bed. Why did she want the servants out of the way? As we'll see very soon, there is strong reason to wonder if it was not to wait—with Eckel? And perhaps Augusta?—for Dr. Burdell's return; wait for him to unlock the front door, and step into the dark and silent house. If so, I don't know what happened the first night the servants were sent early to bed, but on this second night, returning from his visit to Demis with his newly signed paper, Dr. Burdell did come into a darkened but far from silent house.

"It was a severe night," said Mary Donaho, meaning that it was stormy. "We [she and Hannah] were in bed . . . and there was no light burning . . ."; but although they had been sent early to bed by Mrs. Cunningham, they weren't asleep. "I heard a noise downstairs at the door": it was a sudden shouting, cursing, and hammering at the street door, and it scared her. Then the doorbell rang, she knew it was the Doctor, and called to Snodgrass in the attic front room, asking him to please go down.

George didn't much want to go down there either, but he did; taking along with him, however, the Cunningham boys, nine and ten, and his visiting brother, still young enough to be called "little Tom Snodgrass." Down the four boys went, three flights through the darkened house, or perhaps with candles, and Snodgrass let the enraged Doctor in, cursing at Snodgrass because, he said, the door of his own house had been deliberately bolted against him, though Snodgrass said that the patent lock had merely slipped, as it sometimes did.

Next morning at the kitchen breakfast table—John Eckel, Emma Cunningham, her two boys and Helen, with Mary Donaho standing by to serve them—they discussed last night's ruckus at the front door. "They were talking about the Doctor being an ugly man," said Mary—meaning his disposition—and as Mary continues we suddenly see them there at that table, Tuesday morning, January 27, 1857.

"Mr. Eckel was eating cakes at the time, and laughing," said Mary, "when, putting down his knife and fork, he rubbed his hands together just so, like making fun, and saying, 'By jingo! Shouldn't I like to be at the stringing up of that old fellow, if I would not have too hard a pull at the cord!' " A little laugh from Mrs. Cunningham, then "she told me I need not remain in the room any longer." Eckel, said Mary, "looked so leeringly at [Emma Cunningham], I hated to look at him at the same time. . . ."

On that same Tuesday morning Dr. Burdell was so disturbed that to a mere acquaintance—the wife of a dentist he knew who had come here to see him on a business matter—"He stated to me that he had let his house to a lady, and that she was the most horrible woman he ever met. He said she was very artful, and she was capable of doing anything to accomplish what she undertook. He told me he suspected foul play, and that he did not like the way *they* were prowling about the house at night. . . ."

So frantic had Dr. Burdell become to get free of these people that he now made what may have been literally a fatal mistake. In this same week, with over three months to go until the blessed May Day when he could at least turn Mrs. Cunningham out of his house, he nevertheless showed two women, a Mrs. Stansbury and her mother, through 31 Bond, offering it for lease when May should finally come.

Hannah Conlon, the cook, was present as the ladies and Harvey Burdell moved from room to room; and Mrs. Cunningham stood listening in the kitchen. What did these women want? she asked when Hannah came in. They were looking over the house, Hannah replied; she thought Dr. Burdell was going to lease the house to them, and sign a paper. " 'Perhaps he will not live to let the house, or sign either,' " Emma Cunningham replied, said Hannah.

A day or so later Mrs. Cunningham instructed Mary Donaho to lay a fire—for what purpose she didn't explain—in a seldom used fireplace of an unoccupied attic room. It would not be used immediately, she said, but she wanted it ready to light. In these same last days Mary overheard Mrs. Cunningham say that Dr. Burdell was " 'a very bad man; it was time he was out of the world.' " And on one of these days Mary left 31 Bond: fired for drunkenness, George Snodgrass later said, though Mary denied it.

We have a glimpse of Harvey Burdell in his final despondency. Dr. Samuel Parmly, who lived directly across the street, saw him; he walked past Parmly on the sidewalk, and: "His head was so low that when I recognized and addressed him he did not observe me."

Friday, at about twelve-thirty, Helen went out for her music lesson . . . about half-past one an old friend of the Doctor's, Alvah Blaisdell, came to the house on business. He and the Doctor stood in the front hall talking, and at first it was the old litany from the Doctor: Mrs. Cunningham, Augusta, Eckel, Snodgrass had locked him out of the house one night; had "abused" him, telling him it was nothing more than he deserved; that "he ought to have his head broke." They went through his papers when he was out, had opened his safe—and this was also the occasion when he told Blaisdell of their fearful trick of opening his door to stare at him.

But now came something new. "He wished me to come here," said Blaisdell, "and remain with him till May. . . ." The Doctor always spoke loudly in his odd barking manner, never lowering his voice in conversation, Blaisdell said, and it was his impression that, as they stood in the hall, their entire conversation had been overheard by Mrs. Cunningham on the floor above.

What Blaisdell replied I don't know, but soon after he left, Catherine Stansbury arrived. They sat down in the front parlor, and she said she and her husband had made up their minds: they'd like to lease the house. The two then discussed the terms of the lease, agreed on them, and Dr. Burdell said he'd have it ready to sign in the morning. Then Catherine Stansbury asked: Does Mrs. Cunningham know we are taking the house? Yes, the Doctor replied, and apparently that worried Mrs. Stansbury, for "I asked him if he had told her where we lived. He said not, but that makes no difference, for she would go to every Stansbury in New-York until she found the right one. I suddenly opened the door," said Mrs. Stansbury. "Mrs. Cunningham was going away from the door."

Harvey Burdell was actually a timid man, said a friend: "I don't think he would fight a boy ten years old." And as he sat with Mrs. Stansbury watching Mrs. Cunningham walk away from the door at which she had apparently been listening to them, I wonder if the prospect of overcoming the force of this woman's will with legalistic pieces of paper didn't shrivel. For when Mrs. Stansbury left, he sent word to Alvah Blaisdell to come back—right away! Told Hannah that the instant a tall man arrived he was to be informed. Around four, Helen returned from her music lesson . . . lodger Daniel Ullman came home, went up to his room, and left again soon after . . . and around four-thirty Blaisdell did return, and what his frightened friend said to him now is pathetic. "He said this: 'I want you to come tonight. I am afraid to stay. I am very melancholy and I don't know the reason. . . .' "

But the best his friend Blaisdell could offer was, "I said I would come in the evening, but could not spend the night with him, that circumstances were such I could not leave home." If he'd kept even that promise, things might have been different, but: "Circumstances prevented me," said Blaisdell, "from keeping my appointment. . . ."

He wasn't prevented at all: he was afraid of garroters, as he later admitted when pressed. "When I got home, I had been gone all day, and had been gone for a number of days before," he explained in the rambling way, it sounds to me, of a man who is embarrassed, "and I found some friends at the house, and they remonstrated against my going out. There have been remonstrances against my going out ever since the garroters have been about. I am very much afraid of them. I started once and intended to have come, but so much was said about it that I declined." Anyway, he added, he hadn't really promised: "I told the Doctor I would come if possible."

I think he heard some unfavorable comment on this excuse, because the next day he changed his story. "I have no fears," he now said, "of going anywhere in this or any other city, night or day—not myself. I have no fears of that—of no man living or dead." But when he finished, the people who heard him laughed.

So Harvey Burdell was left alone, among his enemies, as he believed. The day continued routinely. Dr. Luther Beecher came to call . . . and Mrs. Van Ness, Emma Cunningham's dressmaker and longtime friend. Cousin Demis stopped by. A seamstress, Susan Carey, was there all afternoon, possibly helping to get Helen ready for her return to school in

Saratoga Springs the next morning; and she stayed for dinner. In the late afternoon Augusta went down the street to Dr. Roberts to get a tooth fixed. At four-thirty the Doctor's newest boy-of-all-work, John Burchell, left for the day. And at about five, Alvah Blaisdell having promised to return around seven, Dr. Burdell went out for his dinner alone.

Then he came home to wait for his friend. And finally, Blaisdell never having showed up, Dr. Burdell went out again. It's not certain where. He may have visited his cousin Lucy Ann Williams that evening, on "Carrol Place" in Brooklyn. Or he may have just wandered around, because a First Avenue druggist who knew him said he "saw him standing on the north-west corner of Bond Street and the Bowery between nine and nine-thirty." He was alone, "dressed in his usual manner; he had on his shawl and coat . . . a black hat . . . a common silk hat." From George Snodgrass we learn that he also wore "indiarubbers," and he carried something, either a cane or an umbrella. It is also known that he wore a black neckerchief.

Inside 31 Bond, in the back parlor of the first floor, Mrs. Cunningham, George Snodgrass, and her family were busy packing trunks and in general preparing for Helen's journey to boarding school at twelve-thirty tomorrow. We can see them fairly well. Little Willie and George Cunningham sat "marking" their sister's clothes; with her name, I assume is meant. Mrs. Cunningham wore black, as Augusta remembered it: "blade silk basque and skirt," or possibly the material was "black bombazine." Augusta, who, as Snodgrass recalled, wore a red plaid dress, spoke of how sorry she was that Helen was leaving, saying she didn't know what she'd do without her. Helen discovered that she didn't have any writing paper, and that she needed a veil, too, so she and George Snodgrass walked out to buy them: "Up Broadway, over to Fourth-street and down the Bowery," George said. They came back, and Helen "brought in the veil," she said, "showed it to mother, and then folded up some of my clothes, putting them into the trunk." Presently John Eckel came home to join them, having remembered as requested to bring some "figs, oranges, and candy," for Helen, or Ellen as she was sometimes called, to take along to school.

As some of the participants described it, it has almost the sound of a festive evening in a quiet way: the girls chattering; the little boys helping a bit and, no doubt, playing a lot; the men watching, and helping a little; the mother busy herself and overseeing the others, as the long dresses and the capes, the shoes and hats, undergarments, and heavy stockings were folded and laid into the traveling trunks—a mid-nineteenth-century kind of evening of a lost innocence and charm.

Around eight a man named Smith Ely, Jr., a business associate of John Eckel's, came to the front door and gave Mrs. Cunningham a written message for Eckel. Later that evening she remembered it, took it to Eckel's door, and gave it to him.

The packing was finished about half-past eight, and the group then went up, as so often, to Mrs. Cunningham's sitting room, third floor front: "Mrs. Cunningham," Snodgrass recalled, "her two daughters, her two sons, Mr. Eckel, and myself." Around nine or nine-thirty the boys were sent up to bed. John Eckel dozed in a rocking chair, boots slipped off.

But then around ten o'clock, once more, and oddly, Mrs. Cunningham—and this time Eckel came with her—went down to the kitchen and mysteriously ordered Hannah early to her attic bed again; and Eckel joined in the order. Hannah went, she said, "as soon as I washed some clothes out." On her way to her attic bedroom she stopped at Mrs. Cunningham's sitting room to ask what they all wanted for breakfast. "Mr. Eckel was sitting in the rocking chair," she remembered, "and Mr. Snodgrass was sitting at the table, I think writing something or other."

A little before eleven Snodgrass was sent down to the kitchen, he said, to bring back some cider. He took a pitcher from its basin and made his way down. The house was completely dark, he said, so when he reached the second floor he ignited a match and lit the wall gas jet just outside Dr. Burdell's door to light his way on down to the kitchen. In its light he happened to notice, he said, that no key protruded from the lock of Dr. Burdell's office door—which was as it should be. Whether or not the Doctor had yet come home Snodgrass said he didn't know. In the kitchen he found the cider locked up, couldn't find the key, so he brought water upstairs instead—turning off the second-floor gas jet on his way back up. Both daughters had a drink from the pitcher, he said, so did he, but the "old lady" did not. Mrs. Cunningham said she was tired and suggested that they all retire; this was at exactly eleven by her mantel clock, Snodgrass observed. He went up to the attic bedroom where he and the boys slept, and Hannah—still lying awake—heard him say good night to Helen. He went to bed, and all three boys said they slept right through till morning, hearing nothing all night long. Hannah, too, said she slept all night, hearing nothing. Everyone else said the same; no one heard a thing.

But some of the sleeping arrangements were peculiar. Mrs. Cunningham later explained that Helen wasn't feeling well, so she had her bring her things down from her attic bedroom and sleep with her. Augusta then said that she, too, wanted to sleep down here; and for a time she and Helen lay in bed talking. They had never before all slept in the one bed, Augusta said, but did so now because her sister was going away next day. But she agreed that Helen could not have been sick or they would not have planned to let her go away. Whatever the reason, the two girls and their mother all slept in Mrs. Cunningham's bed, Mrs. Cunningham in the middle. It doesn't sound comfortable, and if Mrs. Cunningham had to get up for any reason, she could hardly have done so without waking one of the girls. But they all said that didn't happen; that all night long none of them awakened. And Eckel said neither did he.

Wherever Harvey Burdell spent that evening, wherever he went or wandered from the corner of Bond Street where he was last seen at nine-thirty, the time came when, the dread still in him, this despondent man finally turned toward home.

You wonder why he didn't stay where he was. Or go to Demis's. Or, walking off the night ferry from Brooklyn, if, in fact, he'd been with cousin Lucy Ann Williams, he didn't just walk on over to the Metropolitan or LaFarge, take a room, and *stay* there. Till May first. Going to the Bond Street house only in the daytime to treat his patients, leaving the house with the last of them. You want to shout at him over the intervening century: *Stay away from this house!*

Why didn't he? Blaisdell said, "Nearly all his difficulties have grown out of money matters. He was one of the most extremely penurious men, perhaps, that ever lived: a penny looked bigger in his eyes than a $20 gold piece to some people." It sounds right: it could be what kept him from marrying. Possibly Harvey Burdell couldn't bring himself to contract a three months' hotel bill when he owned a house of his own; and to abandon a valuable piece of property to those who occupied it now.

In spite of his terror at being in this house, Harvey Burdell walked toward it now: along late-at-night Bond Street, possibly hearing his own reluctant steps muffled by the india-rubbers we know he was wearing, along with coat and shawl, black neckerchief, and common black silk hat, and carrying

40

either cane or umbrella. It was a warm night for January, other people who came along Bond Street that night tell us; partly overcast and foggy, with a suggestion of rain to come, the sidewalks damp but clear, and snow and ice, packed hard, remaining in the street.

We have these details of his appearance and that of the street, but still it isn't easy to see Dr. Burdell just now. The houses he is walking past are of a kind our eyes have never seen except as antiques, yet here and now they are comparatively new. There are winter trees set in the walk; they're easy to picture. But the light that touches their bare branches and the wet sidewalk and the iron fencing he is passing is gaslight, and what does that really look like? We have to see him as best we can, moving along that winter street of New York City in 1857—walking slowly, I would think —toward number 31; then turning in to climb the six white steps of his marble stoop; bending slightly to unlock the door, which is painted white —he'd be silhouetted against it as he stooped—then stepping into the dark house; turning to close and then lock the door behind him.

He climbed the dark staircase to his rooms. Whether he had to unlock his door I don't know, but if he did, it seems to me he would have removed the key and, I would also think, have locked his door from the inside. In his office—large dental chair near one end, instruments in a case —he lighted the gas jet over his desk and took off his outer clothes, laying his coat and shawl on the sofa, but did not remove his black neckerchief. He lighted the fire, which he always laid himself, said his work-boy, John Burchell. Then he opened his desk, sat down before it, and brought out some papers, including a bankbook.

It is not quite impossible that this is not what happened; that, instead, he had brought someone home with him who sat with him now discussing those papers, possibly, before betraying him. But there was never any reason to think that, and no one really did think so; in fact, he may even have been seen entering his house alone. And what happened now, everything suggested, is that as he sat at his desk looking over his papers under the gas jet, Dr. Burdell's door was silently unlocked with a stolen key, the key then left protruding from the hall side of the door, to be found there in the morning. And then as on other nights, someone eased his door open to stare in at the back of Burdell's bowed head. Or someone who'd been hiding in the Doctor's adjoining bedroom, or in a closet, now silently opened its door.

A large mirror hung over the Doctor's desk. If he had glanced at it, he might have seen whoever came sneaking across the room toward him now. But not heard—for apparently the figure moved in utter silence on tiptoe or in bare or stockinged feet, because everything indicates that Dr. Burdell did not stand, had no warning. And then . . .

41

this is what happened to Harvey Burdell.

This should not be mistaken for a merely imaginative drawing, even though the unknown murderer is made to resemble John J. Eckel. For the artist who signed it stood in the very room: the wall, chair, desk, the mirror above it, the gaslight, all were precisely as he shows them here. And the evidence of a medical commission is that the moment of attack was exactly as Brightly carefully shows it: neckerchief suddenly gripped from behind, choking him, knife thrusting down fast and hard, hunting the heart.

It missed, wounding him, but a bloody trail across the room showed what happened then. "I traced the blood carefully," said Dr. George F. Woodward of a medical examining committee, explaining the deductions from which Brightly made his drawings. "There was a chair placed in front of the Doctor's writing desk, and the leaf of the desk was down . . . there was a very considerable quantity of blood. The chair that set in

42

front of it was also stained very considerably with blood. While examining the wounds, I desired a gentleman to be seated [at the desk] . . . and with [a dagger] placed directly over the wound on the right shoulder. So that if the assassin held this dagger in his right hand, he would have plainly plunged it over the right shoulder. Now that would run obliquely downward and forward. . . ." From observations like these Dr. Woodward made the following deductions:

". . . My idea is that the Doctor got home about the usual time, threw off his shawl and over-shoes, and sat down in the chair by his Secretary, and in a few moments someone came in, surprised him and gave him that cut on the left shoulder while yet sitting. . . . My theory is that at this time the Doctor made resistance . . . we traced blood from that chair to the door . . . his first impulse would be to go to that door [leading to the hall and the stairs]. After arriving at the door it is evident that a great deal of exertion was made on the part of the Doctor, because on examination of his boots, blood was found to be literally ground into them. While there,

with his hand on the knob [as artist Brightly shows above, and which bloodily marked the knob], they gave him this stab in the neck from which the blood . . . spurted per saltum, as we call it, upon the closet door. My judgment is that the heart wound followed that in the throat, for if the heart had been deprived of its mechanical function it could not have thrown that blood. . . ."

One of those never-ceasing dagger thrusts then cut through "the carotid artery" in the neck, the blood spouting upon the closet door, and Harvey Burdell "threw up his arms," Dr. Woodward believed, and before

he could even fall he received another thrust "under the arm. . . . He then from loss of blood apparently sank down, and while down" the dagger continued to work: two more thrusts into the abdomen, then the body momentarily tilted up for the fatal blow penetrating "the heart at the right ventricle. . . ." His fear turned to fact now, Harvey Burdell lay dead by the door he had tried for.

Fifteen times he'd been stabbed in a savage flurry of blows over a furious fifty or sixty seconds: "random blows," Dr. Woodward said, "given without thought or object, only to kill the man." A stab "one inch from the left nipple, on a line and external to it . . . a second two and a half inches downward and inward . . . a third directly below." More "at the neck . . . above the angle of the jaw . . . touching the lobe of the left ear . . . on the face directly over the malar bone . . . on the right wrist . . . the left hand . . . the left arm. . . ." His blood spurted out onto his desk top and chair; onto the center table as he stumbled past it, struggling to pull away; then onto chests, the wall, and the door as he was literally cornered—and finally turning the carpet under him soggy as he lay motionless at last, alone again.

Because this was the night of Harvey Burdell's murder we have a glimpse of the life of New York's streets on January 30, 1857, which would otherwise be lost; and I have the impression that Manhattan was pretty lively then at night. People on foot, places open late, quite a lot going on.

Even little Bond Street had a remarkable number and variety of people moving along it that night, and nearby Broadway sounds wild.

Across the street from 31 Bond, Dr. Samuel Parmly, who had been reading in his sitting room, stood up about nine-thirty, put on hat and coat, and went out for a walk, as he often did; tonight he turned toward Broadway. The air was warm, he remembered, with a feeling of rain or snow to come, the street coated with old packed-down snow. Approaching him came a couple of "suspicious looking characters," he said, "and I turned off from the walk" because "there was a great deal [being] said about the danger of walking the streets at night." Dr. Parmly walked over to Broadway and turned onto it, heading north, and saw that it was crammed with traffic, so many of the tiny, dome-roofed Broadway omnibuses that pedestrians were finding it hard to cross. Up ahead, at Astor Place, he saw that the windows of "the Mercantile Library" were still lighted. And across the street from it, a Mr. Deane's confectionery store was still open; and therefore, I suppose, other stores too. At Eighth Street Dr. Parmly turned back and as he did so saw the library lights go out, and knew it was just ten o'clock.

That was his first walk, which I report simply for the glimpse it gives us of Broadway. Back home reading again, Parmly felt restless, couldn't sit still, he said, and in about fifteen minutes he called his dog, a year-old "spaniel of the King Charles breed," and went out again, this time turning toward the Bowery. And now, as he came home, a strange thing happened. About to reenter his own house, he looked around for the dog, and saw him across the street standing on the steps of number 31, head lifted, staring up at the house.

He whistled but the dog ignored him, staring up at the windows of the house, all dark. Then Parmly smelled something odd. It was the odor of burning clothes, he thought, and in the same moment, up in an attic window of number 31, he saw a light so bright that "I thought Dr. Burdell's house was on fire." It was the window of the unused room, he later learned, in which Mary Donaho had been instructed to lay a fire ready to light when needed. "The light in the attic was extraordinary," said Parmly, "and"—listen to the care with which this nineteenth-century man uses his native tongue—"likely to excite attention from the fact of the unusual darkness of the rest of the house; from no light ever having been seen previously in that attic; and more particularly from the character of the light and its intensity . . . as though newspapers or some easily combustible substance had one by one been successively thrown upon a fire" (deep breath), "flaring and blazing up, and the light suddenly subsiding and brightening again."

So intent was the dog that Dr. Parmly had to walk across the street, scoop him up, "and carry him away from the steps of Dr. Burdell's house." Tonight, as he walked back into his house, Parmly was merely puzzled: tomorrow he'd wonder if he had seen the flames from and smelled the burning of someone's blood-soiled clothing.

Within minutes, more footsteps along Bond and voices, I imagine, calling good nights; because Mrs. Anna C. Rausch and her husband, visiting friends next door to Dr. Burdell's house, now left. They came down the steps, turned toward Broadway and the Prescott House, where they lived, and Mrs. Rausch, too, "smelled a very disagreeable smell."

Still another person walking through little Bond Street at somewhere around this time: William Ross, an architect. And Ross thought he saw someone enter number 31. He had left a friend's house on Spring Street to head for home on Second Avenue, and: "My general way is to cross Broadway at Houston Street," he said, "but that night it was entangled with omnibuses and . . . I came as I thought by Broadway to Bleecker Street . . . till I got to the corner, and then I knew I was in Bond Street, so I came through. . . ." Up ahead, "a hundred or one hundred and fifty feet," Ross saw a man walk up the steps of 31 Bond, he said, open the door with a key, and go in. "I could hear the key; the street was very quiet."

But "when I got down, two houses further on," Ross said, "I heard a cry like 'murd'—very short—and I turned round and looked behind me, but could see nobody. I turned then, and looked the other way, fancying there was somebody garroted. . . . When I looked toward the Bowery there were several young men there that were kind of roguish, making a noise, and I thought it might proceed from them, and I paid no more attention. . . ."

A second man also heard a strangled cry of murder on Bond Street at more or less this same time; the timings, by both men, recollected later. In the third-story front room of number 36 Bond, this man was just going to bed when he heard the cry. He jumped up on a chest to look out across the tops of the window shutters, but saw nothing. "It sounded as if there was a struggle," he said. "The first syllable was distinct, but the last 'd-e-r' was guttural, such as you heard from Forrest sometimes in the theater, and I immediately thought of garroters."

And still a third man heard a cry on Bond Street that night. He worked at "Deane's confectionery establishment, at 741 Broadway opposite Astor Place." He left the store at twenty minutes before eleven; and five or ten minutes later, he thought, "was passing on the opposite side of the street some three or four doors beyond [number 31], and heard a

46

stifled cry . . . a piercing cry . . . it seemed to come from [31]." He thought the cry "like a person in distress or agony."

Three separate cries, only minutes apart? Or two? Or one, the three men who heard it not noticing the other men? Possible, I suppose, in the street lighting of the time. However many cries and wherever they came from . . . Mrs. Cunningham and her daughters, all crowded into the same bed; George Snodgrass, the two little boys, and Hannah, the cook, in the attic; and John Eckel in his room beside Mrs. Cunningham's . . . heard not a sound, they all said.

The life of Bond Street had not yet subsided. Down at number 16 a young lawyer and some friends were entertaining another friend just home "from the West"; and at something after eleven they all came out of number 16, heading for Broadway and the action. They, too, smelled what they thought was burning clothes, and so even now that long-ago party still faintly persists in our minds.

Past midnight now, and Daniel Ullman, the almost-governor of New York, came home to number 31, and went right upstairs and to bed, in his third-floor room, hearing, seeing, smelling nothing.

And around one o'clock a sleigh turned into Bond, Dr. Stephen Maine of number 32 holding the reins; he and his wife coming home from a party. They, too, smelled something burning.

At about three in the morning it began to snow, thickly enough to cover the walks and streets of New York City, the yellow lights that marked those streets brightening a little from the glitter of whiteness beneath them. I once saw gaslight on new snow as a child, walking with my parents from the home of one of their friends to a suburban railroad station near Chicago, and it's a lovely sight: soft-edged circles of lemony light lying on the fresh and sparkling white—a nineteenth-century sight reaching out into the twentieth to take hold of me forever. I feel sorry for Harvey Burdell because I liked him, I'm not sure why, and yet: the low-roofed city all around him now as he lies dead must have been briefly beautiful.

3

For the rest of the night Harvey Burdell lay like this in his office. The open door at the left leads through a small cupboardlike room to the Doctor's bedroom. The map hanging beside that door is entitled "Histoire de France," and is now spotted with blood. So is the framed chart hanging in the corner; it bears the printed political platforms of the last presidential election. The framed engraving over the fireplace is of Dr. William Harvey demonstrating the circulation of blood.

All night now, his watch ticking in his pocket, Dr. Burdell lay, the fire he'd lighted growing at first, blazing up; then subsiding to flicker erratically, and turn to gray ash; while the gas jet over his desk burned motionlessly, finally paling in the dawn.

At six minutes of six in the morning his watch stopped; and at something around the same time the last ordinary hour number 31 Bond would know began with Hannah Conlon, the cook, opening her eyes in the dark of her attic room. From habit she knew "It was between 6 and 7 o'clock," time to begin one more day, and she got up to dress. "It was dark, and I had a lighted candle," she said.

Dressed, Hannah went down the stairs with her candle, passing directly by the door just behind which the Doctor lay, to the basement kitchen to begin preparing the family's breakfast. Around seven she heard an expected knock at the back basement door. This was locked and bolted, she later said; as it should have been. Hannah opened it, and let in young John Burchell, the Doctor's latest boy-of-all-work. I assume the two spoke some brief good-morning, and I see the boy as stomping slush from his shoes or boots before stepping into Hannah's kitchen.

Young John went to work, the start of his day being to make a fire in the washroom, back of the rear parlor. From here he could see into the backyard, and now there occurred the first unusual thing of this day: surprisingly, John Eckel was already up and about. "I saw Mr. Eckel go out into the yard as I came into the washroom," Burchell said, "about seven. . . . He had his usual dress, his undercoat, black pants and fur cap. . . ." It had begun to rain and: "He had his two hands in his pockets. . . . He went into the last [of several 'water closets'], the one next to the fence." Not only was Eckel up early this day but, speaking to no one, he left without breakfast, something else he'd never before done.

Burchell took about fifteen minutes to make the washroom fire, since he had to clean out yesterday's ashes first. "Then I went down to the cellar, and brought a scuttle of coal up to the Doctor's room." As he climbed, the loaded scuttle pulling at his arm, the boy's cheek moved past the damp marks of new blood along the wall of the staircase, but this was January, early in the morning, the house still not very light, and he didn't see them. At the Doctor's door he did not open it, but set the scuttle on the floor beside it. John did see the key protruding from the lock, another unusual thing this morning. Then down he went for a scuttle of coal for Mrs. Cunningham's room.

At just about that same time, around seven-fifteen, John Eckel arrived at one of his three places of business, his bookkeeper said: this one, on Stanton Street. "Is Mr. Smith Ely here?" he immediately asked the bookkeeper. Ely was the man who'd brought a note for Eckel last night, arranging a business appointment for eight this morning. But since this was forty-five minutes early, of course Ely hadn't even left

home yet. John Eckel picked up the morning *Herald* from the floor, and walked to the doorway for light to read it; he wore the fur cap Burchell had noticed, and also now, said one of his workmen, an outer coat "the color of beer." The *Herald* was delivered daily, shoved through a door slot to fall onto the floor of the room where new hides were kept. The hides being raw, the floor permanently damp from them, John Eckel stands reading now in his cap and beer-colored coat, the front page of the paper in his hands wet and bloody.

Hannah "went up to Mrs. Cunningham's door to call her to come down, as breakfast was ready. She [Mrs. Cunningham] asked me if Mr. Eckel was down at his breakfast. . . ." Hannah said no, she hadn't seen him.

At his chores, young John saw the Cunningham family and George Snodgrass at the breakfast table. Later he recalled—or thought he did— that Mrs. Cunningham "was kind of sad that morning, towards what she was the other mornings . . . kind of downcast as if something was the matter. . . ." Well, maybe.

The family and Snodgrass moved up to Emma Cunningham's sitting room after breakfast, Snodgrass not going to work this morning because he was to escort Helen to the railroad station later. And now once more a touch of the bizarre so often present when Emma Cunningham is: with Harvey Burdell lying in his own chilled blood just below, the happy plinkety-plink of George Snodgrass's banjo began to sound through the house from Emma Cunningham's living room, and you wonder if Eckel's canaries weren't trilling along.

Hearing that rollicking banjo as he climbed the stairs yet another time, John Burchell (wearing his overcoat in anticipation) went up to the Doctor's room "to ask . . . if I should clean the snow off the sidewalk." He knocked; stood listening; heard nothing, of course. He tried the door, from which the key protruded, found it unlocked, pushed the door open,

50

stepped inside, and normal life at 31 Bond Street ended.

The room was lighted by the still-burning jet over the desk and: "The first thing that presented itself," said John, "was the blood on the wall and closet door. I then beheld the doctor lying on his face close to the door and surrounded by blood. I was frightened, and slamming the door after me, I fell on my back outside the door"—I see him as backing out so fast he fell flat. "I then got up, and ran downstairs, and informed Hannah, the cook. . . ."

"I was so frightened," Hannah said, "that I let a plate fall and broke it . . ." though John remembered her as having been ironing, and dropping her iron, exclaiming, " 'Don't tell me that, don't tell me that.' " Hannah ran to the stairs to climb toward the sound of the plinking banjo, crying, " 'My God, my God!' " Daniel Ullman, lying in bed, heard the pounding feet on the treads.

"I ran to Mrs. Cunningham's door," said Hannah, "and kicked it open with my foot. . . . Mr. Snodgrass was playing the banjo. I said 'My God, you are enjoying yourselves all very well, and the Doctor is either dead or murdered in his room!' "

Nearly everyone that day seemed to pay close attention to Emma Cunningham's responses. To Hannah now she "looked very excited, and ran over to the bed. So did Helen, who fainted." John Burchell followed Hannah upstairs, and he saw that "Mr. Snodgrass was holding [Mrs. Cunningham] on the bed, and she was crying." Snodgrass (who remembered Hannah as bursting into the room "with hands covered with dough") said, "They all began to halloo."

It took me a long while to get straight, from many accounts of that morning, what happened during the next few hours at 31 Bond Street: who said and did what in that house, when, and in what order; who came rushing in from outside and with whom, and who had run out to get them; what people said, saw, or thought they saw. But I think you'll understand those hours equally well—by simply knowing that people got excited, and acted only semirationally; that they screamed, cried out, fainted, burst into tears real or false; ran down hallways, up and down stairs, and rushed out of the house for help.

Hannah further reported that Mrs. Cunningham "cried out but did not say much," that she "seemed crazy, and tore her hair." Snodgrass "got some camphor" for the fainting Helen. Hannah rushed out to bring in the next-door neighbor. Ten-year-old George Cunningham was sent running across the street through the rain for Dr. Stephen Maine.

Maine seems a cool, intelligent man. During that first confused hour many of the people who came in and looked at the dead man did not understand what had happened to him. His clothes were so saturated, and by morning so stiff, with blood, that it wasn't easy to make out the slits in his clothing and understand that he'd been stabbed to death. But Stephen Maine, standing with the neighbor from next door, looking down at Harvey Burdell, then stooping to touch him and feel the cold skin, saw that he'd been murdered, and how. He examined the entire room then, and the Doctor's bedroom next door; observantly, remembering all he saw, and that is why we know where the Doctor's overshoes, hat, and shawl had been placed, and that a blood-speckled *Herald* lay on the center table.

Next he set his "student," who'd followed him from across the street, to guarding the door of the murder room. Snodgrass called to Dr. Maine from the floor above, and he went up to see Emma Cunningham. Snodgrass got a hat—it was raining still, and a northwest wind had come up —and ran out, and down Bond toward number 55 for Dr. W. R. Roberts, friend of both Harvey Burdell and Emma Cunningham. Dr. Maine found Mrs. Cunningham "upon the sofa," he said, and "the eldest daughter upon a chair, leaning upon a large trunk . . . the youngest daughter lay partly across the bed, and appeared to be in great agony." In Dr. Maine's opinion, she truly was "in a state of actual fainting, in a state of syncope," which my big dictionary says is "a partial or complete temporary suspension of respiration and circulation," and he loosened her corset.

He thought Mrs. Cunningham "very excitable and agitated; she had a sort of hysterical action as if she felt very bad," and—giving us a clue to his own age possibly—Stephen Maine said of a thirty-five-year-old woman, "The old lady was exclaiming [in a curious phrasing, if these are really her words], 'He is dead, and I always liked him, and thought a great deal of him!' "

But Maine "thought her 'fainting' differing from the others," and now when Emma Cunningham asked him the cause of Harvey Burdell's death, he decided not to tell her. "I knew he was killed," Maine said, "from observing his wounds," but what he told her was that Burdell had burst a blood vessel, causing a hemorrhage; I suppose he wanted to hear her reaction. "She said she was so glad to know that was the case, for she supposed that he was murdered or killed, adding at the same time that Hannah had told her that he was murdered, or had given her that idea. . . ."

More excited running around: Hannah, with the same idea as Snodgrass, ran out to go get Dr. Roberts. He was sleeping late this morning, having been at the Academy of Music last night; they got him up, then the three of them hurried along Bond through a rainstorm. Dr. Roberts climbed the stairs to the Doctor's office, and saw Dr. Maine and the neighbor standing at the door with Maine's student, and Snodgrass sent John Burchell running over to Fourth Street for Dr. Allen Smith, friend and former partner of Burdell's.

And so it went. Dr. Roberts arrived, to stare down at his dead friend, then went up to Emma Cunningham's room, where he found her "crying, and the first remark I think I heard her make was that if the Doctor was dead, she could not live. . . ." Awkwardly, as it seems to me, "I told her that if he was dead it could not be helped." Her reply mystified him: "She made a remark then, 'You don't know the secret.' . . ." The doctor helped Snodgrass lay her on the bed, and went back downstairs to the murder room.

Dr. Maine returned with three cops, a couple of whom had been here before, fetched from Broadway by Harvey Burdell during battles with Mrs. Cunningham. Now one of the cops went right back to the station house to report to Captain Dilk that Burdell had died of a broken blood vessel. Dilk telegraphed this to the coroner's office, where the afternoon papers picked it up.

Daniel Ullman finally got up from his bed, then stood in the bloody office staring at what lay on the floor. Dr. Burdell, the lawyer cautiously decided, was "evidently" dead.

More people hurrying into the house: a dentist cousin of Burdell's named Maguire; a Dr. Knight; a Dr. Francis, sixty-seven years old, which means he was born in 1790, while Washington was President, and who knew why he was called *physician:* "I have been in the practice of physic for 47 years."

Maguire found Emma Cunningham "moaning quite loudly," saying, " 'This is a horrible affair.' " Her daughter, too, "was on the sofa moaning," but Maguire "did not know if [Emma Cunningham's] moaning was sincere; it struck me that it was not," and he left the room.

And then . . . Edward Downes Connery—Coroner Connery—arrived, bringing his son, who was also his assistant, and 31 Bond turned into a different place. Almost immediately, legally or not, Connery made the house a prison for some of its inmates. Thirty-one Bond became a source of sensational news, shouted through the streets every day for weeks; crisscrossing the country by telegraph; moving across the oceans by ship. And finally the house at 31 Bond became a place of inquisition as strange and at times demented as anything yet in Emma Cunningham's life.

They searched the dead man's pockets, finding his watch stopped at 5:54; some "coppers and silver," one of the cops tells us, the silver being "six-pences, shillings, or quarters." Dr. Maine had already seen a big bunch of keys on Harvey Burdell's desk, and now they found still more in his pockets: a key to the safe at the other end of the room, a night-latch key to the house, and others. Keys, keys, keys: it sounds right for this man. Connery's son, John, then brought out his knife, slit the dead man's sleeves and pant legs, and ripped up the backs of his coat and undergarments. Then Drs. Maine and Francis pulled the stiff and bloody clothes off, and Harvey Burdell lay face up and naked now, and, said Maine, they saw "marks of redness around the neck. All of us spoke of that when we were examining [the body]. It was not done with a cord but something larger; we took it to be with his neck handkerchief. He was choked, for his tongue protruded." Dr. Francis "thought of garroting, but said nothing."

The doctors studied the many stab wounds; counted them; probed their depths and measured their widths with instruments Dr. Knight had brought. They speculated on the kind of weapon, and on how the murder had been done. Then Dr. Maine went out to the hall with one of the cops, Davis, and they examined and noted the locations of the bloody marks there, down the length of the staircase, and a bloody print on the inside of the street door just over the lock.

Again Dr. Roberts went up to Emma Cunningham's room, this time to tell her that Harvey Burdell had been murdered. ". . . it was a very solemn time," he said. "I felt very bad to see an old friend cut up so." And now, to the astonished Roberts, Emma Cunningham revealed her secret: she was the dead man's widow.

4

By mid-afternoon of the same day the coroner had impaneled a full jury of twelve men: where and how he got them that fast I don't know. The inquest began immediately, and it was held right here in the house, at number 31 Bond. What's more, Coroner Connery held it in the very blood-spattered room in which the murder was done. They simply picked up the naked corpse, carried it into the front bedroom next door, and laid it out on the bed, "where it presented a ghastly appearance," the New

York *Tribune* reporter thought. Then they brought in chairs for the jury, and swore in John Burchell, the boy who a few hours earlier had opened the door of the room he now sat in, the blood he'd seen then and saw now still not entirely dry.

Outside the house the wind pushed down the long north–south streets, flinging the rain, freezing it. Some pedestrians fell on slick new ice, signs blew down, window shutters ripped loose. Presently the wind subsided, the temperature rising, and then: "At the street crossings the rain and melted snow formed lakes varying from six inches to two feet deep. Along side streets the water rushed like a torrent. . . ." It flooded basements, and drove rats out onto "Washington-street, South-street, the docks and the markets. . . ." Horses strained and slipped, and the cars of the "Sixth and Eighth-avenue Railroad Companies," whose tracks had been scattered with salt, were pulled through foot-deep water, causing waves. At unflooded street crossings "enterprising boys with dilapidated brooms" swept the broad crossing-stones clear for pedestrians, to earn tips.

Up in the murder room I'm sure a fire had been lighted—or possibly rekindled from the fire the Doctor himself had lighted only last night. And Coroner Connery, who spoke with some remnant of an Irish brogue, questioned the boy in the dental chair. Who told them what had happened here this morning, but—only a boy, and I assume terribly excited—forgot to mention John Eckel's unusually early departure. Dentist Allen Smith testified to "angry words" he'd overheard in this house, and to some of Harvey Burdell's complaints. Dr. Roberts, old friend and frequent visitor here that he was, said he knew practically nothing.

About one o'clock a message reached John Eckel at his Stanton Street place, brought by "a boy," his bookkeeper recalled, saying that "a man was dead at his place of residence . . . and Mr. Eckel was requested to come home immediately . . . Eckel seemed much surprised. . . ." Surprised, but when he'd left the house that morning there'd been three men still there: Snodgrass, Ullman, and Burdell. Yet now, as the bookkeeper recalled it, he did not ask which of the three was dead.

He knew nothing at all of the murder, he told the inquest: had heard nothing all night; never heard anyone threaten Dr. Burdell; and: "That is all I know of the matter." Eckel was dismissed, and back at work within a couple of hours.

Several doctors testified on what they'd found here, then Connery declared a recess, and had some cops search the house. They found plenty. On the floor of an attic room, in a heap of ladies' clothes, a bloody shirt mysteriously marked "Charles J. Ketcham." More blood: on a sheet, a towel, a floor matting. In the room of one of the Cunningham girls, a

56

newspaper, dry now but bloody. In this empty attic room, in which Mary
Donaho had been told to
lay a fire, and through
the window of which Dr.
Parmly thought he had
seen fire last night, they
found ashes in that grate
and scraps of woolen cloth.
Still more blood on the
door handle and keyhole,
looking to a reporter "as
if rubbed by a bloody
hand." And in one of Mrs.

Cunningham's bureau drawers they found a loaded revolver and this
dagger, also bloody, said the reporter. So the prospects looked good for
solving the murder when Coroner
Connery and the jury
reassembled; and when Hannah
Conlon began to talk, they looked still better. Sitting under the gaslight
of Dr. Burdell's office, this "genuine-looking Irish girl," which is a reporter's description, told Connery, jury, and the reporters who took down
her account what she suspected of relations between Emma Cunningham
and John Eckel . . . of overheard disputes and accusations . . . of the
Thanksgiving Day miscarriage. She told of being sent early to bed last
night, and other nights; of Eckel's departure before breakfast this morning
. . . "I know no more," she finished, "If I did I would tell it if I was to
go to the gallows for it."

Time now to hear from Mrs. Cunningham. Who showed her usual
determination and propensity to blunder by refusing to come down or
testify. Connery hit the roof, and sent a cop up for her, threatening to have
her dragged down by the collar.

"Mrs. Cunningham presently appeared. She seemed to be very much
moved by the strangeness of her position and the horrid nature of the
events which had transpired beneath her roof." She "shed tears copiously," and was dressed "in black, and wore a fur cape negligently around
her shoulders. . . . Her face is oval, high cheek bones, and slightly sunken
cheeks. Thin, firm lips would seem to indicate decision and firmness of
character. Her bust is full, and her figure good for her age; medium height.
Her face, as a whole, is not handsome, and yet she is prepossessing when
animated; her voice is soft and low, and under favorable circumstances,
she would be an attractive woman. In her distressing situation, her counte-

57

nance only wore an overwhelming expression of wretchedness."

"Your name is Mrs. Emma Augusta Cunningham," said Connery, and she dropped her bombshell.

"My name is Emma Augusta Burdell. I am the wife of the deceased."

"How is that? Your friends say your name is Cunningham."

"I can establish by satisfactory proof that I am the lawful wife of Dr. Burdell," she said, and then explained things.

Yes, Harvey Burdell had accused her of stealing a note, but it wasn't true. Yes, they'd also had other quarrels: about his failure at first to keep his promise of marriage, about females he brought into the house; but she knew nothing about his murder. True, she had spoken to Hannah last night, but not to send her early to bed; she had merely "asked her if she was nearly done with her work. I told her what to get for breakfast. . . ." She'd heard nothing all night, couldn't say who'd killed Harvey Burdell, and she brought out and handed over the certificate attesting to her marriage on October 28, signed by a minister of the Dutch Reformed Church, Uriah Marvine. Why hadn't she mentioned this marriage before? Because she and Harvey had decided to keep it secret till June.

That was enough for one day. Connery adjourned till tomorrow, and sent the jurymen home. Hannah Conlon he placed under arrest as a material witness and, unable to put up $1,000 bail, she was led off to Captain Dilk's Fifteenth Ward station house, and locked in a cell. Emma Cunningham was placed under house arrest, and cops were stationed throughout the house.

The two girls and the little boys stayed with their mother. Eckel came home presently, and I don't know whether Snodgrass had ever left. And so, except for Ullman and Hannah, and with the additions of the cops on guard, the house was left again to the same inmates as the night before, Harvey Burdell now motionless on his bed.

What could that evening have been like? Mrs. Cunningham and her daughters were surely allowed to come downstairs to put together a supper for themselves, the boys, and possibly the two men. What did they say, what did each think, moving up and down the bloody staircase, passing the door behind which the Doctor lay? A cluster of people stood across the street, word that the death here was murder having spread through the compact city by word of mouth. Did the Cunninghams move the drawn blinds of their rooms to peek out and down at the people standing before Drs. Parmly's and Maine's houses, staring over here to catch a glimpse of them? Did their eyes meet for a moment?

That same evening Eckel and George Snodgrass were taken to the Fifteenth Precinct station house, as witnesses, and locked in a cell near Hannah Conlon. She saw them come in, and remarked to Eckel that "it was too bad to lock me up for no cause," but got no sympathy; it was too bad for him, too, said Eckel. Hannah said she was sorry she'd ever come to 31 Bond.

Only one cell away from the men, Hannah sat hearing them talk, not paying much attention or feeling like talking herself, she said, but she noticed they didn't seem very upset. "In my opinion they seemed to be very happy. They seemed to have no trouble in their minds for being there. I only wished I could have felt so happy. They didn't seem to be down-hearted at all at being locked up there. I didn't like to be locked up there." Resentfully, it sounds, Hannah said, "Mr. Snodgrass appeared to laugh and sing the whole night. Mr. Eckel didn't sing, but he laughed. Snodgrass *hollered* at me, and asked me how I liked being there. I felt very bad to be there, and was very sorry for the deceased. I said how could they be so merry. Snodgrass asked me what there was to be sorry for. I said on account of the murder of Dr. Burdell. . . . After a while he stopped [singing]."

Daniel Ullman sat in the front parlor of 31 Bond that evening talking to the police. During this the undertakers arrived, and went on upstairs. I don't know whether they did any sort of embalming, but they'd come to make the corpse presentable. Soon after they arrived, Mrs. Cunningham sent word down to Ullman that she wanted to see him. He went up to her room, and "she asked me if she could not be permitted to direct the manner in which Dr. Burdell should be dressed. That she did not wish him to have a shroud, but to be dressed in his usual clothes. She seemed to be greatly agitated and excited; she said that he was hers, alive or dead. She hoped that I would speak to the undertakers."

At the jail, said Hannah, "Snodgrass sung out to me in the night if I was asleep. I said I could not sleep, I was cold and wet," which meant, I suppose, that she'd been walked to the station house in the rain.

In the morning Ullman packed and moved out of 31 Bond forever, taking a room at the St. Nicholas on Broadway. On the same morning a cop, stationed here in the house, came to Mrs. Cunningham's room, and offered a word of advice: Stop talking about the murder.

Newsboys were out with the Sunday papers and the news that Harvey Burdell—a prominent man—had been murdered. And by afternoon: "The street in the neighborhood of the house was crowded with persons attracted thither by curiosity, but who were denied admission. The hall and staircase were also thronged by those, who obtaining admittance were unable to proceed any further. The room in which the examination was held was filled to its capacity by lawyers, reporters, and acquaintances of the deceased man. . . . A. Oakey Hall, Esq., was present. . . ."

This was the district attorney, here perhaps at the coroner's request; or, with a politician's instinct for what's big, here on his own. For A. Oakey Hall was a politician above all else, well known here and now, and to become notorious in a decade or so when Thomas Nast, greatest political cartoonist of all, began endlessly caricaturing Hall in *Harper's Weekly,* along with Boss Tweed and the others of the infamous Tweed Ring.

Also here in the crowded room were Mrs. Cunningham's lawyer, B. C. Thayer, and a new man, attorney Henry L. Clinton. These two were "employed as counsel for all the defendants," and whoever brought in Henry Clinton made a smart move. For Clinton was a formidable lawyer, as he would gradually demonstrate, and Eckel and Emma Cunningham needed just that. The *Times,* calling them "defendants," had picked the right word: Coroner Edward Connery almost immediately revealed that in his mind and ambition this inquest was really a trial, that he knew Eckel and Mrs. Cunningham were guilty, and was going to prove it.

Did Harvey Burdell really marry Emma Cunningham? That was the first question in Connery's mind, and he immediately subpoenaed this man to find out about that. He is the Reverend Mr. Marvine, and he took

the stand now, at two-thirty Sunday afternoon. Marvine turned out to be as Dickensian as his first name: a Uriah Bumble, a Mr. Addlepate. Whom had he married on October 28?

"A person came to me," Dr. Marvine replied carefully, "calling himself Burdell." Helpfully he added, "I married him to a lady." Would he recognize the man? "I might. . . ."

They took him into the bedroom, and Marvine stood beside the mahogany bedstead looking down at the pale, drained face, its eyes closed; stood for some time, but could not recognize in it the living face of the man he had married. "The Coroner then had Mrs. Cunningham brought into the room, and again asked the minister the question as to the marriage. He scanned her features, but said he could not positively recognize her or the deceased." During the conversation between the frustrated coroner and the minister, "Mrs. Cunningham gazed at the deceased, and became much affected—her tears flowing copiously. Stooping, she took the cold hand of the deceased and kissed it, when she was led from the room by the officer."

Captain Dilk had converted a back room on the second floor into a holding cell for witnesses, and now they brought in a young med student who'd known Burdell, and had been in and out of the house.

He didn't have much to tell them except that he'd never heard Mrs. Cunningham referred to as Mrs. Burdell. But now the coroner left the narrow path of his official function, expanding the inquiry into matters, and in a way, that soon got him into trouble.

"Did you know that improper conduct was going on in this house?"

"I had very strong suspicions. . . ."

"Did you not know that there was a certain intimacy, a *matter of congress* [the paper set that in italics] between Mr. Eckel and Mrs. Cunningham?"

But the young man "did not suspect it."

A bit later: "By the virtue of your solemn oath, do you think this is a regular, moral virtuous house?"

"I had suspicion that something wrong was going on between Mrs. Cunningham and Dr. Burdell."

This kind of dirty talk worried one of the jurors, who spoke up to ask whether evidence like this "of a very delicate nature" ought to be published in the newspapers.

More witnesses, including ex-landlady Margaret Jones. "A portion of the evidence of this witness relative to the miscarriage of Mrs. Cunningham," the *Times* told its readers, "was unfit for publication."

It was Sunday night, the coroner had got nowhere, so he adjourned till ten in the morning, and now the undertakers went to work. In the matter of dress they seem to have followed Mrs. Cunningham's request of the night before. For: "The corpse of the deceased, attired in a new suit of black, was placed in a handsome rosewood coffin, with silver mountings, and lined with white satin. A black cravat and high short collar concealed the wounds in the throat. The cuts in the face were very visible. On a silver plate on the coffin lid" was engraved an inscription. When the undertakers had finished, artist Brightly of *Frank Leslie's Illustrated Newspaper* was allowed in to sketch the result of their work.

This is what he saw as he stood in the doorway between Dr. Burdell's

office and bedroom, sketch pad and pencil in hand. Then he walked on in, stopped at the foot of the coffin, and drew this.

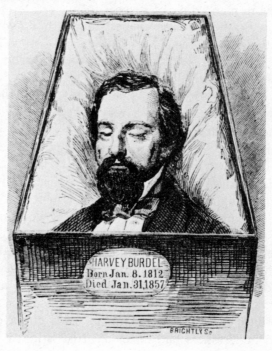

5

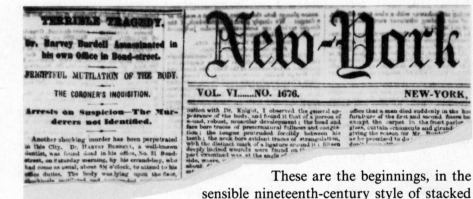

These are the beginnings, in the sensible nineteenth-century style of stacked

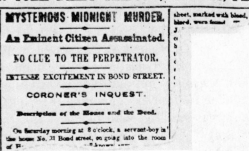

headings that summarized at a glance these two great dailies' coverage of a story that would run for months. But *Times* and *Trib* were two days late: already in type Saturday when this biggest story of years broke, and with no Sunday editions. It must have been frustrating to their editors, hearing newsboys peddling rival papers that weekend, but they made up for it; their reporters seem hardly to have slept during those two days, talking to everyone they could discover who had anything to add or thought he did.

On Monday they were ready, their stories beginning with the headings you've seen, and to continue thereafter in a remarkable daily coverage, the *Times* occasionally printing full-newspaper-size supplements containing nothing but pages of spillover. I certainly haven't counted, but *Times* and *Tribune* must have printed millions of words on the Burdell case; or so I believe, having read them all in the countless columns it finally took to tell the story whose eventual ramifications those editors didn't yet even imagine. Big columns, too, wider than today's, and on larger pages. The only thing smaller was the type.

On this same day, before resuming the inquest, Coroner Connery invited everyone—jurors and reporters, too—to join him in again searching the house, and I'm glad he did. Because although the *Times* of Tuesday treated the result a little contemptuously, both the *Tribune* man and I thought what they found was pretty interesting.

"In the room of Mr. Snodgrass," said the *Trib* man, "his clothes were hanging upon the wall, and a couple of bronze statuettes stood on the drawers. There was no washbowl. The bed was in a very topsy-turvy state —bolsters and pillows being mixed with feminine underclothes in the greatest confusion. The drawers—all but one—were filled with all sorts of knick-knacks, articles of feminine wearing apparel. A dozen or so replies to the party given [by Mrs. Cunningham on Augusta's birthday in January] on the 14th were mixed up with the rest. On a piece of paper were these lines traced in a delicate hand [Helen's, I suspect, and I'm grateful the *Tribune* man took the trouble to copy them]:
" 'What would the rose, with all her pride, be worth,
Were there no Sun to call her brightness forth?
Maidens unloved, like flowers in darkness thrown,
Want but that light, which comes from Love alone.' "
Downstairs on the piano in the front parlor the search party found "a little lulu book [Don't ask] entitled The Boat Builder, published in 1852 . . . 'Miss Georgiana A. Cunningham, 10 years old and 3,900 days,' was written on the fly leaf in a child's hand. The leaf containing the 79th and 80th pages was cut out; blood was visible on the edge of the leaf not cut off. The two leaves containing the 91st to 94th pages were torn out; the 95th was smeared with blood. These three leaves were the only leaves missing." As the *Times* man said, "Scarcely anything of importance . . . can be attached to this discovery," but the *Tribune* man knew what we wanted, and found some more: "A few blotches on the walls of the

rooms, and along the halls, some of them as high as one can easily reach, evidently produced by killing mosquitoes or other insects, attracted considerable attention."

Some cops arrived from the station house with Eckel and Snodgrass, Connery had them taken up to a second-floor room, and the two men were made to strip in the presence of Dr. George Woodward, the assistant coroner, and another witness. This was to see if they had any marks or bruises consistent with having been "engaged in the fearful tragedy of Friday night." They hadn't.

In his zeal the coroner then did something really dumb: he had Emma Cunningham examined. According to the *Tribune* she was forced to strip, too, by the same witnesses. "Why Mrs. Cunningham was compelled to submit to so degrading an examination at hands of men when there were a dozen ladies in the house competent to perform this duty, we cannot conceive. No marks of any kind were found. . . ."

Cousin Demis Hubbard arrived, "and the scene of her visit . . . to the coffin of the murdered man was enough to wring tears from a heart hard enough to take the life of such a man as her gashed and scarred relative lying before her."

A busy morning, and now—it was cold today, the murder room chilly—Connery moved the inquest here to the first-floor back parlor, and

we get a little further view of the interior of 31 Bond. They moved in tables and chairs for reporters, in the foreground and at left; chairs for jurors by the windows; and next day carried down the Doctor's dentist chair. In the later view, on the previous page, you can see it.

Today it was George Snodgrass to the stand first, and he sat for a long time answering the coroner's questions about how he'd come to live here, how well he knew the Cunninghams, what he could say about relations between Emma Cunningham and the Doctor, and between her and Eckel, and what everyone had done the night of the murder and the morning after.

He said nothing harmful to Emma Cunningham, Eckel, or himself; as for the bloody shirt marked "Ketcham" found in the attic, that was "mine, Sir," Snodgrass told them. He'd borrowed it when staying with a friend on Twenty-third Street, whose name and address he provided. Here at home he'd tossed it into a storeroom for washing, as he did with all his soiled linen. The small marks of blood it showed must have been picked up from clothes already there.

Once in answer to a question about who had told him something or other, Snodgrass answered, "Miss Helen Cunningham," and a reporter said, "The tone and manner of the witness in pronouncing this name— a tone which told the tenderness he could not hide—immediately enlisted sympathy in his behalf." He was later asked, "Did you think . . . that if you could marry one of [the Cunningham girls], you would do it?" And "Mr. Snodgrass's face grew very red."

Smith Ely, Jr., "in the hide and leather business," confirmed that he'd left a note for Eckel on Friday evening arranging a business meeting Saturday morning; which did seem to explain Eckel's leaving early, even if somewhat earlier than necessary.

If Connery was trying to pin the murder on Eckel and Emma Cunningham—and he was, as he would thoroughly demonstrate—he wasn't getting anywhere today. But a juryman had an idea. "A juror then stated that it had been demonstrated in France that the object last seen by the deceased would be found impressed on the retina of the eye, and that it would be well to have an oculist or some other competent person make that examination in this case.

"The Coroner had no objection at all.

"The District-Attorney said that . . . he had got a friend to make certain observations to test the theory, but the result did not increase his faith in the theory. All these experiments, however, were worth trying."

Everybody up to the murder room then, reporters included, and they searched Dr. Burdell's desk and safe, finding nothing useful.

Up to Eckel's room, where they unlocked his "secretoire" and "found in a large envelope various papers endorsed in Burdell's hand 'private papers.' " Among these: Harvey Burdell's affidavit that he had never made a will up to October 8, 1856, "and that if he had made such a will it was a forgery," as the *Trib* put it; in Burdell's handwriting a release from Mrs. Cunningham of all claims she might have against him, but unsigned. And Emma Cunningham's lease on the house; her note to Burdell, signed last September, "for $109 for ninety days"; and the famous paper in which Dr. Burdell promised Emma Cunningham his friendship for life.

One thing they didn't find—hadn't found in the dead man's pockets, and didn't find now in his room, his office, his safe, or anywhere else—was the lease which in May would have transferred this house from Emma Cunningham to Mrs. Stansbury, and which he'd said would be ready for signing on the morning he was found murdered.

Mary Donaho was called to the stand, and in his excitement over what she now told them, Connery began making remarks that added up to the worst mistake of his career. As Mary sat there in the back parlor, which she'd probably dusted more than once, talking about quarrels she'd heard in this house . . . of the night Dr. Burdell had rushed out to bring back the police . . . of the hullabaloo the night he was locked out . . . of her suspicions about the conduct of Eckel and Mrs. Cunningham, Coroner Connery couldn't prevent his pleasure and bias from showing.

Examples: When Mary described how she and Hannah had been sent early and mysteriously to bed, Connery cried, "Aha!" When she referred to Eckel's canaries, Connery said, "Yes, he was a bird himself!" getting a laugh. Mary said she'd never seen Emma Cunningham in the Doctor's room at an "improper hour," but Connery interjected, "I don't know about that; propriety don't depend on an hour. . . ."

And then the coroner popped out the remark that would dog him for months. Had Mrs. Cunningham ever threatened the Doctor? Yes, said Mary, ". . . she said it was time he was out of the world, for he was not fit to live in it . . ." and in his elation Connery cried, "I knew, Mary, I knew that you carried your tail behind you, by gracious!" Undoubtedly poor Edward Connery knew what he meant by that and that he meant it harmlessly, but no one else seemed to understand it, and it didn't sound like a proper remark. Once he got started, the excited coroner didn't stop. When Mary apparently spoke too fast or confusedly, Connery said, "Tell it easy, Mary," nodding at the reporters busy taking it down, "they want to get it. Those men are not going to annoy you. Some of them are old stale bachelors, and their hearing is bad. If you asked one of them to kiss you, he wouldn't hear it. (Laughter) Go on, now, and tell it out." When Mary quoted Eckel's breakfast-table remark that he'd like to string up Dr.

Burdell, Connery cried, "Aha! Good for him!"

Mary said Helen Cunningham had told her of looking through a keyhole and seeing Eckel leave her mother's room "not dressed as he should have been."

"Dressed in a state of Nature, like Timon of Athens?" said the now irrepressible coroner, getting a laugh, and it took a juror to straighten out what Mary meant: "With his nightgown on, you mean?" and Mary said yes.

This kind of goofy remark, which he continued for days after, made Connery suddenly famous or at least talked about throughout the city. Artist Brightly got a Mathew Brady ambrotype, and from it drew this portrait of Connery. I think that's an amiable face, and I think Connery

comes through the years and old print as a likable man in spite of his deficient sense of constitutional rights and his bad jokes: a very human man. And in spite of the *Times*'s increasing criticism of Connery from this day on, I think someone on that paper liked him, too: for in a story headed *"Who is Coroner Connery?"* they said:

"People are asking eagerly about the antecedents of Coroner Connery, who by his singular mode of conducting the Bond-street investigations, and queer, classical jests, has forced himself so suddenly and prominently upon public attention. Edward Downes Connery is somewhere in the vicinity of 50 years of age. He is an Irishman by birth, and though he has resided in this City the past twenty years, still retains a rich and resonant Irish brogue, which he always delivers with a startling emphasis. His r's are peculiarly emphatic and thrilling. He is married and the father of a large family. He is about the medium height, stout build, and of florid complexion [which the portrait doesn't suggest, to me]. He practices medicine at times, and is a good printer, we presume, from the fact that he formerly superintended the job-printing department of the *Herald*. . . ." He had been elected coroner two years earlier, said the *Times*, "ahead of his ticket by a great many votes. . . .

"Dr. Connery is a general favorite," the *Times* man continued, "being regarded by all who know him best as 'a jolly fellow, and good company, always fond of a joke,' which, as those who have read the pending Burdell investigation well know, he never fails to crack, be it good or bad, and upon all and every occasion.

"The Doctor, too, is up in his classics, as no one who ever had five minutes' conversation with him, can for a moment doubt.

"He is always ready with an extempore speech, many of which he delivered in the suburbs during the last campaign, to crowds of the unter-rified.

"In a word, E. Downes Connery is E. Downes Connery, and walks a little lame."

"The City is in a fever of excitement. Nothing is talked of or apparently thought of except the murder," said the *Tribune*, "and from a few hours' observation one would reasonably conclude that the entire adult population had resolved themselves into an immense Coroner, with a million sleepless eyes and five hundred thousand tireless tongues, each . . . having no other earthly function than to search out the perpetrators. . . ."

But the *Tribune* seemed to think this great public coroner needed guidance in reaching a decision, and they provided it. "It has been ascertained," they said, referring not to any testimony yet heard but merely to some gossip their man had picked up, "that on the morning when the murder was discovered, Mr. Eckel left the house at an early and unusual hour [and] Mrs. Cunningham followed in a carriage, and he stood talking with her half an hour or more at the carriage door, opposite his factory. He was seen to give her a roll of bills. This transpired before breakfast." No speculation about why, if the lady in the carriage were Mrs. Cunningham, Eckel hadn't simply handed over the money at home.

"The head waiter of Mr. Peteler, the confectioner," they continued, said that "Mr. Eckel, for several months past, was in the daily habit of visiting the establishment of Mr. Peteler, where he used to meet a lady whom he, the waiter, considered to be one of the nymphs of the pavé, about noon, and partaking of refreshments with her." This time it was the lady, said the waiter, who would slip Eckel the money to pay the bill.

In contrast to Eckel, Dr. Harvey Burdell had been an honorary member of the Philadelphia Medical Society, member of both the city and county medical societies, and of the New-York Historical and Statistical Society, a director of the Artisans' Bank, a prominent and well-to-do member of the dental profession, and coauthor of a book on dentistry published by Scathard & Adams, the same Adams who was later "murdered by John C. Colt in the house situated at the corner of Chambers and Broadway now occupied by Delmonico," this industrious reporter added.

69

The *Tribune* was Horace Greeley's paper, and I hope he paid that man well; on this kind of supplementary stuff the *Trib* usually left the *Times* at the post.

Burdell's reputation was apparently impeccable, but of Emma Cunningham, whose "maiden name was Hempstead . . . It is reported that she has lived in Twenty-Fifth-street in this city, in Saratoga and elsewhere, under the name of Mrs. Cunningham, Mrs. Gatouse, and Mrs. Douglass. Strange stories are told of the character of her establishments; but"—a nice touch—"such rumors are not sufficiently well grounded to warrant their publication. That she went to Dr. Burdell's house in the capacity of his mistress is obvious. . . ."

Harvey Burdell had "several cousins," the busy *Tribune* man or men had discovered, "one of whom—a fine, hearty, good-looking young lady," he said admiringly (surely my girl, Demis), "was very warmly attached to the Doctor, and very familiar with him, and frequently interchanged visits. She was at the house on Friday afternoon before the murder, and heard his expressions of disgust toward the woman who now claims to be his widow. . . ."

The *Tribune* also informed the great public coroner that "Dr. Burdell met Mrs. Cunningham and her daughters at Saratoga, and as he had been acquainted with her husband, and as she was a widow and engaged in the usual business of Saratoga widows, it was not hard to make her acquaintance. It is not impossible," the *Tribune* man speculated, "that as he had no very exalted opinion of female virtue, he may have made proposals of marriage or something else." Later, the *Trib* man said, "the widow met with such a mishap as widows have met before. . . ."

Unnamed friends, the *Tribune* continued, "are very emphatic in their declarations that he never could have married Mrs. Cunningham, and that the whole affair was a fraud—a plot with someone to represent himself as Dr. Burdell, so as to enable her to claim a portion of his property as his widow. . . ." Who this someone might have been the *Tribune* didn't say, but did suggest that Eckel's "associations, both male and female, have . . . been of the kind to initiate him into [iniquity]. His female correspondence found in his trunk is most scandalous. A few months ago, when he used to be in the habit of visiting a certain Broadway restaurant in company with a woman from Georgia, his hair and whiskers were thin and light-colored. The man that was married to Mrs. Cunningham had dark whiskers, and some of Mr. Eckel's former acquaintances are surprised to find that his turned dark about the same time. . . ."

As for George Snodgrass, "the wild son of a respectable minister

. . . it is evident that this youth is very much enamored of one of the Cunningham girls, and scandal says that if there is not a secret marriage between them, there ought to be. A free supply of her toilet articles and garments found in his bedroom is thought to afford evidence in this respect. . . ." Play that on your banjo, George.

The supplies for Mrs. Cunningham's party of January 14 "have not yet been paid for—the lady promising that when her rents came in, from the 1st to the 10th of February, she would have plenty of money. It is said that these rents are as mythical as the hundred thousand dollars worth of property which the same woman represented herself to Dr. Burdell to be worth. This Mr. Eckel"—the obsessed reporter continued without pause or paragraph—"seems to have been, if nothing more, a very proper companion for that class of man about town of whom Dr. Thrasher Lyons was a living example. His position in this family is not exactly defined, but it certainly appears to have been a free and easy one." Thrasher Lyons was a name in the recent news—and a splendid name for this—because of his many affairs with women.

All this pretty well took care of everyone at 31 Bond but the servants and Eckel's canaries—except for Daniel Ullman. But Ullman was a practicing attorney, had been a nearly successful candidate for governor of New York, and the *Tribune* handled him with care. ". . . though it appears that the Hon. Daniel Ullman had a room in the house . . . he cannot, of course, be expected to throw any light on the subject."

The *Trib* wrapped things up by offering its citywide jury a choice of motives: ". . . feelings of enmity independent of getting possession of [Burdell's] property might be a sufficient inducement for unprincipled people to take a fellow-creature's life, particularly if it could be done in a quiet way with the garrote, so that his body could be hung up and represented as that of a suicide. If this was the intent, the unexpected resistance and overpowering of the garroter, so as to require a resort to the dagger frustrated the plan. . . ."

Or the motive might have been vengeance by "a most vindictive rascal" who "swore that if he lived to get out of prison he would be revenged. . . ." This referred to a Sing Sing prisoner convicted of a forgery by Dr. Burdell's persistence. Had he finished his term, and returned to the city? the *Tribune* wondered.

Or maybe—and by now I think the *Trib* was reaching—the murderer was one of the guests at Emma Cunningham's party in January because: "It is charged by public rumor that bad women and worse men were among the guests; and the same busy tongue charges that Mrs. Cunningham's antecedents are not such as belong to a strictly virtuous woman. . . ."

Finally the *Tribune* warned its readers that they must not prejudge these people, because "we repeat that nothing yet developed tends to implicate any individual sufficient to warrant detention for trial."

The *Times* took it a little easier, though what they said about the people of 31 Bond Street would give a present-day libel lawyer fits. In the village where young Snodgrass grew up, they said, he "never established a reputation for remarkable steadiness of demeanor, or refinement or delicacy of sentiment; in fact was looked upon by the village as a young gentleman whom sharp discipline would benefit."

And "Emma Augusta Hempstead in her youth was remarkable chiefly foi a well-developed, voluptuous form, and more than ordinary powers of fascination. She drew within her toils Mr. George D. Cunningham who . . . some years ago abandoned his legal spouse . . . and connected himself with Miss Hempstead." When his wife finally died, "Miss Hempstead, with her offspring, several in number, of which he was the reputed father, again domiciled herself with him." Three years later he died "in a fit," and "it became known that the life of the deceased had been insured for $10,000, which fact, connected with other facts, caused considerable speculation at the time.

"With the death of Mr. Cunningham, the validity of the claim Miss Emma Hempstead made to his effects was discussed, and she then as now produced a marriage certificate to substantiate such a claim. Many of Mr. C.'s friends had heard him say that he was not married. But others had heard him relate how he was married while intoxicated, and was not aware of the fact until the next day when the evidence of it was placed before his eyes. He, it would seem, did not trouble himself much about it afterwards. Mrs. C., released from her alleged tie by death, and with $10,000 at her command, was lost sight of by the public until Saturday last."

Letters had been coming in to the *Times*. ". . . The case of Dr. H. Burdell is one in which an investigation of the last impression on the inner coat of the eye ought to be thoroughly made . . ." wrote J. H. A. Graham.

Mr. W. D. Porter wrote to say that "several months ago—or just after the murder of Burke—I published in the New-York Herald a method of detecting murders by an examination of the *eye of the person murdered.* I have also addressed several other letters to the Herald on the same subject, which that paper has not published. If Dr. Burdell's murder took place at any time when the room was lit by gas, or by daylight, pass the eyes of Dr. Burdell through the process recommended by me, and the image of the murderer will be seen in the eye—much more perfect than any daguerrotype. Yours truly."

"The juryman's suggestion about the retina of the eye was a good one," wrote "Detector," "but the best way to arrive at the truth is to call up Dr. Burdell's spirit and get him to name his murderers at once. . . ."

Down on Bond Street today, Tuesday, more than a thousand people crowded the walks and streets before number 31, the *Times* judged; even more people than yesterday. The back parlor where the inquest was about to resume was crowded with "many doctors and chemists . . . in attendance to learn the result of the proposed examination of the eyes of the murdered man, and of the blood on the sheets, [Ketcham's] shirt, and the towels found in the store-room."

They began the resumed inquest with Burdell's work-boy, John Burchell, back on the stand to say all over again what had happened the morning he'd discovered the murdered Doctor; but also, this time, to be questioned about Eckel's unusual early departure that morning. John was small, like many a hardworking child of those times, I imagine, and the room was crowded: people couldn't see or hear him well, and it was now that they carried the operating chair down, and the "boy mounted it so that all could see him."

When they'd heard the boy, Coroner Connery made an announcement: an analysis would be made of the blood found on the clothing and sheets found in the attic; but: "The physicians with whom I have conversed upon the propriety of an examination of [Burdell's] eyes . . . all agree that the matter is a farce, that it will amount to nothing." One of the doctors then told the jurors that even if an image of the murderer had been retained in Harvey Burdell's eyes, "it would be impossible so long after death, in consequence of the opacity of the humors of the eye, to detect. . . ." Besides, they had no reason to think such an image had ever existed.

But some of the jurors didn't want to give up the attractive hope of a picture of the murderer's face lying like an undeveloped film inside Burdell's closed eyes upstairs; a couple of them said they didn't see any harm in trying to find it. But a difficulty occurred to a third juror. He said, "The question may arise if the image of a 'dear one' is not likely to be imprinted on the eye as of the person seen in the moment of death." That danger seemed to finish the discussion, and the doctors went upstairs—using Daniel Ullman's old room—to test for blood.

What they found was leaked to the papers that same day. The bloody

73

dagger found in Mrs. Cunningham's room wasn't bloody at all; the spots turned out to be rust. All of Eckel's and Emma Cunningham's clothes that could be found in the house, including boots and shoes, showed no trace of blood. The heap of soiled clothing, sheets, towels, and the like, including Ketcham's shirt (which I'll bet he never got back), was marked with blood spots, but they were "pronounced without hesitation of menstrual origin."

No blood on table cutlery, the marks on the little lulu book weren't blood either; no blood anywhere but in the murder room, the hall outside it, and the staircase down, and the smear on the downstairs door. If Emma Cunningham and John Eckel, and possibly George Snodgrass and maybe even Augusta, had murdered or helped in the murder of Harvey Burdell —as most of New York believed, and as Coroner Connery seemed certain —not a shred of hard evidence had yet been found to help prove it.

Connery kept hunting. While the doctors were making their tests, he had Cyrenius Stevens on the stand. Stevens had been taken to the station house to stare in at John Eckel in his cell, and now Connery tried to get him to say that he recognized Eckel as Van Dolan. But Stevens wouldn't quite do that; Eckel might be "Van Dolan," but he would not say for sure.

At one point while Stevens talked about a visit to Dr. Burdell, at which Burdell explained the innocent nature of Sophronia Stevens's visits, Connery cried, "Stop, Sir, was Mrs. Cunningham present?"

"She was not."

Up to his old tricks, Connery said, "Probably she was peeking through a crack, and having a view of the elephant. [Laughter]." To "see the elephant" was nineteenth-century slang for seeing the world, widening one's experience: a joke well up to Coroner Connery's usual standard.

A Mr. John T. Hildreth of Brooklyn, who was next, contributed absolutely nothing to Connery's search for the murderer, but I'm grateful anyway. He was "an impulsive gentleman," said one reporter correctly, "past middle age, wearing spectacles, and anxious to speak his mind. . . ."

"What do you know of Dr. Burdell's death?"

"Nothing but what I have read in the papers."

"Very important testimony!"

"I may have known Mrs. Cunningham in Brooklyn, if her name was Emma A. Hempstead . . . I knew her before she was married, and after, too—that is, if she ever was married, but I don't believe she was; she had the reputation of being a prostitute."

"Have you any reason for saying so?"

74

"I have a great many reasons for saying so. I know there was a difficulty with a certain gentleman in Brooklyn, who was likely to get into a scrape—"

"To whom was she married?"

"To Cunningham, the distiller."

"You see," said Connery, "I am a queer fellow: I can get something out of nothing after all. Her husband was a distiller?"

"Yes, a distiller; a manufacturer, as I call it, of liquid death."

"A man-u fact-tu rer of li-quid death?" Connery replied, getting his laugh, "I will put that down for the benefit of the Temperance Society."

"Put it down, it may do some good."

"How long was she married before his death took place?"

"I don't know."

"Did you hear that he died very suddenly?"

"I did, and I wish they would disinter his body, and examine it, for I believe he was murdered by his wife. I do think so, and have always thought so. She was a bad woman, and had no better example from her mother. Her father was as good a man as ever lived."

"How did you know she was so bad?"

"A lawyer in New York addressed a letter to a certain gentleman in Brooklyn," Hildreth explained confusedly, "threatening him unless he did something to retrieve her character. I went to that lawyer and told him he had got his head in the lion's mouth."

"Well, this amounts to nothing," the coroner finally decided.

But Hildreth, "getting more excited," said the *Times,* now said, "I have no doubt but that her marriage with Dr. Burdell is a fabrication."

A juror spoke up. "What evidence have you that Mrs. Cunningham was a prostitute?"

"I have many evidences; I have had bills of hers handed me in for collection—"

Connery cut him off: "Have you any proof she was a strumpet?"

"I believe her to have been as much so as ever Phoebe Doty was." (Sorry I can't help with the identification of Phoebe Doty, as fine a name for a strumpet as Thrasher Lyons for a roué.) "I have no regret," Hildreth added of Emma Cunningham's alleged strumpetry, "that I do not know it personally."

"Did you ever give her the wink yourself?" asked the unquenchable Connery.

"I can't say I ever did. . . . A gentleman told me," Hildreth went on, piling hearsay upon hearsay, "that he overheard a conversation between

Mrs. Cunningham and a man in which they were to meet in the evening on the corner of Nassau and Washington Streets, Brooklyn, at a certain time, and he was to take out his handkerchief as a signal."

"Who was the man?" a juror asked.

"It was not me."

"Gentlemen," said Connery to the jury, "this is not evidence; I must stop this here." He indicated a written summary of Hildreth's testimony: "Will you step up here, and sign this?"

"Is it my death warrant?"

"Yes, sir, your death warrant."

"And so," the *Times* said, "the witness was fitly put from the stand."

Sophronia Stevens described the same events her husband had. She, too, had been shown Eckel, sitting in his cell, and now Connery asked her if "by virtue of the solemn oath, Madam, which you have taken," she could identify him as "Van Dolan."

This time he got results: "Yes, sir, very much so," said Sophronia Stevens, and Connery adjourned for lunch.

After lunch, more hearsay on hearsay: a Seventeenth Ward cop said "a certain party down in Stanton Street" had seen Eckel hand Mrs. Cunningham a roll of bills as she sat there in a carriage the morning the murder was discovered. And then an actual witness: he lived on Stanton Street near Eckel's hides-and-fat business, and had actually seen Eckel hand over the money to the woman in the carriage. They whisked him right upstairs for a look at Emma Cunningham, brought him back, and now he told the jury that Mrs. Cunningham was not that woman.

"Was that lady tall or short?" said a juror.

"Short."

"Gaily dressed?"

"Rather."

"Was she alone or did she have a little boy?"

"She had a little boy."

"I know her very well," the juror said—surprisingly, in view of what followed. "It's not Mrs. Cunningham."

"The juror whispered it about," said the *Tribune,* "that this woman used to go by the name of Prosser; he always had an impression that Eckel kept her. She was a short woman with very black eyes and a white face —a pretty woman." It eventually turned out—showing what a compact town New York must have been—that the juror was quite right.

Another witness, and then, walking toward the stand, came my favorite among all the many inquest witnesses: the Honorable Daniel

Ullman. Apparently his manner could have been appropriately accompanied by drum roll and trumpet, for both *Times* and *Tribune* reported it tongue in cheek. The *Trib* man actually wrote his account with irreverent stage directions:

"(Enter Daniel Ullman) Your name, if you please.

"(Deliberately and emphatically) Daniel Ullman."

And in his reply when asked where he lived the *Tribune* reporter inserted a comment in Latin: ". . . since Saturday morning I have taken up my old quarters *(con dignitate)* at the St. Nicholas Hotel again."

"You were familiarly acquainted with the family, Sir; Mr. Burdell, Mrs. Cunningham, Mr. Eckel, and others?"

But this was no man for a simple Yes or No, sir. "Will the Coroner permit me to make a statement which I suppose will cover most of the points which his interrogatories will reach?"

"Yes, Sir, certainly."

"After I have done that, I shall be ready to answer any questions he pleases."

"All right, Sir."

"I will endeavor to state concisely all my connections with this house."

"Go on, Sir."

"Some time in the month of October last, my friend Mr. Anson Wolcott of Lockport, who intended to reside permanently in this city—"

Connery tried to stem the tide: "I beg, if you please, that all extraneous matters . . ." He paused, then added, a little desperately maybe, "We want exactly the transactions in the house, if you please."

Too late. "That is exactly what I wish to give the Coroner; and by this course I suppose I will reach it better."

"Yes, Sir, but this seems rather remote."

"I wish to show how I came here, and what I saw, so far as I am concerned with this matter."

"Very well, Sir."

"Mr. Wolcott wished me to take lodgings with him out of the St. Nicholas, as he wished to be away from the City considerably. I told him that if he would find a suitable floor in some respectable house near the hotel . . ." But we can cut short all that Connery, jury, and the reporters had to sit listening to now: Ullman's monologue ran over nine inches in the wide column and small type of the *Tribune,* its only apparent purpose to demonstrate his own respectability. His friend Wolcott had found a place in Bond Street, and had heard "a high character given of the persons

77

who kept it. . . . I then told Mr. Wolcott that if he would make satisfactory inquiries as to the character of the house, the lady and the family . . . he came to me a few days after and said . . . that respectable persons have given him an excellent character of the lady and the family. . . ." Etc. The many good reasons for Ullman's belief in the complete respectability of the house in which he rented his rooms took about half his monologue; the rest went to show how remote were his connections with anyone in this house. He had, however, been invited to the January 14 party—and went.

"You came to the party?" said the coroner, sounding to me as surprised as I was.

Well, yes; but just barely: "I came to the party, and passed half an hour at it. Saw some persons whom I recognized to be very respectable persons." In fact, this was the first time he'd ever had any conversation with anyone else in the house, "and then for not over two or three minutes." Didn't even know the daughters' names till the party. Saw someone whose name, he learned only later, "was John J. Eckel, so little notice did I take of him then, or have I since." Didn't think he'd recognize Eckel even now. He also met "a young man whose name I afterward learned was Snodgrass." Ullman didn't even know where anyone else slept; he'd been a kind of ghost, apparently, unseen and unseeing, hardly actually there at all.

Connery finally got a question in, to which Ullman replied, and then, said the *Tribune,* "Mr. Ullman yawned, and looked ennuyé."

Coming finally to more recent times: ". . . on Friday last I came to my room about 4 o'clock in the afternoon (yawn)," says the *Trib.* And that night "returned to the St. Nicholas Hotel," where he "took supper with Mr. Douglass, Colonel Looney and his family. On leaving the dinner I met my friends, Mr. Van Dusen, of Hudson, and Whiting of Kinderhook. . . ." Who sound to my ears like a pretty respectable bunch.

In response to questioning, Ullman described events of the morning the murder was discovered, and of that evening, which is how we learn of such things as his conversation with Mrs. Cunningham about how the corpse was to be dressed. And then, pompous though Daniel Ullman may have been, and anxious to disassociate himself from the murder, which isn't hard to understand, I think he redeemed himself. He would not go along with suggestions of Connery's that Emma Cunningham and others had failed to exhibit proper grief; and he concluded by volunteering "that the conduct of all these persons impressed me with an idea that they could scarcely have had anything to do with this, and I have been pondering on it ever since." So maybe he deserved the "Honorable."

"Mr. Ullman," Connery said, "that will do. Will you please sign this now?" referring to the written summary of his testimony.

"I have made it a practice since I was Master in Chancery to read everything I sign. I made it a point to read the whole testimony over to a witness before he signed it."

But Connery wasn't going to read all that back to Ullman. "Very well, Sir; I have not the time. You can read it if you like . . . I have only taken an epitome of your evidence. There's a number of matters you said that I didn't think worthy of . . ." He didn't finish.

Ullman took the paper, the *Times* said, looked at it for a moment, and the notion of reading it may have seemed too much to him, too. "I believe I will sign it."

"Yes, Sir," said Connery, "you may depend upon it as much as if it was verbatim et literatim. (Laughter) If you are hung, Mr. Ullman, I will be the executioner. (Laughter)"

"Well, Sir, so pleasant a gentleman would perform an execution in an exceedingly gentle manner; no doubt of it, Sir. Do you want anything more with me, Mr. Coroner?"

"I believe not, Sir."

"I am very busy, Sir, but you know that I am at your call when you wish for me."

"Yes, Sir," and not to be outdone in grace, "You have done the State some service, and the State knows it, Mr. Ullman. (Laughter)"

"The witness withdrew," said the *Times,* and I was sorry to see him go.

When Susan Maine, the doctor's wife, was recalled, and gave her name, Connery said, "This is a *main* chance of making a conquest, anyway. (Laughter)," the *Times* reported.

They adjourned presently, and now another cluster of doctors climbed the inside stairs of number 31: this included Dr. David Uhl, a man who in time would wish he had never heard of this case. The group walked on into the bedroom where Harvey Burdell lay in his coffin, for tomorrow was to be the funeral, and this was the last chance to make certain they had complete descriptions of the wounds—and to perform an autopsy.

With the group was Mr. A. Berghaus, a *Leslie's* artist, here to make drawings that might be needed after the burial and after the murder room had been cleaned up. I suspect—*Leslie's* was a pretty hustling paper—that it had volunteered his services, because not long afterward they selected from Berghaus's works of this afternoon (as I've done also) those they felt their readers would most appreciate. These included drawings (the captions are theirs) of:

79

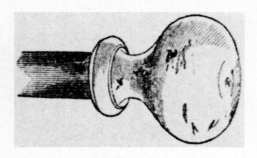

"Handle of the
door of attic
room with the
spots of blood."

"Appearance of
some of the
holes in the
Doctor's shirt."

"Shirt sleeve
showing the
spots of blood."

"Doctor Burdell's
heart showing the
two wounds."

6

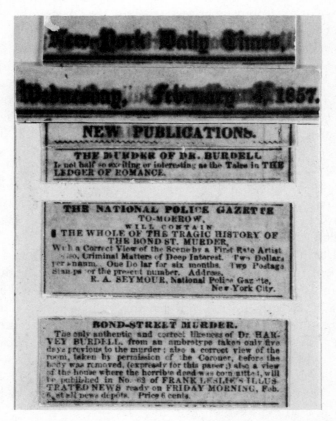

A cold nasty day, said the *Times,* speaking of Wednesday, February 4, but soon after daybreak a crowd began to gather on Bond Street, and presently it "far exceeded that of previous days," for today was the funeral, and they were waiting for the hearse.

All morning the crowd continued to grow until: "It gathered as a huge black spot around the door of the house," 31 Bond. ". . . The street . . . so blockaded that vehicles could scarcely pass." "In Broadway another crowd was . . . watching for the funeral cortege."

About noon the hearse turned into Bond Street, "drawn by four white horses caparisoned in black," the street now "a complete mass of human beings, almost every window . . . filled by the inmates of the . . . houses on both sides of the street." Inside number 31 "the Coroner's investigation was going on," the street "lined with spectators all anxious to see the coffin. . . ."

The hearse stopped at the curb, the undertaker and his assistant climbed down, made their way across the crowded walk, up the steps of 31, in past the cop at the door. I see them then as tiptoeing by the downstairs parlor, from which, very possibly, the voice of the coroner or a witness could be heard; then moving quietly up the stairs.

In her room Mrs. Cunningham, "learning that the funeral was about to take place, and that the coffin was about to be taken from the house, requested that she might be permitted to pay her last respects to the deceased. This having been granted, she was conducted to the room where the coffin was, and having clipped a lock from Dr. Burdell's hair, kissed his lips with a more than ordinary impress, and exclaimed, 'Oh, Doctor! Oh, Doctor!' and wept. She was conducted from the apartment. . . ."

The undertaker and his assistant fitted the lid over the dead man's face. I believe coffin lids were screwed down then, though this isn't mentioned. Then each picked up an end of the box, and carried it down the stairs, working it around the turn. Past the parlor door and the voices of those futilely trying to discover who had put the Doctor here. Then out the door, and: "Immediately the coffin was removed from the house . . . a violent rush took place from all directions, each individual of the crowd being anxious to get a sight of the coffin. The undertaker and his aide quickly placed it in [the] neat hearse. . . ."

The reins flicked, the four horses in their black draperies pressed into their collars, and "at a quick pace" the loaded hearse rolled ahead toward Broadway. The crowd moved with it, looking in at the coffin—standing high and visible, I believe, behind the etched glass panels of a hearse of the time. "The multitude moved on and into Broadway, where they were preceded by a strong force of police. . . ."

Practical cameras had been around for eighteen years as that hearse moved slowly up Broadway; and Anthony, Meade, Brady, and others had their studios right *on* Broadway. Did anyone trundle a big camera over to a Broadway window, aim it down at that thronged street, bring it to focus, and get an actual photograph of the black rooftop of Harvey Burdell's hearse, the white heads of its horses, the flat caps of the police, and the shawled heads and shoulders, the fur caps and stovepipe-hatted heads, of the crowd swarming around them? It seems possible, the kind of impulse that should come to a photographer looking down at Broadway that day. If it did, his photo may be around: daguerreotypes were metal, and survive. I won't find it, of course, in the kind of semi-antique, semi-junk store where such things are sometimes discovered. But you might.

The police "marched up to Grace Church and opened up a passage through the crowd . . ." and at twelve-thirty the hearse stopped at the curb before the church, and "notwithstanding the unpleasant state of the weather, a larger crowd than was ever known was gathered around the church, and blockaded Broadway from Union-square on one side nearly to Bond-street on the other. One half of the crowd was composed of the best-dressed ladies known to Fifth Avenue and its circumjacent localities. Since the funeral of Poole, nothing has been in the way of a funeral cortege like that. . . ." (Poole was a famous pugilist, shot down a couple years earlier in the Stanwix Hotel on Broadway, across the street from the Metropolitan. His last words a few days later were, "I die a true American." His funeral, attended by sports, toughs, and thousands of members of the "Native American" party, the coffin wrapped in an American flag, was enormous. Plays were produced in New York, says one account of the murder, "in which the hero, encircling his limbs with the star-spangled banner, departed this life to slow music and red fire, exclaiming: 'I die a true American!' ")

At the church door, waiting for Harvey Burdell's coffin, stood: "A strong detachment of police . . . detailed by Captain Dilk—the enterprising Captain of the Fifteenth Ward—to prevent the incursion of unauthorized parties." The coffin was carried in past them, then the doors were locked against the crowd.

At the curb the hearse and four horses stood waiting, as they must now for hours. The horses, I feel sure, would be covered by blankets over their black drapings; and would be fed, canvas or leather feed bags strapped to the long, munching faces. Around them the great crowd would move slowly, overflowing the walks and filling the streets, waiting. Well-dressed ladies, many in hoopskirts, many carrying muffs—the "fair multitude," the *Tribune* called them—waited in the crowd, too, out here in the cold before the church, for the next hour and a half.

At 31 Bond the witnesses came and went, nothing much being learned. A cop walked in with a scuttle of fresh coal for the fire, and made considerable noise pouring it on. Connery spoke up "grandiloquently, as if reading from a newspaper," the *Tribune* reported, saying, "Here a terrible confusion arose from a box of coal being put on the fire. Put that in, gentlemen of the press," and they did.

83

I take Connery's remark as a reference to the editorials in today's papers; I think he was hurt and possibly shocked by them. They are, in fact, the most outspoken attack I can recall seeing in print anywhere: no paper ever referred to Nixon at his worst the way they did this morning to Coroner Connery.

The *Times* referred to his "most extraordinary unfitness . . ." and said: "If anything ever occurred in a Court of Justice more shocking than" Connery's jokes and his "obvious attempts to pin the crime" on Mrs. Cunningham and Eckel "it has not fallen under our notice. . . ." Only yesterday the *Times* had referred to Emma Cunningham's "voluptuous form, and more than ordinary powers of fascination. She drew within her toils Mr. George D. Cunningham. . . ." Today, not hesitating to heave a stone through the open window of their own glass house, they spoke of Connery's "low chuckling over the disclosure of everything throwing doubt upon the relations of the parties . . . ," and they had a stone left for the *Tribune,* which, the *Times* said sanctimoniously, had a "remarkably free and easy style of dealing with private character. . . ."

The *Tribune* couldn't "understand why . . . the office of Coroner . . . should so often be bestowed upon silly, ignorant and otherwise incompetent persons. . . ." Connery, they said, had "the knowledge of a hedge-school-master and the perspicacity of a beadle . . . a bad heart, a loose tongue, a limited intellect and a coarse nature."

The *Tribune* today was remarkable; at two cents, this issue of Wednesday, February 4, was a steal. Yesterday they had quoted unnamed friends of Harvey Burdell who were "very emphatic in their declarations that he never could have married Mrs. Cunningham, and that the whole affair was a fraud—a plot. . . ." Today it seemed unlikely to the *Trib* that anyone living in the house had done the murder, for: "How bold the act, if done by an inmate of the house, at an hour when [Ullman] might walk in and find him in the very midst of the struggle!" It seemed, the *Trib* thought now, "altogether possible that [the inmates of the house] are guiltless. . . ."

In yesterday's *Trib,* Harvey Burdell had been a member of various important societies, a bank director, coauthor of a book, "prominent and well-to-do. . . ." Today the *Trib* threw its readers another curve by reprinting from the *Herald* that, while living in his brother's house, Harvey Burdell "began to manifest a very licentious and loose character. At last he had a quarrel with his brother, during which they had a severe fight, John [Burdell] alleging that Harvey was too intimate with his wife." With Harvey's help she got a divorce, Harvey then cheated John out of a lot of property, and during John's "last illness, and just before his death,

84

Harvey Burdell got out an attachment against him . . . and with it and a Sheriff went to John's room and took possession of everything he had, even the furniture of his death chamber, leaving him to die on a sofa." Not even a little embarrassed, "Harvey Burdell frequently told of this deed among his acquaintances." He also got his brother to sign a will, presumably before yanking his deathbed from under him, making Harvey his executor. Harvey then gave the ex-wife nothing. "Honesty was by no means a characteristic of his dealings, and his moral character was far from being above reproach. His reputation among good men was bad, very bad." It's true he had "considerable talents and spent most of his time in reading, the pursuit of his profession, and money-getting." But: "He had been a very licentious man, and had a great many difficulties in consequence of it; his name is found in the books at the Tombs, in the law courts, and he has been known to the head of the police for many years. . . ."

And that's not all. When a young man, he'd been engaged "to a respectable young lady, but her father peremptorily refused to permit the marriage; at which Burdell got angry, struck the father and gave him a black eye." Engaged to still another girl, "the day and hour was set for the wedding, the wedding party assembled, the bridesmaids and the bridegroom were present, the clergyman was ready to perform the ceremony, when Dr. Harvey Burdell entered the room of the old man and told him that before he married the girl he wanted a check for $20,000." The father refused, the wedding broke up, and later "the young lady married the person who was to be groomsman on the former occasion, [and] he received the check for $20,000. The check on the previous occasion was made out for Burdell, and would have been given him immediately after the marriage ceremony was performed; and when he heard about it, he is said to have become greatly excited, and declared that he would never get married."

That wasn't the half of it, either. "Dr. Burdell had a very curious servant girl, called Biddy, who was with him for five years," two of them "at No. 31 Bond Street, during the whole of which time she never went to bed. He never furnished her with a bed, or anything to sleep upon. She was poorly clad, and hardly ever had anything to wear on her feet. He never provided her with anything to eat, but gave her a small weekly salary, upon which she supported herself, buying her food at the groceries. This is an example of the doctor's penuriousness. The girl could speak four languages fluently—namely, the English, French, German and Spanish. She had a great passion for studying and learning languages. She was an Irish girl, and a most faithful servant. She frequently saved the doctor

85

from being beaten, for if a fight occurred, she would run between him and his assailant, and stand there till she stopped the fighting. She slept on a stool below the hall door. . . ."

And besides that: "There was a wealthy widow lady of this city who used to visit Dr. Burdell every day for two years. On occasion she called on him in the afternoon to go to the theater with him in the evening. On the way to the theater, she said she would like something to eat, and entered Thompson's saloon and called for what she wanted. Dr. Burdell refused to call for anything for himself, saying that he had been to tea. She told him to call and be decent. He refused—when she called for him. He would not eat; and on coming back for her would neither pay for himself nor her. The Doctor is represented by those intimately acquainted with him to have been a very peculiar man. He hates children, and never had any pets except some Guinea pigs. His brother, Lewis Burdell, is now in the Lunatic Asylum, on Blackwell's Island, having gone mad from the effects of a nameless habit. . . ."

What's more: "The dentists represent that Harvey Burdell never held a high position in the dental profession; that the most respectable portion of that profession would have nothing to do with him, that he was dishonest in his practice, that he has filled twelve teeth in an hour, when an honest dentist could not do that amount of work in less than twelve hours, that he was willing to do anything for money, that the greatest portion of his patients while [his office was] in Broadway were disreputable characters. . . ." He hadn't even written any of the book he signed as coauthor; the work was really done entirely by a brother, and a medical work Burdell claimed to have translated from the French was translated by someone else.

He was never connected with the American Society of Dental Surgeons, having been proposed for membership but not elected. He had been president of "the New-York Society of Dental Surgeons—more popularly known as the Amalgum [sic] Society because they were in favor of using [a compound of mercury and silver] to fill the teeth with . . ." but: "It was under his Presidency that the Society collapsed. . . ."

And now for Mrs. Cunningham's *mother.* "A leading physician of Brooklyn yesterday gave a correspondent the following facts in elucidation of the antecedents of Mrs. Cunningham." Her late sister, "known as Mrs. Williams, understood to be the kept mistress of a Wall Street lawyer of that name," had been very sick a dozen years before. "A male relative expressed great anxiety for her recovery; 'for,' said he, 'she has been a very bad woman, and is not fit to die.' " She did die, though, "of disease of the heart, attended with such peculiar symptoms that [the doctor] was very

86

desirous to make a post mortem examination of that organ." Her mother okayed this, and: "The doctor being unattended by any professional friend, and no one else being willing to aid or be present at the operation, the mother held a candle while he took out her daughter's heart, without exhibiting the least tremor or emotion." The doctor had kept, and he showed the reporter, that very heart, by now "partially ossified. The doctor became acquainted with Mrs. Cunningham as well as her sisters, and was fully convinced that from example and training they grew up wholly destitute of character or principle."

Well, I'm not convinced; that mother had all the character she could use. And so did daughter Emma, I think. To me the doctor sounds a little ungrateful for that unwavering candle.

"It appears, gentlemen," Coroner Connery said to his jury before adjourning for lunch, that "I have received a castigation . . . from some of the papers." He then made a heartfelt speech in rebuttal and a speech is what it was: it took the *Times* fifteen column inches to report it.

About half his speech looks like a buildup to producing a paper refuting the *Tribune*'s criticism of him for having Mrs. Cunningham stripped. Now he read it aloud: "This is to certify that the examination of my person by Dr. Woodward was conducted in the most delicate manner. There was no indecent exposure. . . ." Mrs. Cunningham had signed this, however, in a way Connery was now obliged to repeat: "E. A. Burdell." But he added, "This is Mrs. Cunningham, who signs her name 'E. A. Burdell.' "

Uptown from the inquest, at Grace Church, a little later: "Shortly after two o'clock, Rev. Dr. Taylor, Rector . . . took his place in the chancel." Relatives and friends of Harvey Burdell had already been seated, and now the doors were unlocked and opened for the waiting crowd.

"The somewhat corpulent sexton . . . did not like the idea of his carpet and the mattings being used in so common a manner as was likely to be the case by a promiscuous congregation such as now presented itself to him," and he tried announcing that no women would be admitted. But "the denunciations which were then poured out upon the Sexton's head were of every variety. One lady, in particular, said that 'his boiler ought to be bursted.' " He had to let the ladies in, but did his best to filter out "pickpockets and other low characters." As the ladies pushed in, some of them "expressed anxiety as to whether they should occupy a seat in the 'pit' or in the 'dress circle' [terminology of the day for certain theater seats]. The preference was given to the pit, for, as they remarked, the church was 'all pit.' "

Every seat in the church was quickly filled, and the aisles filled with standers, "ladies as well as gentlemen. On no occasion do we remember an equal excitement attendant upon any funeral occasion."

The funeral began with the reading of the burial service. This was to be followed by the choir . . . a reading of the epistle . . . the choir again. . . .

While this was going on, the jury reassembled down at 31 Bond. Connery, having apparently learned nothing at all from the intense newspaper criticism, now produced two remarkable letters, leaving to the jury whether they should be given to the press, although he himself was always in favor, he said, of doing "anything in the world to aid the press."

It was okay with the jury, and Connery handed to the reporters, to copy first, an astonishing example of his notions of proper procedure. "No. 4 Barclay Street, New York. Coroner Connery," it began; and then detailed a long argument in support of a fake groom and that John Eckel was the fake. None of Burdell's actions after the marriage was that of a husband, or of a man who even knew he was married; nor did Emma Cunningham behave as though married. So: "Might not [Eckel] be the person who represented" Burdell at the supposed marriage? And: "Why did the man that was married wear false whiskers as a disguise . . . ? If it was her motive to get Dr. Burdell's property, such a plan was well calculated to accomplish it . . . and then [the writer's speculations now surpassed anything anyone else had even imagined] getting in the family way . . . and then getting rid of the Doctor. If in the family way the child would be supposed to be his, and she and it would get all the property. . . . In respect of her former husband it would save a great deal of trouble to get a gouty old man out of the way, and especially if by doing so she would realize $10,000 on his life. . . ."

Incredibly, this long argument for the guilt of Eckel and Mrs. Cunningham, running nearly eight thousand words, was listened to by the entire coroner's jury, and then published for a city full of prospective trial jurors. Even more incredibly, the letter was anonymous: "Respectfully, OBSERVER," it concluded.

That one out of the way, Connery handed over his second letter, also anonymous. "Sir: Wishing to assist in the ends of justice, I beg to state that a lady dreamed twice last night that Mrs. Cunningham had left the house early on the morning of the murder, met Mr. Eckel at a bath-house, and there washed off together some offensive marks on their body.

"This is perhaps all nonsense, but it may lead to some opening." Signed, "JUSTICE."

The next witness, a woman, took the oath and the operating chair, and Connery asked her business. "I am a clairvoyant," she replied, and the inquest was once more on its way.

The clairvoyant neither knew nor divined anything useful, and Eckel's bookkeeper then testified in German, a juror translating; and I mention him only, since he has nothing new to tell us, to quote a reply he made because I think it gives us another momentary glimpse of how it was once in a vanished New York. Asked when something had happened, he said, "It was at candlelight, about 5 o'clock."

At Grace Church the choir finished its final selection, and the organ pipes sounded the ponderous tones of the "Dead March" from *Saul*. Eight pallbearers, Drs. Stephen Maine and Samuel Parmly among them, then lifted the coffin together, and carried it down the aisle, and out to the waiting hearse. The watching crowd by now, said the *Times*, "could not have fallen short of 8,000 persons, of all colors, ages and sizes."

Carriages stood waiting at the curb, many of them hired; people, some of whom would have been wearing full black mourning, came down the church steps, and climbed into them. The procession—hearse first, pallbearers next, then relatives—began moving down Broadway, "hearse and 50 carriages." Half the carriages were empty but "gave character to the affair."

As the procession rolled south, "the crowd gathered along the sidewalk, and every window was filled with gazers anxious to behold the last trace of the deceased. Especially at the end of Broadway the crowd was very dense, and the carriages had great difficulty in making way. . . . It was not until nearly at Canal Street that the pressure of the crowd diminished—and even until it reached Hamilton Ferry the sidewalks were thronged with people. . . .

"The river at this point being free from ice no impediment prevented the speedy crossing of the water. It was generally understood in Brooklyn that the procession would cross at Fulton Ferry, and those who were drawn together by curiosity to witness the scene were thus disappointed. On arriving at Greenwood Cemetery, a lady named Williams and calling herself a relative of Dr. Burdell's joined the funeral party. She entered the reporters' carriage and stated that she herself had selected the lot in which the remains of the unfortunate man were to be interred. Not altogether the mourner did she appear there. Her excitement bore evidence of strong animosity toward Mrs. Cunningham. She said, in tones loud enough to be heard by all who were present, and with very impulsive gestures, that 'The doctor's sentiments toward Mrs. Cunningham were well known to his *friends*—that he always expressed the utmost aversion to her, and, to use his own words, would rather be torn in pieces with hot pincers than to marry her.'

"This lady, after subduing her emotions," the *Times* continued, "inquired if any will had been found. She said that to her certain knowledge Dr. Burdell had made a will, and she thought it had been stolen or altered. The lady after this demonstration said no more, but simply subsided into grief."

Surprisingly, the *Tribune* reporter seems either to have missed cousin Lucy Ann Williams or, more likely, I think—the *Tribune* having an afternoon edition—he did not go out to the cemetery. But the *Trib* man rarely let his readers down, and didn't now: he filled out with fine writing.

"The body was conveyed to Greenwood Cemetery," he wrote, "where now lie the remains of one, who having worked assiduously to acquire a fortune, lost it; lost life, lost all the pleasures in which he was wont to indulge; lost them all in the twinkling of an eye. Surrounded by circumstances of his own choice, or at least arising out of the elements which he had once chosen as his social enhancers" (whatever that is intended to mean; he may simply have gotten carried away by the beauty of his own prose, which I can sympathize with) "he was involved in embarrassment by this course, and his life came to be in jeopardy every hour, at least so it is said in testimony of what he himself stated to different individuals at different times."

Relieved, I suppose, to have made it alive out of that sentence, the *Tribune* man, pen dipping frequently, took off: "He dies! not as the patriot dies. He dies! not as the cherished husband, not as the fond father, not as the philanthropist, not as the benefactor of his race . . ." Etc.

Finally he finished with a paragraph that I quote not only for its splendid prose but because we are the answers to his question: "Who will think of this funeral, now it is passed? Who will permit themselves to think of the why and wherefore of the occasion, and then [this may also apply to some of us] turning from diverse ways which lead to ruin and death, arrest their downward career, and turn to those associations which are developed in the true family circle, which is a sacred altar upon which are laid all that we hold dear in life, surrounded by hands ever ready to repel the assassin, push back the invader of social dignity and virtue, protect the public peace, and send out into the world men and women whose virtue is a tower of strength and whose moral courage is a terror to those who demand the right to luxury without the effort to obtain it honestly." This was immediately followed by a full reprint of the scurrilous account of Harvey Burdell's life that they had published yesterday.

The *Times* man did go out to Greenwood, and there is the feel of eyewitness reality in the conclusion of his story: "The coffin enclosing the remains of Dr. Burdell was taken from the hearse and placed in a strong deal case. The grave was dug in a spot on Locust Hill, in section No. 44 —the number of the grave being 3,799."

If cousin Lucy Ann Williams had indeed selected this lot, she had done so at least seven years earlier, for this was the Burdell family plot —a large circular area of the kind chosen then with the intention of erecting a tall center monument inscribed with the family name, and the whole encircled by a low wall on which individual names would from time to time be carved. There was no monument yet, no marker of any kind, but Dr. Burdell's brother John already lay here, buried in 1850.

"There was no address from any individual," the *Times* man continued, "a few relatives stood mourning around—many strangers looked on with mere curiosity. The snow lay deep and untrodden in the vicinity of the grave, while the remains of him who five days before trod the streets of the City in health and strength, were lowered to their last resting place."

There is no way of knowing it, but the dead man lying out in the blackness of Greenwood Cemetery that night surely touched the minds of Emma Cunningham and her daughters as they sat in their rooms in his house. And if so, it could explain their near-panic at a sudden sharp sound, an explosion on Broadway a short distance away. It was nothing: only a "salute" set off by exuberant friends of a man whose election as chief engineer of the Fire Department had been announced that evening. But "Mrs. Cunningham and her daughters were much alarmed. The elder one almost fainted, supposing it was the mob coming to pull down the house."

7

The coroner's case against Emma Cunningham was collapsing. A *Times* editorial writer spelled it out: ". . . with every successive step in the inquiry, one after another of the suspicious circumstances is explained." Emma Cunningham had sued Harvey Burdell, but the suits were "withdrawn, and . . . all their differences . . . amicably and finally settled." The supposed falsity of the wedding "is by no means proved. . . ." The Cunningham girls' sleeping with their mother on the night of the murder "is absolutely incompatible with the supposition that she took any personal and premeditated part in that murder,—except on the incredible supposition that she voluntarily admitted those daughters to a knowledge of her share in that transaction, or the still more monstrous hypothesis that they also shared in her guilt. . . . Nothing that she has said or done since the murder . . . seems to us to furnish even presumptive evidence of her guilt."

As for Eckel, "nothing whatever is shown that indicates him as the Doctor's assassin. . . ."

There was nothing left. "The bloody clothes found in the garret have been accounted for; the dagger found in one of the rooms . . . was not large enough to have inflicted the stabs;—the papers found in Eckel's room were in Mrs. Cunningham's desk, and they belonged properly to her. . . ."

The *Tribune* also gave Connery unshirted hell. It was an outrage, they said, the way the coroner arbitrarily clapped witnesses, particularly women, into jail "who could not give bail in the sum of $1000 each for their appearance at the Court of Sessions to prove Mrs. Cunningham guilty . . . and this, too, before the Jury have found that there are any grounds for detaining her to stand such a trial. . . . Mrs. Seymour [the clairvoyant], whose testimony, our readers must judge after reading it, is not worth a thousand straws, and yet this woman was ordered to give $1000 bail or go to prison. She declared to the officer who took her to prison that she had been kept two days without a mouthful to eat, and now must go to jail of course, for she could not give bail.

". . . This course adopted by this stupidest of Dogberrys," the *Tribune* concluded, meant that anyone, especially a woman, who might come forward with useful information would now not do so lest she be put in jail for her trouble.

Connery now seems to me simply to react to whatever the newspapers criticized as though he could get them off his back by complying. That same afternoon he ordered all witnesses except Mary Donaho and Hannah Conlon released from the Fifteenth Precinct station house jail. He also gave in to Henry L. Clinton, Mrs. Cunningham's formidable lawyer, and Eckel's counsel, William R. Stafford, who'd been fighting him about this, and allowed them to consult with Eckel, who had been moved to the Tombs.

It didn't help. "A monomania seems to have seized the Coroner in regard to the inmates of the house," the *Times* said on Friday. "Even if they are the guilty parties, it is not at all essential that their guilt be established now . . . the main thing *now* is to discover what *other* parties are open to suspicion. . . . The Coroner will find this quite useful, if not so congenial a field for the exercise of his peculiar talents, as an inquiry into the antecedents of Mrs. Cunningham, Mr. Eckel's demeanor toward his mistress, or the feelings and opinions of Hannah, the cook."

Almost obediently, Connery began the inquest that morning by telling the jury, in a kind of knee-jerk paraphrase of the *Times*'s scolding, that they'd heard enough about what had gone on in the house before the murder, and "I trust that your questions will be confined solely to when Mr. Burdell left the house that evening, where he dined, who dined with him, when he left dinner, when he went to dine, and every matter tracing him up to the period when we suppose the murder to have been done. . . . I am anxious . . . that nothing should be left undone in regard to finding out the perpetrators. . . ."

I feel a little sorry for Connery. And I miss his jokes. The trouble with his instructions to the jury was that they didn't have anybody to ask those questions of. Connery tried Alvah Blaisdell again, learning nothing much that they didn't already know. He tried the Reverend Uriah Marvine once more, and things went from bad to worse. Connery had sent Marvine to the Tombs yesterday to take a look at Eckel, with and without wig. Now he asked Marvine if he'd seen Eckel, and got a typically Uriah Marvine answer: "I went yesterday to see a man in prison whom they called Eckel," he said scrupulously.

Did he recognize him as the man he'd married to Emma Cunningham? And this time got a remarkably positive answer. "I would say as far as this," the Reverend boldly replied, "that the body I saw upstairs resembles the man I married more than the man I saw yesterday, called Eckel," and that was the end of that.

I think poor Edward Downes Connery hardly knew whom to call, or what to do next, and he didn't redeem himself with anyone but me by bringing out one more nutty letter for the reporters to copy:

> "to mister Conorery esq.
> coroner off
> new york city
> Mr. Croner it is with pleasure that i writes to you about
> mises cunningham i noed wance a man that was kilt and the
> peple went and lef thre hands on him and wen the man the
> man that kilt ham put his hand on him he begun to blead
> and the man confesd and was hangd, if the same was dun wid
> the docktur it wud serve justis
> from your servent
> games donoly"

At the noon recess the coroner had a cop go get a chimney sweep, who then swept all the chimneys of 31 for evidence of burnt cloth. He had the cesspool and privies searched; had the yard dug up and turned over; had the ashes in the cellar sifted. And all he found was a trunk of John Eckel's, some of whose clothes were packed inside it, but not a speck of blood in the lot. "It may have significance to some," the *Times* said mystifyingly, "that at the bottom of the trunk were found a quantity of capsules of balsam of copaiva." This reference was cleared up by my family doctor, John Lee, whom I asked about it: the stuff was once used to treat gonorrhea.

A Reverend Cox took the stand, interesting everyone because he'd been sued for divorce last year in a sensational case, "the complaint being," said the *Times,* "repeated and aggravated infidelities." (I understand "repeated" but I wish they'd explained "aggravated.") Cox said that

94

only last Friday Burdell had told him he wasn't married, and never would be.

Then a big fight with attorney Henry Clinton, who demanded to be allowed upstairs to see Mrs. Cunningham. Connery refused, defending his decision, then seemed to forget the argument, drifting into what is eating away at him. "I can bear all the scourge I get; I am thankful to the press; it is a liberty which the press has a right to possess. *That* liberty I do not wish to deny. I esteem the press for more reasons than one, and I wish the press to have very full powers. They are at liberty to chastise every man when he departs from strict rectitude and honest deportment of conduct. But I trust anybody who has been listening to me here, and to the manner in which I have been conducting this investigation, will do me the justice to say that if I may not have the most towering talents in the world, there is honesty of heart for the protection of the accused and the development of crime." (This is correctly copied.) The *Times* adds: "(Applause, and cries of 'Order!' from the police.)"

Connery then changed his mind, and allowed Henry Clinton to see Mrs. Cunningham; he went right upstairs, and got her signature on a writ of habeas corpus.

Charles Ketcham testified that the bloody shirt was his. Mrs. Stansbury talked about the lease she and her husband were to sign here last Saturday. But they hadn't come that morning, because the weather was bad, and: "On Saturday evening," Mrs. Stansbury now told the jury, "my husband was sitting in the parlor reading the paper, when he dropped the paper, turned round to me, and said, 'Mr. Burdell is dead!'

"I said, 'What Burdell?'

"He said, 'Harvey Burdell, Dentist, Bond Street.' Then he said, 'He broke a blood vessel, and the blood is on the door.'

"I said, 'It is very strange that a blood-vessel should fly on the door.' I thought then that something perhaps was wrong, knowing how the parties felt. And I says, 'This morning the writing was to be signed, and last night he was murdered or died. . . .' " Impressive, chilling; but proof of nothing, and not even evidence.

The inquest went hopelessly on. Mrs. Cunningham's hairdresser raised her hand, laid the other on a Bible, swore to tell the whole truth, then told the jury that all she knew was that she dressed Mrs. Cunningham's hair, and that Mrs. Cunningham owed her money. "I wish you luck till you get it," someone called out, and when she stepped down, Connery said, "Gentlemen, that is a very important witness." He could have said the same for his remaining witnesses today, such as a livery-stable owner whose testimony was simply that he had sometimes rented carriages to Dr.

Burdell, to Eckel, and to Mrs. Prosser.

A bad day for Edward Downes Connery, who "walks a little lame."

After he and the jury had left, the house empty except for the Cunninghams up on the third floor and the cops on guard duty, the *Times* reporter was left without much of a story for the day. So instead of leaving, he climbed the stairs to Harvey Burdell's office, hunting for something to liven up his account. It was after six, early February, as he stepped into the room, so I expect he had to light the gas: possibly the jet over the Doctor's desk. Then he wandered the room, but nothing had changed: walls, carpets, furniture, the doors in the far corner still marked with spilled blood; turned black by now, I would think. Why this room hadn't been cleaned up I don't know; maybe Connery still hoped some kind of clue would turn up here; or maybe he was afraid to do anything irrevocable that the papers might criticize.

The *Times* man picked up the Doctor's bloody boots, surprisingly still there, and looked at them. But all he found to say when he wrote about it later was that the blood ground into the soles showed how the Doctor must have struggled for his life, and that had already been said by others.

He put down the boots, and walked over to the corner of the room where Dr. Burdell had died. There, he wrote later: "By the side of the closet door which is thickly splashed with blood, hangs a political chart, on which were printed the names of the candidates and the platforms of the three great parties to the last Presidential struggle." Desperate for material, I suspect, and possibly imitating the generally lively reporting of the *Tribune,* the *Times* man now discovered, or says he did, that: "Curiously enough, upon that sentence in the Republican platform which reads: 'Murders, robberies, and arsons have been instigated, and encouraged, and the offenders have been allowed to go unpunished,' a blood-spot had fallen on the word 'murders,' and another on the word 'unpunished.' The sentence proceeds, 'and that it is our fixed purpose to bring the perpetrators of these atrocious outrages, and their accomplices, to a sure and condign hereafter.' This passage is marked significantly, as by an index finger, by a long spurt of blood!"

I like it, and hope he got a raise for initiative, imagination, and fine creative writing.

8

Augusta Cunningham walked into the downstairs parlor of 31 Bond Street next morning, and laid her palm on the Bible: an eighteen-year-old girl "in a dark-plaid silk [dress] and a Russian sable coat." Here at last was a witness who might be expected to know something of what had happened in this house the night Harvey Burdell died; and Connery and his jury, the reporters and spectators crowding the room, watched as she raised her other hand, and swore to tell them the truth. We see her now from the reporters' table, through the eyes of the *Times* man: "rather tall . . . her features . . . regular and decidely handsome. Her air and manner . . . dignified, confident and self-possessed. Her eyes are mild in expression, but her mouth is rigid, hard and indicative of firmness, not unmixed with peremptory arrogance of character."

The *Tribune* man, possibly more alert to color, also saw her eyes: "light blue, and . . . somewhat dimmed, as if the result of excessive weeping." He saw her hair, too: "light brown." And like the *Times* man he also saw strength in that face: "She very much resembles her mother . . . and looks as if full of determination of purpose. . . ."

They were right. The oath given, Augusta sat down in the dentist's chair, at which Dr. Burdell had once stood fixing her teeth: you wonder if memory of that now stirred in her mind. Then the questions began: and Augusta stonewalled them.

". . . she answered only such questions as were put to her,—volunteering nothing and remembering less than was deemed desirable. Throughout her examination she was evidently inclined to make out the most amicable relations between her mother and Doctor Burdell, and ignored all the difficulties which have been shown by other witnesses. . . ."

In fact, Augusta seemed hardly to know the answers to even innocuous questions. "What was the period of the first acquaintance of your mother and family with Dr. Burdell?"

"I do not know; I was at Cleveland at that time."

"As near as you can guess?"

"Nearly two years; I am not certain."

For how long had the Doctor visited her mother?

"I cannot say. . . ."

Upstairs Emma Cunningham and Helen sat waiting: for their turns, so Edward Connery thought, to be called down to the witness stand when Augusta was finished. Except for his brief questioning of Mrs. Cunningham on the day the inquest began, when she was not yet a suspect, no one knew what the three women could tell of the murder. Now, finally—a full week later, during which the coroner had questioned several prostitutes, a livery-station owner, a clairvoyant, and Mrs. Cunningham's hairdresser —he was ready for the Cunninghams.

But Emma Cunningham hadn't waited for Coroner Connery; she was waiting now for something else, for at just about the time Augusta had taken the oath downstairs a Judge Brady took his seat at the bench of his City Hall courtroom, and began listening to Emma Cunningham's attorney, Henry Clinton. Clinton had a signed application from her for a writ of habeas corpus, and now he handed this up to the judge, and asked him to order her brought here along with Eckel and Snodgrass, all of whom, he said, were being illegally imprisoned by Edward Connery. Judge Brady agreed, and sent Deputy Sheriff Crombie up to 31 Bond. And before Augusta's questioning was even well started, Crombie arrived to snatch away the coroner's principal witness by serving "a writ of habeas corpus upon the Coroner, in behalf of Mrs. Cunningham." What's more, she was to leave right now: Crombie had a carriage waiting.

There was nothing Connery could do. All week he'd delayed; could even have questioned Mrs. Cunningham this morning by starting earlier. But now she was upstairs getting into her outer clothing, putting on a veil; and Connery could only hope she'd soon be brought back and delivered over to him again.

His troubles grew: two judges came visiting the inquest now, Recorder Smith and Judge Capron, and he politely made them welcome. Why they had come I can't say, but it seems possible to me, or even likely, that someone with the power to make it stick had decided Connery's fumbling inquisition badly needed experienced help. "The Deputy Sheriff at this moment called the Coroner out, [and] the rest of the examination was conducted by Recorder Smith. . . ."

Who had no better luck than Connery. Did Augusta's mother have a lease on the house?

"That I cannot say."

"Why can't you say?"

"I never asked her anything at all about it; I am not of an inquisitive nature. . . ."

Wasn't she in "the habit of talking with her mother about her affairs?"

"I never thought anything about the house—whether she was going to live here another year or not."

"Never even asked the question?"

"No, Sir, never did."

"Felt no interest in it," Smith continued doggedly, "whether you was going to remain here or was going away?"

"No, Sir, I did not."

And so on. But when the questioning turned to the marriage, Augusta knew plenty. She'd been a witness, she said, to the marriage between her mother and Harvey Burdell; and it had taken place on Tuesday, October 28. She remembered that date because the Doctor himself often spoke to her of it in a joking sort of way; saying such things as you won't forget the 28th of October, and: "He would often joke about my having another father."

It was he, not her mother, who wanted the marriage kept secret. As soon as they'd left the Reverend Marvine's, in fact, out on the street, "I said, 'Doctor, what would you say if I should tell of it?' Says he, 'Augusta, if you ever tell of it I'll take your life.' I don't know whether he said it in jest or not, but that's the remark." As to why the marriage was secret: "He said because he said he was going to be single, and they would laugh at him if he told of his marriage. But he wished it to be known on the first of June, as they were going to leave here for Europe."

Pretty positive testimony, but it turned out she hadn't actually heard all this from Dr. Burdell. "Who told you that?"

"Mother. . . ."

They'd walked to the Reverend Marvine's because: "The Doctor said it was nonsense to spend money on a carriage," and here the *Tribune* added: "(Miss Cunningham could not repress a smile as she said this.)"

"Any merry-making" when they got home that night?

"No, the Doctor didn't wish anything of the kind. He was very close with his means, and didn't want any money spent that could be avoided." Persuasive; it sounds like the Doctor.

Her mother and the Doctor, Augusta continued, had occupied the same room on their wedding night, and had continued to do so until about a month ago when her sister took sick and her mother had begun sleeping with Helen. At least, the Doctor and her mother had slept on the second floor: whether in the same bed, she couldn't say.

There was much more. Recorder Smith, Connery (who'd returned now), and even a juror questioned Augusta about everything any of them could think of. As they hunted for something, anything, the questioning grew so prolonged that to report it, along with the testimony of others, the *Times* had to publish a "Special Supplement" containing nothing else. Augusta's question-and-answer testimony alone took more than a full page. I read a sample of it aloud, timing it (strange to hear spoken aloud, even in my own voice, words spoken by Augusta a century and a quarter ago); and I believe she was on the stand for nearly an hour.

"During the course of her examination," the *Tribune* said, "she bore the gaze of the spectators with remarkable firmness, though at times she exhibited emotion." The *Times* man thought: "She was pale and evidently controlled the agitation she felt only by strong effort."

But the stone wall held. Had she never heard of the note Dr. Burdell said her mother stole? No. Well, didn't she know police had come to the house? "My little brother once told me there was a policeman there; I didn't know what it was about."

"Not a word between you and your mother as to the subject of [their] visit?"

"No, Sir."

Yes, of course she'd been curious, but her mother, she said, wouldn't tell her why.

"Did [Eckel] spend time in your mother's room?"

"Only when he went up to fix the birds."

Her mother never went out alone with Eckel, only with a group. Yes, she'd seen the dagger in her mother's bureau; they had had it for years; it had belonged to her father.

A big question: "Did you hear any noise that night [of the murder]?"

"Not the slightest."

100

I think they finally ran out of questions. A juror stood up to try his luck, eventually asking things like, "Did your mother usually wear much jewelry?"

"No."

"Did she wear braids in her hair?"

"Yes."

"Did she wear bracelets? . . ."

Presently Connery said to the juror, "I think, Sir, that you have gone far enough . . ." but the juryman didn't want to give up, insisting on more questions, and finally both he and Connery were asking Augusta about a Mr. Todd whose only connection with the case seems to have been that, along with a Mr. Coe, he called at the house for some reason or other on the afternoon before the murder. The long session dwindled to this:

"Do you know where Mr. Coe lives?" the juror persisted.

"I do not; he boards in New-York somewhere. I think he is now at Dr. Wellington's water-cure Establishment."

"What is his appearance? Is he as tall as myself (about 5 ft. 4)?"

"I think he was; he is rather short. (Merriment.)"

"Had he black hair?"

"Not very dark."

"Does he wear considerable beard?"

"No."

"What is the color of his whiskers?"

"I do not know."

"Are his features sharp or full-faced?"

"Rather sharp."

"I think I know that gentleman," said the juror, and that was too much for Connery. "That may be," he said, "but it seems to me that we have had enough of this."

"The juror sat down," wrote one reporter, "to the relief of his own legs, and the patience of his fellows." And Augusta, dismissed at last— it was now one o'clock—stood up from the Doctor's chair. If she knew who had killed Harvey Burdell, as she walked from the room in her plaid dress and sable coat, she took the knowledge with her.

Down at City Hall "the curiosity to see Mrs. Cunningham and Eckel was . . . great," said the *Times* reporter. He stood watching an "immense throng gathered about and within City Hall, to see them as they passed," and I try to imagine what the man who put those words down on paper was actually looking at. I can see City Hall because I know what it looked like. Then I try to add women in hoopskirts, shawls over their heads against the winter air; men in tall Daniel Webster stovepipe hats; boys in short-peaked little wool caps; and the girls are miniature women. And there could still be seen on New York streets occasionally old men unwilling to adopt the newer heavy dark clothes of the nineteenth century, and who continued to wear the outmoded knee breeches of their younger days and worn felt hats whose brims tipped up to form a tricorne. Possibly even one of those old men stood in that crowd.

All this can be managed in the mind, you can see the crowd thus far. But I think there'd be more than merely a difference in clothing style if you could really go back somehow and stand among those people, listening and sneaking looks at their faces. Because I believe their faces are also different from ours; that you can see this when you study the old photographs. Faces different because the people are different. In their minds lies the knowledge that the name of the President-elect is Buchanan; California is far more remote for them than any place on earth is for us now; and possibly some of them suspect that a civil war may be coming. Those boys in their caps, free of school today, are going to fight it.

Even greater than the differences in what they know are the differences in the way they see the world and in the ideas that move them; their faces are formed by their own times, and I think that's why movies and television of other days are so often unpersuasive. They get the clothes right, sometimes, but the faces of the people wearing them are today's; they're us, and you can see it. Unless directors search out the rare throwback faces, which they don't generally bother to do. Sometimes the English will, and then you get the sudden sharp thrill of glimpsing what Dickens saw.

To somehow join that crowd and stand silent beside the *Times* reporter, seeing what he saw, would be almost unimaginably different from watching a crowd of today. I think the fascination of it might be nearly unbearable, just too much to take, though I'd be glad to give it a try.

But of course they're exactly like us in the fundamental ways: they push, gawk, and lift their chins, trying to see "Eckel walk from the prison, through Centre-street, in company with . . . one of the officers of the prison. Not many recognized them. . . ." "The greatest anxiety was manifested to see the unfortunate woman who claims to be the wife of Dr. Burdell. . . . She was brought from her house in Bond-street in a closed carriage to the City Hall, and there kept in the Sheriff's office. . . ."

Inside City Hall: "The room was crowded, the lobby in a great measure filled, and the stairs, portico, and City Hall steps were occupied by a large number of expectant spectators."

John Eckel and Snodgrass sat in the courtroom "in the vicinity of their counsel, in charge of two Sheriff's officers. The prisoners attracted general attention. Neither seemed very much annoyed. Snodgrass conversed freely if not jocularly with his friends. Eckel remained impassive. . . . Eckel's appearance, it must be admitted, fails to give any serious indications of a murderous nature. Indeed he is rather good looking. The only unpleasant feature about him is his eyes. They are small, greyish-blue —rather protuberant and bloodshot."

Henry Clinton came forward, and offered his arguments as Judge Brady listened. And then agreed. He discharged Snodgrass altogether: no one any longer seriously thought he'd had anything to do with the murder, and Connery had already examined him as a witness; twice, in fact. As for Eckel and Emma Cunningham, Brady called in a messenger boy, and sent word down to Connery to put into writing—right now, today—on what grounds they were held. While Clinton was at it, he obtained and sent along with the messenger writs of habeas corpus for Helen and Augusta.

Helen was on the witness stand, following Augusta, when the messenger arrived at 31 Bond: they weren't even well started with her testimony when Recorder Smith had to explain to the frustrated spectators that " . . . it would be contempt of court to detain this witness. The cheated crowd cried, 'Shame! Shame!' " but they had to let her go. And as she and Augusta put on their veils upstairs, Coroner Connery's big plans for this day were reduced to bringing down nine-year-old William Stuart Cunningham—and Connery couldn't even stick around for that.

He went off to write his appeal to Judge Brady, and as Connery worked, Willie satisfied Recorder Smith that he understood the significance of an oath, was sworn, and climbed up into the dental chair, his legs certainly not reaching the footrest, possibly even sticking straight out as he sat there. Then even nine-year-old Willie demonstrated that he, too, as a reporter said, was a "cool and self-possessed" Cunningham. After Smith had questioned the boy about the evening before the murder as the family got Helen ready to leave for boarding school in the morning, Smith got tricky, even sneaky. "After you went to bed that night how long was it before you heard the noise?"

And got nowhere. "I heard no noise."

A little later Smith tried again. "Did your little brother speak to you about the noise when you woke up in the morning? Don't you recollect him speaking to you about that?"

"No; when he woke up in the morning, he told me something about my cousin, and then I got up and got dressed."

Smith abandoned it. ". . . When you went to bed where did you leave [Snodgrass]?"

"I left him marking my sister's clothes. He said he wanted to go down and wash his neck."

"What did he want to wash his neck for?"

"It was dirty."

Learning nothing helpful from Willie, they put on his older brother, ten-year-old George. His was a different nature, and: "He sobbed and cried very much, and was evidently greatly frightened." They quieted him, and presently Smith tried again: "Who woke up first when the noise was heard in the night, you or your brother?"

"I never woke up. I did not hear any noise in the night."

"You did not?" Smith went on, beginning to make Coroner Connery look good.

"No, Sir."

"You did not hear any noise?"

"No; I sleep very light, too."

Presently: "The boy burst into another fit of crying." Smith tried to continue but: "The witness did not reply . . . his sobs increased, and . . . 'Oh! do let me go, I want to go upstairs. I feel as if I want to puke,' " the *Times* quoted George (". . . want to be sick," said the *Trib*), and that was the end of the day's testimony from the Cunninghams.

The drama was downtown now, Emma Cunningham waiting in the sheriff's office of City Hall to find out whether she'd be forced to return to 31 and face questions about the murder, or be freed of them forever. In the street outside: "An immense assemblage congregated in the vicinity of the Court-room at 3 o'clock, for the purpose of seeing the prisoners.

"The anxiety was increased by the knowledge that not only Mrs. Cunningham and Eckel, but the lady's two daughters would be produced in court, writs of habeas corpus being sued out, and served on the Coroner for their return in the interval before the Court resumed.

"A strong posse of policemen and sheriff's officers kept guard at the doors of the Court-room," then, all three of them veiled, "Mrs. Cunningham, Miss Augusta and Miss Helen Cunningham were brought into Court about a quarter past three o'clock. Their entrance was the signal for a general neck-stretching rush, accompanied by an excited murmur from the officers.

"While entering the Court-room, Mrs. Cunningham met with a slight, though for a time painful, accident. Walking with her head bent to evade, probably, the piercing glances of those congregated, she struck her head with great violence against one of the half-open doors. The blow stunned her for a moment, and she seemed as though going to fall, but one of the attendant officers caught her and conveyed her to her seat, where she soon recovered.

"The ladies took their seats by the side of Mr. Clinton, their counsel. Mrs. Cunningham removed her veil. She looked pale and exhausted, but gave no indication of nervousness or fear . . . [and her face] wore its usual decided and masculine expression. . . . Her daughters remained closely veiled."

Connery had made an awful mistake: his written orders for the confinement of Eckel and Emma Cunningham were now read aloud; and, the coroner had said, he wanted to hold Eckel as witness and suspect both. But of course this was a flat legal impossibility: an arrested suspect cannot be made to testify against himself as a witness.

Henry Clinton exploded. He did not ask, he now said to Judge Brady, that Eckel actually be discharged "on a mere technicality on account of the blundering inefficiency of this officer, Coroner Connery. . . ." Confident as they were of the final outcome for Eckel, "they did not wish that he should escape on account of the stupid, the miserable, the wretched, the contemptible, the disgraceful blundering of this man who had [just now] given them another written evidence of his stupidity, as though it were not plainly enough established already." He asked that the court adjourn once more, and another message be sent to Connery "that he no longer trifle with the Court, but . . . take the one ground or the other in reference to Mr. Eckel."

Brady didn't even bother: he simply discharged Eckel as a witness right then and there, ordering him held as a suspect only—exactly what Clinton had hoped for, I think; he could hardly have expected that a prime suspect would be turned completely loose. But now Eckel was free forever, if he chose never to talk, from questioning by anyone about Harvey Burdell's murder.

Clinton asked for the same decision for Emma Cunningham and, for good measure, "that the decision in her case include . . . that her counsel should have the right to consult with her whenever they pleased . . . without the august presence of our great magnate, the Coroner, any of his officials, his policemen, or his dignified son, John. (Laughter.)"

He got it. Brady ordered: "That the said Emma A. Burdell be remanded to the custody of the Coroner . . . at No. 31 Bond-street . . . until the rendition of the verdict of the Coroner's jury . . . on the ground solely of being held as a party implicated . . . and not as a witness." And Emma

Cunningham, too, was forever free of Connery.

While he'd had her and Eckel, Connery could have questioned them at any length: about the quarrels at 31 Bond, the alleged thefts from the Doctor's safe, the strange marriage, the threats; and about how it could be that a man in their midst could fight for his life, his cries apparently heard out on the street, while they'd slept through it all, hearing nothing. Too late now; he'd given Emma Cunningham time, and she'd used it to beat him.

Brady ordered Augusta discharged from custody on any ground, and ordered that while Helen's interrupted examination could be resumed, she would appear "as a witness only, and not subjected to detention."

The Cunningham women went back to 31 Bond, taken there in the enclosed carriage that brought them, I would expect; but "Eckel was taken to the Chief's office below, where an arrangement was made by which he might escape the annoyance of the curious throng who waited impatiently outside for his appearance."

Who thought up this arrangement, I don't know, but I wonder if it wasn't Eckel himself, the man who loved disguises. "His hat and coat were exchanged for the hat and coat of Mr. Wetmore, of the City Prison, who then, in company of Officer Masterson, proceeded across [City Hall] Park, and down Centre-street to the Prison. The crowd followed after, pushing and struggling madly to get a sight of Eckel. Those fortunate enough to get a 'good look' left satisfied, while their places were quickly filled by others. It was discovered, however, before he reached the Prison, that Mr. Wetmore was a counterfeit, and not a very good one either, for Eckel had large black whiskers and light hair, while he, Wetmore, had black hair and no whiskers. The sell being quickly learned, the crowd retraced their steps in haste to the Chief's office, where they learned that they had indeed been sold—for Eckel had a few moments before left for the Tombs in charge of Sergeant Murphy, *via* Broadway and Franklin-street, unrecognized and undisturbed."

At 31 Bond this wreck of a day finally ended for Coroner Connery. He adjourned till morning, further from pinning the murder on anyone than he'd been a full week before. Just before everyone left the room he stood up to say forlornly, ". . . I wish it to be understood that I had a witness sworn and under examination at the time she was removed from my jurisdiction. . . . I have submitted to every order that came to me. . . . And now, notwithstanding all the barbarity that has characterized this atrocious murder, I am informed that Mr. Snodgrass is walking about Broadway. . . ." It was worse than that, of course, and I expect he learned so soon afterward; that he would have waited around to hear.

As Connery finally walks out into the winter evening, it's too bad it's not possible to let him know, across a dozen decades, that help is coming. That, in a sudden melodramatic development surely better than even his gaudiest daydream, everything will suddenly go his way, even the newspapers swinging around to applaud. Be nice to do that; he'd have something better to say to his wife than he does now, walking along Bond Street through the dusk toward home.

9

"Feb. 9, 1857. Dear Sir," a man sat writing somewhere in New York Monday morning. "I have to-day heard that a man of the name of McFarrell, employed in the Appraiser's Store, under Mr. Graham, has said that he was in Bond-street at the time of the murder. . . ." He continued writing, then concluded, "He assigns as a cause of his not making it known that he was afraid he might be kept from his family and inconvenienced by his appearing as a witness, as he is a poor man." Then, having just blown the other man's cover, he hung on to his own: "I am yours respectfully, ONE WHO SEEKS FOR JUSTICE," and sent the note off to the Coroner by messenger.

This same morning, first thing, Connery sent a cop down to the Tombs to bring Eckel here—in a closed carriage, he ordered, so that the crowd outside wouldn't see who it was as he arrived. Over the weekend, Helen Cunningham had finished her testimony, stonewalling them as effectively as Augusta had; little George finished his testimony, from which they learned nothing helpful; and the inquest had dragged on. But today Eckel arrived, they put him off in a room under guard, and swore in Emily Sallenbach, the piano-playing girl at whose apartment on Broadway Mrs. Cunningham and Augusta had waited for the man who met them there on the night of the wedding. They took Emily into the room where Eckel sat waiting, and she stood there staring at his face. Then she returned to the witness stand: "Yes, Sir," she said in reply to the question, "that is the gentleman that was at our house."

But of course they couldn't question him. Not now. Or Emma Cunningham. These were "by all odds the most important witnesses yet produced in this case," the *Times* said later. "They *must* know something of the murder. . . ." But: "Their mouths have been closed. . . . Why is it that these parties have not been examined before?"

Well, they hadn't, and Connery was reduced to what surely seemed a forlorn hope. He'd sent someone to investigate, after receiving the anonymous note, and learned there was nobody named McFarrell working at the Appraiser's Public Store. There was a man named Farrell, though, and Connery sent out a subpoena for him now, to appear in the morning. His final order of the day was "to the police officers, to have all the carpets in the house taken up and all the floors examined," which shows, it seems to me, how desperate he felt.

In the morning—of what turned out to be the most spectacular day of the inquest—things began in a typically farcical way. The first scheduled witness was A. DeWitt Baldwin, one of the passersby in Bond Street who had smelled burning cloth the night of the murder. And Coroner Connery—conceivably out of excitement because by now he knew what was coming later—got things rolling by calling out, "Officer, call DeWitt Clinton!"

". . . DeWitt Clinton not appearing," the *Times* said (Clinton had been a well-known New York political figure, now thirty years dead), Mrs. Jane Miller was sworn and examined by visiting Judge Capron. She was merely an acquaintance of Dr. Burdell who had happened to drop in and see him on what turned out to be his last day. And again typically, she knew nothing to help the inquest.

But today this didn't matter: by now Connery knew what his main witness was going to say, and the first few witnesses were merely pre-

THE BOND-STREET MURDER.

ELEVENTH DAY OF THE CORONER'S INQUEST.

THE CURTAIN LIFTING.

Eckel Identified as the Murderer

Mrs. Cunningham tries to buy a Sword-Cane on the Day of the Murder.

Mrs. Cunningham Committed to the Tombs.

THE MURDERER SEEN AT THE DOOR.

TREMENDOUS EXCITEMENT IN THE CITY.

EXCEEDINGLY IMPORTANT TESTIMONY.

The investigation before Coroner Connery was resumed yesterday at 11 o'clock. Two hours before the doors were opened for the admission of Jury and witnesses, a large crowd gathered in the street, who satisfied their curiosity, as usual, by gazing with great intentness at the outside of the house.

The hour named for resuming the Inquest was 11 A. M. The Coroner was on hand at 10, but it was nearly 11½ before the proceedings commenced. Judge Capron again assisted the Coroner. The crowd was larger than on any previous occasion. It increased every hour, and at the time when Eckel was reconducted to the Tombs, numbered about two thousand persons. When he was led back in the custody of Captain Dilkes and three officers, and placed in the carriage in waiting for him, the crowd set up a dismal

New-York

VOL. VI......NO. 1684.   NEW-YORK,

liminaries: once again Eckel had been sent for from the Tombs, and they were just marking time till he got there, because this time keeping his mouth closed wasn't going to help. Eckel arrived, was taken to an upstairs bedroom; and then to the witness stand, to be sworn and examined by Judge Capron, there came the inquest's most sensational witness. He was John Farrell, thirty-two years old, married, and with three small children. He lived in Mott Street near the corner of Houston, at number 274, "at the rear of a small groggery, the keeper of which is his landlord."

Farrell sat down, looking like this to newspaper artist Brightly; and then the big question. Had he been in Bond Street, Capron asked him, on the night of the murder?

"I was."

"Where were you?"

"I was on this stoop that night," he replied astonishingly.

"At what time?"

"It might have been half past ten . . . it was between ten and eleven. . . ."

"How came you to come there?"

"Can I tell?"

"Yes, tell your story."

"I started from my house likely about half past nine o'clock that night. I have a disease of the back, and I work at a business which requires my sitting bent over, and I have frequently to get up and exercise myself. . . . Sometimes it takes me an hour to straighten myself, and sometimes more." He made ladies' shoes, he said, working at home, and: "This night I had some particular work for the man I worked for, a particular kind of customer gaiters which he wanted done next day, and they having heels on which was rather troublesome, I concluded to go out and walk, till my back got straight and did not ache so much, and come back and see if I could not do something at night. And I did work for an hour."

Farrell walked around for a while, he said, and presently came "up the Bowery to Bond-street, [and] came down this side of the street. I got within a few doors of here, and I stepped on the string of my shoe—the same that I have [on] now—and drawed the string nearly out, and I stooped down. It was sloppy, and I set down on this stoop here, and I took the shoe off, and was trying to fix the string in at the proper place. The string, I found, had not the tin usually on the end. It took me some time. While sitting there a man came along—two men. . . ." They were walking west, but were not together, Farrell said, and the second man walked on. But the first, who was wearing a shawl, he remembered, turned in and came up the stairs, "on the right-hand side . . . I set on the left, close to the railing."

Did this man wear a cap or a hat? Farrell couldn't recall. But: "You remember the shawl?"

"I remember the shawl because it was on the same height with my head when I first looked at it. Then I threw up my eyes as he got on the higher steps."

The man with the shawl walked on past him, climbing the stairs of the stoop, said Farrell, entered the house, the door closing, and "I heard the footsteps retreating from the door." The man had been inside only a short time—a minute, minute and a half, two minutes: he wasn't sure—when "I heard a cry of murder. I said to myself, 'There is a muss in this house, probably. . . . I guess they have been drinking. . . .' " Farrell said: "The cry that I heard was of a man being choked, for I remarked that especially, for I thought that the man that went in had caught hold of some person and choked him, inside."

Farrell heard no other sound, he said, "with the exception of some men talking on the corner of the Bowery and Bond-street," and he resumed trying to fix his shoestring.

Another witness, an architect named William Ross, had testified here last Thursday that he had walked along Bond Street on that same night . . . at about the same time . . . and with another man walking ahead of him. This man had turned in at number 31, unlocked the door, and gone into the house. So far, exactly what Farrell had just described.

However, Ross said they'd both come from the direction of Broadway, and so were walking *east;* and had also walked separated by a hundred feet or more. While Farrell said the two men he saw came from the opposite direction, and only a few feet apart. Otherwise their testimony agreed; for Ross had said that within a very short time after the other man had entered number 31—"when I got . . . two houses further on"—he, too, had heard a cry of murder. He looked behind him, saw nothing, and looked up ahead toward the Bowery. And there, like Farrell, Ross saw several young men, "that were kind of roguish," Ross had said, "making a noise." He decided that the cry of murder had come from them, and walked on.

If Farrell had incorrectly remembered from which direction the two men he saw had come . . . and if one or the other was mistaken about the distance between the two walkers . . . then Farrell's testimony now and that of William Ross last Thursday seem otherwise to agree. It's true that if Farrell had been sitting on the steps of number 31, shoe in hand, when Ross walked by, then Ross somehow failed to see him there; but Farrell testified that the steps were quite dark. Of course, it is also true that Farrell had had the chance, like everyone else in New York, to read William Ross's testimony in last Friday's papers.

The man in the shawl entered the house, Farrell sat trying to fix his shoelace, he said, and then: "Probably a minute might have passed . . .

[when] I heard the door open . . . [and] a man came to the door. . . . He said to me, 'What are you doing there?' He spoke in a very rough manner. I was afraid; I thought the man that went in had ordered him to put me off the stoop. . . . The man . . . was in his shirt sleeves. I saw his head, his shoulders, and a part of his left hand.

". . . He said, 'What are you doing there?' I said, 'Nothing.' . . . I had my shoe off . . . wetting the shoe string in my mouth, and trying to put it in the holes." Shoe in hand, "and thinking there was a row in the house, and fearing he would probably kick me," Farrell got to his feet, "and in rising I kept my face to the door. At the time I was bent; I could not straighten myself very well on account of this complaint in my back, and I retreated down the steps sideways for fear . . . that he might assault me."

At some time along in here Connery sent eight or ten spectators and some reporters up to Harvey Burdell's bedroom.

Farrell continued: walking on his toes because the sidewalk was sloppy, he moved down to another stoop "three or four doors below." He sat down again, put on his shoe, and went home, where he worked "for an hour on the ladies' gaiters." Farrell thought nothing more of the incident on the stoop of number 31 Bond, he said, until he began reading about the murder in the papers.

They tested him. On the night all this happened, "Was you sober?" a juror wanted to know.

"I was."

What were his "habits as to drink?" An occasional drink when his back hurt, but he wasn't in the habit of getting intoxicated. All he'd had to drink that night was "one glass of rectified spirits; about half an ounce." Of whiskey? "No, what we call spirits. It is such as is usually sold in Dutch groceries." But that's all he'd had in twenty-four hours.

How was his sight? Shortsighted, but could easily see short distances. Thought he'd be able to recognize the men at the reporters' table, if he saw them again.

Was he sure this was the house? Yes; he'd seen the house numerals that night; seen a one and a three, that is, but couldn't remember later whether the number was 13 or 31. So last Thursday night he'd walked down Bond Street again, had looked at the stoop of number 13, and that wasn't the one. It was number 31.

And so they came to the final question: Was the man who had frightened Farrell from the stoop of 31 on the night of the murder . . . John Eckel? Connery sent some of the jurymen up to join the spectators and reporters in Dr. Burdell's bedroom; and had Eckel taken in to join them. Then Connery walked in, and told the men, some twenty-five of them, to take off their coats, including Eckel—because the man who'd come to the front door the night of the murder, said Connery, had been in shirt sleeves.

Henry Clinton seems to have briefed Eckel, who sat "occupying a chair near the foot of the bed, dressed in a shaggy brown overcoat, with a pointed plush cap on his head"—because Eckel refused to take off his coat "by advice of counsel." The other men then put their coats back on, and "formed themselves into an irregular circle, Eckel standing by the head of the bed with nothing in his position or manner to distinguish him from the rest. . . . All had their heads uncovered."

Connery returned to the inquest room, where it was "announced that the witness would be taken upstairs," said the *Times,* and "there was an instant rush to the door which the policemen guarded jealously." But Connery said, "Gentlemen of the Press will be permitted to go upstairs," the cops let the reporters through, and about a dozen of them, "pencils and paper in hand, wended their way up. . . ."

His stage set, the reporters ready, Connery brought Farrell upstairs. Through the murder room, and into Harvey Burdell's bedroom, where the waiting men made "a pretty good roomful." Eckel now stood "behind the chair on which he had been sitting, leaning against the footpost of the bed; his appearance indicated considerable nervous trepidation, although his feelings were under strong control.

"Witness had been directed to look and see if he found any person that resembled the man that he had seen on the night of the murder come to the door of the house. . . ." Farrell walked slowly around the irregular circle of silent men, "peering into the face of each individual as he passed, but did not at first pay any particular attention to Eckel; a moment afterward, *he turned and looked at Eckel fixedly.* Eckel's eyes winked incessantly, but he gazed steadily at Witness while undergoing this scrutiny. The absorbed attention with which every person in the room watched this proceeding was actually painful in its intensity. The bystanders scarcely breathed, and a pin might have been heard to drop. Mr. Farrell, after glancing at Eckel in an uncertain, hesitating way, turned twice, evidently struck by something familiar in Eckel's countenance, and the third time he looked, continued to gaze. We observed Eckel's countenance attentively," said the *Times* man. "The lines about his mouth were even more deeply set and strongly marked than usual. He had the appearance of a man who had made up his mind to undergo examination, and had steeled himself to the task. It was impossible, of course, that he should have known the precise object for which this scrutiny was instituted; he had undergone several interviews with different parties who were called to identify him, but it could not have escaped the notice of the most unobserving that he had arrived at the conclusion that there was something more than usual in this particular investigation. Although, therefore, he was probably unaware of the precise object of this examination, he had put himself under severe restraint, in order that no movement of a muscle and no change in countenance should betray his emotions. But if the expression of Eckel's face was that of stoical indifference, that of the witness Farrell was the epitome of hesitation, doubt and reluctance. He gave a very slight start, so slight as to be almost imperceptible, when his attention was first arrested by the expression in Eckel's face. Unwilling to swear positively that Eckel was the man, yet he evidently struggled with a conviction which seemed to force itself upon his mind, that the person who appeared at the door on the night of the murder and this man were one and the same. He put his hand to his head, and appeared lost in thought for a moment or two,—then turned and walked away."

Farrell came back to Eckel then, and stooped to one knee, "so as to

bring the suspected man's face in the same relation that it stood on the fatal Saturday night; this done, much doubt seemed to vanish from Farrell's face."

" 'Well, which is the man?' " a reporter quoted Connery.

" 'I don't *know*,' " he replied; this is the reporter's italicizing. " '*I think that is the man.*' (pointing to Eckel)."

On the witness stand again, Farrell said "he was sorry [to be] the means of putting any man's life in jeopardy . . ." but in replies to Judge Capron's further questions he said, "*I had no trouble in selecting him from among the others,*" and "as soon as I looked at him, he attracted my attention; I should have known the man again who came to the door had I seen him twenty years afterwards."

Outside the house the crowd had been growing all morning, and now two thousand people, the *Times* estimated, stood waiting as Captain Dilk and three cops brought Eckel out of number 31 and down toward a carriage at the curb. As they stepped out the door onto the stoop, "the crowd set up a dismal howl, which was prolonged until the vehicle reached Broadway, and was lost among the crowd of stages." The *Tribune* said: "A number of men and boys followed the carriage a short distance, booing and hissing as they went," and the *Times* concluded: "For many years in this City, there has not been such a burst of execration respecting any

suspected criminal as that which jarred on Eckel's ears as he was taken
. . . from the premises in Bond Street."

Inside the house the inquest was exploding: a new witness had arrived
whose testimony on any other day would have been a sensation of itself.
She was Isabella Banford, she told them from the witness chair, "a young
and quite handsome woman of fine personal appearance and great intelligence." Another reporter liked her, too: thought her "handsome and
intelligent." She was "a Jewess," he said, and when "Connery advanced,
holding the Bible, she said, 'I do not swear; I am not a Christian,'" so
they let her "affirm."

She lived at 401 Broadway, she told them, and worked for Clyde &
Black, retailers of umbrellas, parasols, canes, etc.

"Have you any recollection of a lady and gentleman calling at your
store, lately, to purchase a sword-cane?"

"Yes, Sir."

"When?

"It was Friday, a week ago." This was the day of the murder night;
a man and woman had come into the store between eleven and noon, and
"asked to see some sword-canes."

It was a triumphant day for Edward Connery, and he wanted no
word missed by the reporters. "Not so fast," he told the witness, and Judge
Capron explained, "These gentlemen wish to write, and they cannot write
as rapidly as you and I can talk." Slowly, making certain the reporters got
it all, they let Isabella Banford tell them how she'd brought out a selection
of sword canes, how the couple had looked them over, and how "the lady
took one in her hands, and said she did not think it would suit, to the
gentleman that was with her."

"Wait there a moment," said Connery. He gave the reporters time
to catch up, then: "Now go on."

"Then what?" the witness was asked. "Did she try it at all?"

"Yes, Sir, she tried it against a corner of the table. . . ." Then she
"held it in her hand, and bent it so." But the kind of sword cane the couple
wanted, they told Miss Banford, must be "'short, sharp and strong.'" She
could get one made, Miss Banford told them, but: "They said it would not
answer, they must have it to-night," and that "they would look further
and see if they could find one."

"Is it a frequent occurrence that a lady comes into your store to buy
a sword-cane?"

"No, Sir, that is something a lady had never asked me before. . . ."

How old was this lady?

". . . about 35 or 36."

116

They took her upstairs for a look at Emma Cunningham, but she came back to say, "I should not like to swear it was her." The lady who'd wanted to buy a sword cane had been wearing a bonnet, so they took the witness upstairs again, and made Mrs. Cunningham put on a bonnet. Back to the witness stand, but Miss Banford still wasn't sure: Mrs. Cunningham's features, she thought, "are very like her, but I would not wish quite to swear." How strong this resemblance? "She looks very much like her, indeed," and her voice "was like as it was in the store."

They sent Miss Banford to the Tombs in a carriage for a look at Eckel, and while they waited, a man spoke privately to Judge Capron. He was Dr. J. B. Morton, described later by the *Times* as "a German, of unprepossessing features." Miss Banford's testimony worried Dr. Morton because, he said to Capron, a friend of his had told him that a gentleman and lady he knew had tried to buy a sword cane at Clyde & Black that same Friday; and they were not Eckel and Mrs. Cunningham. They were merely people going to a party that evening, and the lady wanted him to have a weapon from fear of the garroters. Just as Miss Banford had said, this couple looked at several sword canes, couldn't find one they liked, and the clerk had suggested having one made. No, the lady had said, they wanted it that night. Capron listened, then told Morton to wait till Isabella Banford came back.

They used the waiting time to hear a man who lived at number 32 Bond; he'd heard a choking gurgle the night of the murder. They'd sent a juror to examine the minutes of the meeting of the directors of the Artisans' Bank; now he returned to say they showed Dr. Burdell present, here in New York, on October 28, the day Mrs. Cunningham said they'd been married. But Judge Capron suggested that the entry might have been made by proxy, that it didn't prove a thing. A tailor who'd made clothes for Eckel was shown the clothes he had here, but couldn't say whether any were missing. And so on.

Isabella Banford came back, and they put her on the stand immediately. Had she seen Eckel?

"Yes, Sir."

"Well, what do you say?"

"I cannot recognize him at all."

"That is bad," Capron said, and questioned her again, but she would not identify Eckel. They had her wait to see if she could recognize the sword-cane customer Dr. Morton had talked about. But Morton didn't know the lady, and couldn't produce her; he'd only heard about her from a friend. So they wouldn't allow his testimony; it was only hearsay, they said.

Henry Clinton pointed out that this was exactly the same kind of hearsay testimony "that you have occupied ten days with," but it didn't do him any good. ". . . I hope you will introduce testimony," said Clinton, "that tells in favor of my client, as well as I observe you do that which tells against her." That started a wrangle which ended with Connery threatening to have a cop put Clinton in jail if he spoke one more word.

Connery then announced that because of "important testimony which connects [Emma Cunningham] this day, more or less, with being the cause of the death of Harvey Burdell, I have, gentlemen of the jury, ordered her to be sent to the Tombs, to be imprisoned tonight, and to be kept there until the issue of this grand inquisition. (Applause)."

Darkness had come, they adjourned, and Emma Cunningham was escorted to a carriage by Officer Smith of the Fifteenth Ward. "The crowd around the house was immense, but night enveloped her removal, and but little notice was taken of her as she entered the carriage. . . ."

At the *Times* I think the typesetters must already have been at work, because the paper came out with an "Extra *Times*" that very evening, containing the "leading parts" of today's stunning testimony. The Extra "created an immense sensation," they said next day. "Our office was densely crowded, and 10,000 or 12,000 copies . . . were sold as rapidly as they could be struck from the press."

In another part of the *Times* offices that evening, a man began writing tomorrow's editorial. "The Curtain Lifted—the Mystery of the Murder Dispelled," he headed it, then: "The Bond-street drama approaches its close," he began; and couldn't have been more mistaken. "Yesterday's proceedings . . . substantially fastened upon John J. Eckel and Mrs. Cunningham the guilt of the bloodiest and most awful murder that has startled this City for many years. . . . There seems little reason to doubt that Eckel did the deed—and he cannot be implicated without it implicating Mrs. Cunningham.

"A remarkable feature of the case is that the witness by whom this consummation has been reached, has been entirely unknown and unheard of until the last moment. An anonymous letter . . .

". . . the very precaution which Eckel took against being observed, —his going to the front door and looking to see if anybody was in the street, proved the means, and thus far the only means, of his exposure!

". . . Mrs. Cunningham is also identified as having, in company with a gentleman, on Friday purchased a sword-cane in Broadway. . . . This leaves it impossible to doubt her complicity in the murder,—or that the whole affair *was deliberately and systematically planned* . . . it will be very difficult to convince the public that no noise was heard by any of the inmates on that night. . . ."

On this same busy evening a lithographer named Robert Mathews walked into the chief of police's office, and handed the sergeant there "a small, square piece of paper, smutted and creased as though carried some time in the vest pocket." A man on the street, a stranger, had handed it to him, Mathews said. "Upon one side of it was written in a large bold hand:

> "John M. Smiter,
> Wm. L. Butkins,
> *alias* Wm. Pike,
>   and
> Joseph M. Hathorn,
> are the murderers
> of H. Burdell.

"and upon the other side:

> "The writer of this
> is one of the
> murderers."

At four o'clock in the morning, George Snodgrass showed up at the Fifteenth Ward station house, and asked for a place to sleep.

The inquest wound down in only a couple more days, as though Farrell and his spectacular shoestring had been a climax it was no use trying to top. Mostly they wrapped up loose ends.

On Friday they didn't meet at all, and the house was cleared out, no outsiders admitted except the cops guarding it. For the first time since the murder, Helen and Augusta and their little brothers were left alone in the house.

What these four Cunningham children had to say to one another throughout that day can only be guessed at; wrongly, I'm sure. At some time during the day and again on the next, the girls went down to the Tombs to visit their imprisoned mother. At the prison: "Their deportment was such as to astonish the warden, doctors and officers. . . . They were dressed in rich silks, with very valuable fur capes, heavy gold bracelets, and other expensive jewelry. While waiting for admission in the outer corridor, they carefully arranged their apparel, and altogether behaved very little like persons about to enter the cell where their mother was confined on a charge of murder."

Well, maybe. You wonder just how they should have behaved to suit the reporter's idea of correct conduct while visiting one's mother in jail.

Possibly they were only toughing it out.

On the last day, Saturday, George Snodgrass was identified by a still-indignant lady witness as the young man she'd quarreled with at her store a few days before the murder. He had bought "a dagger-knife," she said, "a four-cornered blade." Snodgrass denied this just as indignantly, and the lady's own clerk failed to support her identification. But Dr. Woodward was given a dagger the store owner had brought along as being a duplicate of the one she'd sold. The doctor left with it, then returned in the afternoon to report that he'd *tried it on a dead body* (this time the italics are all mine) and that it could have made the wounds that killed the Doctor. That was enough for Connery: he ordered Snodgrass arrested as an accessory to the murder.

Still another man testified that he, too, had been passing through Bond Street on the night of the murder; that he'd seen Farrell sitting there on the stoop fixing his shoe; and that he'd also seen the man in shirt sleeves open the door.

And the *Times* got a letter from the Dr. Morton who'd been turned down as a witness on Tuesday. He said, "The 'German, of unprepossessing features'—the 'would-be' witness, presents his compliments to the Reporter of the Daily Times, and begs his acceptance of the inclosed [a daguerreotype of himself]; trusting that he will be truly grateful for it, as furnishing him with the means for a prompt vindication of his skill as a physiognomist.

"The undersigned begs to state for the information of the sagacious Reporter, that he was born in this state, and of New England parents—studied medicine in this city, and has practiced medicine here for the last five years; that he is upheld from despondency, in view of the expressed opinion of the Reporter—by assurances from several sympathizing friends, that he does not look especially like a villain. . . ." Signed, "J. B. Morton, No. 119 Tenth Street."

The *Times* replied: "We cannot help thinking that Dr. M. is unduly sensitive. . . . We permit him, however, to make his own explanation . . . adding our own certificate that, from the daguerrotype of himself which he inclosed in the letter, our Reporter's opinion of his personal appearance is entirely mistaken. We regret our inability to present an engraving of this picture for the assurance and satisfaction of the public. We must ask them to take our own statement that the Doctor is a very good-looking man. Those who doubt it can see the portrait he has sent us, on application at the Times office."

Then they turned serious. Only two days earlier the *Times* had editorialized: ". . . Mrs. Cunningham is . . . identified as having . . .

120

purchased a sword-cane" (although in fact she had not been identified).
". . . This leaves it impossible to doubt her complicity. . . ." Now they
denounced Connery and Judge Capron for refusing to allow Dr. Morton
to testify that maybe it wasn't Emma Cunningham "who bought the
sword-cane, and said it must be 'short and sharp.' . . . This testimony is
permitted to go through the length and breadth of the land, while proof
that would completely explode it is ruled out. . . .

"This may be the law," the *Times* huffed, "but it is not justice."

And then finally, on Saturday afternoon, two weeks to the day from
when Harvey Burdell was found murdered in his office, the inquest was
over. Except for the verdict.

And the coroner's summation. He'd written it out, and would read
it aloud, he said, so that he couldn't be misquoted. I don't suppose that
under the circumstances it was actually too long; it took forty-five minutes, the *Tribune* said. A few selected phrases may suggest the flavor of
the coroner's address: ". . . I may assert without fear of contradiction
. . . the perpetrators of the foul deed . . . eyes of the public riveted upon
us . . . unparalleled in the annals of crime," and "I do not shrink from
the task. . . ."

Of course, it wouldn't have been the coroner if he hadn't got at least
one laugh: ". . . I saw it predicated in one of the public journals of this
City on Thursday last, that I should probably consume *an entire day* in
my summing-up of the case, and as that prediction will not be verified,
I shall await with calm resignation the castigation that awaits me for
presuming to falsify the prediction referred to. (Laughter.)"

My reading of the coroner's charge to his jury is that he virtually
directed a verdict naming Eckel and Mrs. Cunningham as the probable
murderers, and Snodgrass as possible accessory. His logic: it was the
inmates of number 31 who had the opportunity: and who were they? He
listed their names (ending with Daniel Ullman, but adding, "This latter
name we may exclude . . ."). So, if we can also eliminate the small boys,
the daughters, and the servants, that left Eckel, Mrs. Cunningham, and
Snodgrass.

As for their motive, it was: "To reap the fruits" of the crime. Because
if you believe, said Connery to the jury, that the October 28 marriage of
Emma Cunningham was to an impostor claiming to be Dr. Burdell—and
no one afterward ever behaved as though a marriage had really occurred
—then the motive is the inheritance as widow of the Doctor's estate by
Emma Cunningham, Eckel sharing in the proceeds for his part of the
crime.

And, he said, we have Farrell for proof, for if you believe, "as I do,"

121

that it was Eckel who came to the door and ordered Farrell away immediately after Dr. Burdell entered the house and then cried out, it eliminates the possibility of an unknown from outside who did the deed, leaving a bloody trail down the staircase, ending in a splotch on the front door, as he fled the house. If Farrell's identification is correct, the man who left that trail is Eckel.

But why would Eckel murder Dr. Burdell, then stick his head out the front door? Well: "For what purpose he came to the door we cannot positively say; but it may be inferred, and I think the inference is a natural one, finding that his victim was dispatched, and having a murderer's fears that the cries may have been heard by some person outside, he ventured to the door, to satisfy himself that they had not been heard, thereby furnishing the strongest possible circumstantial evidence against himself, that he was the murderer or one of the murderers, . . . in this horrid tragedy. Thus, gentlemen, by what *man* terms *accident,* but which may more fitly be termed the just and wise interposition of that Being who guides and governs all, and from whom no secrets are hidden, was the witness Farrell on the very spot at the *needed moment,* and was there made by the murderer himself a witness of his guilt."

Farrell's testimony also meant that, if he could hear the cry of the murdered man from outside the house, those inside the house surely heard it, too. Therefore they lied when they said they didn't. For further corroboration, add in the peculiar sleeping arrangements of the Cunningham women on the night of the murder, suggesting a clumsily arranged false alibi; and also add the sending of the servants early to bed as though to get them out of the way. In addition, there was the smell of burning wool and leather on the night of the murder, suggesting the burning of clothes. The fact that no bloody clothing was ever found led—by the coroner's logic—to the inference, not that maybe there was none to find, but "that the murderer proceeded . . . to destroy the garments he wore, spotted and besmeared and in all probability saturated and baptized as by immersion in the blood of his victim."

There was more: ". . . the blood of the murdered man cries out to Heaven for vengeance . . ."; there were "arrows of retributive justice," and "pandering to the morbid appetite of the public . . ." and, he said: "The attacks on myself personally, past and yet to come . . . have been but as 'dewdrops on the lion's mane. . . .' "

Toward the end the coroner told the jury that: "*My opinion* ought not to weigh a feather in the scales of justice now in your hands. The verdict is to be *yours,* not *mine,* or influenced by me." At about a quarter to five, the jury retired to think it all over.

If the coroner's logic was a little shaky at times, and if he suggested that things had been proved that really hadn't, I don't know that he did too badly nevertheless. Things certainly didn't look good for Emma Cunningham and John Eckel, anyway. So what could the coroner suggest to his jury: to let them go? This wasn't a trial, even if he himself had made it seem like one; he was telling them only that there ought to *be* a trial, and surely he was right. Just the same, hours passed and they stayed out, unable to make up their minds.

But I enjoyed the wait. "The large crowd which had occupied the street in front of the house during the day, the throng of more fortunate spectators who crowded the front parlor, and the changeable detachment of hangers-on who succeeded, by one pretense or another, in obtaining admission to the Coroner's room, lingered pertinaciously for two or three hours in the hope of hearing a verdict. As 9 o'clock approached, however, and no sign was made by the jurors indicating that they had agreed, the patience of even the most patient began to tire, and people dropped off, one by one, until the crowd outside had dwindled down to half a dozen, and the assemblage inside, exclusive of members of the press and police officers, had so far diminished as barely to exceed a score. After the tedious task of transcribing the Coroner's charge had been completed by the reporters—and the event was celebrated with sundry jokes and numerous hearty congratulations—the scene within became unusually animated, and assumed a free-and-easy air strangely at variance both with the occasion and the place. Groups of five or six were scattered here and there through the room, discussing the probable terms of the verdict, the probable chance of the ultimate conviction of the accused, the probable disposition of the house, the probable fate of the children, the probability of success in raising a fund to buy drinks all round, and a perfect litany of other chances, speculations, probabilities and reflections. At fitful intervals appeared the Coroner, and no sooner would his good-natured face show itself within the door, than he was beset by a torrent of queries as to what the jury was doing, and whether they had agreed. 'Gentlemen,' said he, on the first occasion, 'I have just been up there; I rapped at the door and told them that if they thought they could not agree before 12 o'clock I would go home, because I'm completely done up, and come back in the morning. They informed me, gentlemen, that they are drawing up a verdict, and so we'll have it in a short time.'

"The next time he reported progress, which was about an hour later, the Jury had but five lines to write—which took them half an hour more.

"In the meantime, the jollity increased downstairs. One enterprising individual raised a supply of crackers and cheese which was extensively partaken of by the five-cent contributors who clubbed to provide funds for the purchase. Another heightened the pleasure of the repast by relating queer mistakes into which the reporters or printers had fallen in giving the testimony of witnesses examined during the inquest. Among the other singular errors that occurred he stated that one had been brought to his attention that morning by Dr. Garish whom he had heard implore, with choking voice and eyes full of tears, the reporter of the Herald to correct that portion of his evidence, as published in that paper, in which he had been made to say that he had examined the wounds in the body of Dr. Burdell, and 'found one in the heart under the navel.'

"Towards the close of the entertainment the Coroner again entered, and was magnanimously presented with the fragments, to-wit: a cracker and a half and the cheese crust. Somebody suggested that he should treat 'the press.'

" 'No, by George,' said he, 'I think the press should treat me. I have been giving them food for a fortnight—filling their rapacious maw, almost to choking, for two whole weeks, and I think they ought to give me food for one night.'

" 'Well, but, Coroner,' said a third, 'you know the press has treated you already.'

" 'Yes,' says the Coroner, 'I know what you mane.'

" 'D——d badly,' said a fourth.

" 'Exactly,' was the general response.

" 'Well, gentlemen,' said the Coroner, 'notwithstanding all the Press has said against me, I can say that I never used an indiscretion at this table. I never thought of using one—but in the case of that little Irishwoman, Mary, I adopted the plan of extracting what she knew from her, which I thought most likely to succeed. But, as for indiscretions, I never meant them—I protest solemnly to God—(and here he reverently removed his hat)—I never meant them.'

"Everybody agreed with the Coroner, and the feeling was universally expressed that he had done as well as he possibly could, and was, in fact, entitled to the distinguished consideration of being regarded as a genuine old brick.

"Time gradually wore on. The last cigars were smoked down to the smallest possible stumps. The last jokes were cracked. Some of the officers had dropped asleep on the sofas. The conversation had subsided into little more than an occasional whisper. Little Georgie Cunningham crept silently in and out of the room. . . .

"Another quarter of an hour passed, and the suspense was at length relieved. Capt. Dilk entered the room and ordered the jurors' seats to be cleared. The buzz of excited conversation was at once renewed. The jurors entered, evidently much exhausted. Silence ensued in an instant. The Deputy Coroner called over the roll, and each juror answered to his name.

"Coroner—Gentlemen, have you agreed upon your verdict?

"Foreman—Yes, Sir.

"Coroner—Read it.

"Mr. Hall read as follows:"

What the foreman then read was a verbal drum-roll beginning, "State of New-York, City and County of New-York. An inquisition taken at the house of the late Harvey Burdell, No. 31 Bond Street, in the Fifteenth Ward of . . ." and continuing for 160 more words such as, ". . . in the year of our lord, one thousand eight hundred and fifty-seven . . . upon the oaths and affirmations of twelve good and lawful men . . . duly chosen and sworn or affirmed and charged to enquire . . . said Harvey Burdell . . . 30th day of January, 1857 . . . feloniously murdered, and came to his death. . . ." And then finally it reached "the jurors believe from the evidence, and therefore find, that Emma Augusta Cunningham and John J. Eckel were principals in the commission of said murder; and the jurors aforesaid find that George Vail Snodgrass either joined . . . in the commission of the said murder, or was an accessory . . . and the jurors aforesaid further find that Augusta Cunningham and Helen Cunningham . . . have some knowledge of the facts connected with the said murder, which they have concealed . . . and that it is the duty of the Coroner to hold them for further action of the Grand Jury. In witness, thereof, we . . ." and they'd signed their names.

Helen and Augusta, Connery then decided, were to stay under police guard here in the house so that they could take care of the boys. Hannah Conlon and Mary Donaho, the jury also advised, should be held as witnesses for the grand jury or made to post bond; and so must Farrell, whose original fears at coming forward as a witness were now realized.

Said Captain Dilk, "I would state to the jury that Mr. Farrell's family are in very destitute circumstances. His wife has nothing to maintain herself with, and he has had nothing except what he has received in the way of food I have given him from the hotel. We had a regular subscription yesterday at the station house for the support of his wife."

"Coroner—Oh, I think the city would act in a matter of this kind. The city ought to do it.

"Capt. Dilk—While the city are thinking of it the woman would starve.

"A juror—I suggest that the jury make a suggestion to that effect to the city, that is, that it take care of his family during the time he is in custody."

125

Several others in the room agreed, the jury was at last discharged, and "Mr. E. Robinson, Jr., made a collection for the benefit of Farrell's family, to which the Jurors and others contributed. It amounted in all to $5.50, and was handed over to Capt. Dilk to be given to Mrs. Farrell."

Nothing I found suggested that anyone remembered that today was Helen's birthday, her sixteenth, but maybe Augusta and the boys did.

10

For a short time now the murder moved to a back burner, though the city's news hunger remained. But the grand jury's deliberations, which began only three days later, were secret and the newspapers had to wait.

They managed to keep the pot simmering, though; and the day after the inquest ended, both the *Times* and *Tribune* reporters showed up at the Tombs to see how Emma Cunningham, in her cell above, and how

John Eckel, in his, were taking the verdict.

I think the *Times* sent the wrong man, or maybe he didn't feel good today. All he found to report was that "Mrs. Cunningham maintained . . . the same stolid indifference which has marked her demeanor throughout the whole of the proceedings since the first day. . . . She remarked that she would prosecute the editors of all the newspapers immediately she regained her liberty." (Starting with the editor of the *Times,* I'd think.) "Her daughters, she added, would not be confined in the Tombs one day, as she would send for friends and get them bailed out."

But the *Tribune* man found a different Emma Cunningham, or possibly she responded differently to another reporter's manner or questions. When he arrived, Mrs. Cunningham had left her cell—to get a little exercise, and "as our reporter entered the corridor in which her cell is situated, she appeared walking toward him; but she no sooner perceived the presence of strangers than she retreated to her cell."

He talked to her there, then wrote: "She bears her trying situation with remarkable fortitude, and receives visitors with an ease and dignity that would seem to convey the impression that she felt conscious of her innocence. . . . She was attired in a mourning dress and dark shawl, and her head was uncovered. . . . She seemed more calm and collected than [she had when the inquest began]." His questions had to do with her guilt or innocence, and "she maintains her perfect innocence of the crime. . . . and scoffs at the idea that she could have committed it. . . ."

Of John Eckel in his cell, the *Times* man said his "conduct has not much varied since the verdict. He was a little graver . . . than at any previous time, but still insisted that everything would 'turn out all right.' He was supplied with all the Sunday papers, and spent the greater part of the day reading them."

It seems uninspired. The *Tribune* man found a lot more to interest him: a good picture emerges from his report, a new look at another kind of Eckel. Eckel was standing outside his cell talking to a couple of officials when the *Trib* man arrived. The officials left, the reporter introduced himself, and Eckel "willingly entered into conversation on the all engrossing topic. He said he was very comfortable, and seemed marvelously calm and self-possessed. . . . His meals are sent in from a restaurant, and he has the privilege of a light at night if he wishes it. Newspapers, cigars and other luxuries are allowed him, and he says that with one exception he has experienced none but the kindest treatment. . . ."

In the interview that followed, the reporter asked what I wanted to hear, and got some pretty good answers. Eckel "admitted that the circumstantial evidence against the family was rather weighty, but he asserted his entire innocence and his full belief that the others now charged with the crime would be proved innocent . . . he denied that he went to the door that night, as Farrell charges. . . . The public excitement at this murder, he thinks, leads people to snatch too eagerly at every little circumstance that goes to substantiate their foregone conclusions, and . . . in their eagerness they lose sight of all probability, and cast aside whatever does not chime with their own opinions. In reference to Farrell's identification . . . he says that his picture had been hawked about in the streets, and his person described until he believed nine-tenths of the community would have no difficulty in pointing him out. . . .

"Mr. Eckel . . . said that perhaps there were few men whose morality would stand the test of a rigid scrutiny; but he argued that they were not therefore to be set down as murderers. . . . Where was his motive . . . ? He never knew Dr. Burdell or Mrs. Cunningham until . . . he saw by an advertisement that he could obtain room and board at No. 31 Bond Street. . . ." Even then he hardly knew Dr. Burdell beyond "the usual forms of recognition when they passed each other in the hall. The idea that he could have personated Dr. Burdell in the marriage with Mrs. Cunningham, in two weeks after he entered their house was simply absurd. And as to his murdering him for the sake of a middle-aged widow with five children, and the chance of a fortune of only $33,000 at furthest, why, it was so absurd that were people not blinded by excitement and prejudice, they would scout the idea as preposterous. All of this was said in a frank, manly way by the accused, without any bitterness or anger, and when our reporter bade him adieu he felt impelled to believe that his innocence would yet be established."

It could be that the *Tribune* reporter was young, Eckel able to impress him more than he should have been. But I think Eckel sounds persuasive, to some degree, and when I'd finished reading the interview I had the same doubts.

Neither *Times* nor *Tribune* seemed to take Snodgrass or the possibility of his having been involved very seriously. The *Times* said: "Snodgrass . . . was removed from the Fifteenth Ward Station-house [where I guess they'd been allowing him to sleep] to the Tombs [yesterday] afternoon. When he left the Station-house he was very desponding, and we were told by the officers present asserted his innocence, and attacked the character of . . . the witness who swore to his purchase of the dagger, in language so gross as to be quite unfit for publication."

"He seems to have laid aside his devil-may-care manner," the *Tribune* man wrote, "and realizes that he has got himself into a serious scrape. That he had no hand in the murder, nor knows anything about it, is very generally believed. He is altogether too shallow to conceal it if he was in any way concerned in the crime. . . . Mr. Snodgrass is confined in the third corridor of the male prison, above Mr. Eckel. His cheerfulness seems to have departed with his banjo and his liberty."

A few more bubbles from the back burner. When the grand jury met on Tuesday it took the advice of District Attorney Hall, and solved the problem of how Farrell's wife was to feed her family for the next couple of months on the five and a half dollars which had been collected for her: it let Farrell go home, "relying on his honesty to reappear when needed." It let Hannah and Mary go, too, and said that Augusta and Helen would be free as soon as it had heard their testimony.

A reporter went around to Mott Street and learned that: "The neighbors give Farrell a most excellent character, but they seem now to have some jealousy of him. He has had money subscribed to him—he had been

130

before the Grand Jury, 'and shure he's goin' to hang the man that killed the Doctor.' So Farrell has got a lift in life, and his old companions watch him narrowly to see if he is getting proud."

And, hunting for something, anything, to print, a reporter dropped in on Emma Cunningham again, learning nothing much, but ". . . the two sons of the unfortunate woman were in the gallery, outside of her cell-door, and their presence alone must have been sufficient to unnerve her. They are very handsome children, the oldest is but eleven [ten, actually], and the younger but nine years old. It was a touching sight to see the little fellow looking around with wondering eyes upon the strange scene."

At 31 Bond: "Some wretched vagabonds" had been "persecuting [the Cunningham girls] by sending to their address obscene valentines." And there were rumors going around town that the girls had been seen promenading Broadway with George Snodgrass. Strumming his banjo, no doubt.

Two days before the grand jury returned its verdict, the *Times* apparently got so desperate for something to print about the case that they published "Midnight in the House of Murder," by Elizabeth Oakes Smith. It was prefaced by this fragment of testimony:

"Mr. Ullman.—The hall was very dark—the gas turned off.

"Coroner.—Had it never been so before?

"Mr. Ullman.—Oh, yes; *but it seemed unusually dark.*"

Then the poem:

"Up the staircase—slowly—slowly
Walked the weary feet that night;
Hollow echoes answer lonely
To the feet, however light.
Up the staircase, to the broadstair,
Turns he sharply to the right,
There is anguish in the still air,
There are shapes athwart the sight.

"No, the eye has only treasured,
Diamond-like, a hidden ray;
And by this, the darkness measured,
Shows it darkest ere the day.
Was that sigh a human sighing?
Was that groan from human heart?
Was that sob from lips in dying?
There's a whisper—'We depart.'

"Murky thick, the blackness seemeth," began the next stanza, and Miss Smith's poem continued for ten more.

131

"Coroner Connery Impeached," the *Tribune* headed a story saying Connery had been served with papers from the governor ordering him to answer charges of conduct unbecoming a public officer during the inquest. This followed by only a week the grand jury's indictment of Emma Cunningham and John Eckel for murder (the girls discharged, Snodgrass held as a witness, but out on bail). Tough-minded attorney Henry Clinton hadn't waited for a trial to defend his clients, but attacked immediately. And now, long before his clients' fate could be left to a jury, he took their case straight to the public from which the trial jury would be selected: it was Henry Clinton who made the complaint that now meant Edward Downes Connery would be attacked first.

And then—Clinton was given still another forum in which to swing public opinion around, if he could, before his clients' trial for murder began. Some of Harvey Burdell's relatives went to the court of Surrogate Alexander Bradford, and asked to be given control of Burdell's property. But Bradford pointed out that if Burdell had a widow she had rights to the property, too. And Emma Cunningham, waiting in the Tombs to be tried for her life, insisted she *was* the Doctor's widow and she wanted his property: all she could get. So now Surrogate Bradford had to hear testimony, and then decide whether Harvey Burdell had really married Emma Cunningham. If Henry Clinton could prove or even strongly suggest that the marriage had happened, it could not only bring his client a widow's share of a lot of money and property, but go a long way, it seems to me, toward a verdict of not guilty at the trial.

He made a good start, by getting Uriah Marvine, the minister who'd officiated at the supposedly false wedding, to say that the more he thought about it, "the more I am convinced that the man I married was Harvey Burdell." While even before Connery's hearing could begin, Mrs. Cunningham announced to an *Express* reporter visiting her cell for an interview that Connery *had* ordered her stripped naked during the inquest. What about the note she'd signed, which seemed to deny this? That was a misinterpretation: what she'd meant was that Dr. Woodward had taken no indecent liberties, but she *had* been forced to strip "to her toes."

At the surrogate's hearing Henry Clinton—who apparently had been scouting around looking into a lot of things—said that the inquest witness who had confirmed Farrell's testimony was insane. His whole story was "the morbid concoction of a diseased brain." A *Times* reporter now went to the man's house—as he could have done long since; as Connery could have done—and talked to the man's sister and daughter. It was true, they said; he'd been insane for years, and they didn't believe his story of seeing Farrell on the front steps of number 31 the night of the murder; didn't even think he'd been out of the house at all that night.

A day or so later, Henry Clinton began the Connery hearing by reading aloud the charges he was bringing: to be printed in the newspapers where prospective jurors could read them. His charges concerned Connery's "gross impertinence and bestiality to the witnesses, illegal detention" of Mrs. Cunningham, "witticisms and indecorous remarks . . . repeated with grins and grimaces," and usurpation of police powers.

Every lighthearted remark of poor Edward Connery's now showed up in Clinton's formal charges: "I knew, Mary," he had said to Mary Donaho, "that you carried your tail behind you . . ."; to Mr. Cyrenius Stevens, "Probably [Mrs. Cunningham] was peeking through a crack, and having a view of the elephant"; to the witness who said Mrs. Cunningham's husband had been ". . . a manufacturer of liquid death," the coroner had "echo[ed] the words, syllable by syllable, 'A man-u fact-tu rer of li-quid death? I will put that down for the benefit of the Temperance Society"; and "Did you ever give her the wink yourself?" . . . " 'Is it my death warrant?' 'Yes, sir, your death warrant' " . . . ; and to Mrs. Stephen Maine, when she gave her name, "This is a main chance of making a conquest, anyway."

Apparently no courtroom procedure involving Connery would be without its weird moments. Dr. Maine, in reply to questions about the coroner's famous remark to his wife, said Connery had looked over at the reporters when he said it, and winked his eye, and laughed.

"How often did you see the Coroner wink . . . ?" Connery's lawyer asked. "As often as I do now? (Mr. Jordan winked several times)."

"Yes, but the wink I referred to was a different kind of wink. . . ."

". . . a long wink or a short wink?"

"I can't understand the question. Whether you mean by closing the eye and keeping it there, or quick."

"What was there peculiar in that wink?"

". . . It was a cunning shrewd wink. . . ."

What kind of wink was that?

"Closing one eye quick, with a contraction of the muscle at the same time."

The *Times* thought that these "proceedings, if not very interesting, were at least very funny. Whether they will redeem the lack of dignity complained of in the aforesaid inquest, or add fresh ridicule to that investigation, may, at present, be considered a doubtful matter."

The New York *Sun* now reported that George Snodgrass had been seen playing his banjo in Cienfuegos, Cuba; and Snodgrass wrote next day —from New York—denying it. While out in the streets, said the *Times:*

133

"The mud . . . grows deeper and more like putty every hour. The people, finding indignation entirely ineffective, are trying to shame Ebling [the city official responsible for cleaning the streets] into a sense of duty. In scores of places, yesterday, they had piled the mud into tombs, mounds and graves, out of which the hats and boots of effigies protruded, and over the heaps placed inscriptions in shocking verse, commenting on the undiscovered virtues of Mayor Wood, and the wretched inefficiency of Ebling. . . ."

On March 31 at 31 Bond the furnishings of the house were auctioned off. Once more the street outside was jammed, "more impassable than in the best days of the inquest, when Coroner Connery wore the mask of Joe Miller." (I think Miller was author of a joke book.) The ladies "outnumbered the gentlemen, three to one, and were determined to get in. They pushed, they elbowed, they squeezed, they fell back on their prerogative, and asserted their women's rights, they strongly went in for going in, and in they went. For a long time nothing was visible but a mass of ladyhood, crowding in, to see the blood stains on the wall of the room where the murder was committed, to talk and to listen to the bids for the furniture. . . . only three ladies made bids, while seven or eight hundred talked, and the rest, a dozen or so, listened. Many a man . . . thanked the Fates . . . that there were not more than five dozen of metallic hooped petticoats.

"The gentlemen . . . were as eager to get in as the ladies, and many a lady's dress suffered in consequence." In fact, "some of the women . . . came out in a form ludicrous in the extreme, their dresses hanging in all manner of zigzags, from the bending of the hoops in their skirts."

Up on the top floor, barred to visitors by cops at the foot of the stairs, the Cunningham children sat waiting it out, and the auction began with the sale of the hair mattress from Dr. Burdell's bed, which went for eight dollars. A shout was heard, cops moved in, nabbed a pickpocket, then the auctioneer sold the Doctor's bedstead for nine dollars. His bureau brought $9.25, and they put up his books, one of the bidders giving his name, whether truthfully or not, as Ebling, the city official who was failing to keep the streets clean, and "there rose cries of 'turn him out,' 'put him in the street,' 'smother him in the dust.'" Then they sold the Doctor's blankets and sheets, "bringing good prices." And "a pair of glass shades, covering sections of the human jaw modeled in wax," and "purchased for five dollars and three shillings [auctioneers do not recognize the decimal currency yet], and then Mr. Ebling, or the audacious imposter usurping his name, purchased a foetus in a glass case for eighteen shillings. Again, at the sound of the hated name, the cry burst forth, the windows were forced open, and for a few moments there was a terrible suspense. Were

134

the indignant crowd near the windows about to hurl Ebling forth into the streets he had left so dirty?"

They sold off a couple of skulls, Dr. Roberts bought a bottle of chloroform for one dollar, they sold the bureau with looking glass, and the bedroom carpet "went for six shillings and sixpence a yard. Dr. Roberts bought the Doctor's electrical machine for three dollars and one shilling, and somebody gave fifty cents for the Doctor's flesh brush. . . ."

Chairs, a rosewood secretary, a mahogany dental work case, the operating chair used by the inquest witnesses, and the Doctor's dental tools went next, including some "scrapers," and when these were announced "a cry was raised for Ebling, but he, or the individual representing him," was gone. " 'He is gone to scrape Broadway,' said the crowd."

The marble center table past which Dr. Burdell staggered as he fought for his life brought seven dollars, and a "dental case, filled with teeth," brought six.

The front-hall carpet, worn by hundreds of feet during the inquest, went for its cost when new. They sold mirrors, and "some wretched landscapes," all for good prices. It turned out, however, that a lot of the bids were fake, the stuff uncalled for, and they had to hold a second "cash-down" auction later. But: "The blood-stained carpet of the room where the mysterious murder was committed . . . was among the first articles removed after the sale."

Once the furniture and the crowds had left 31 Bond, Mrs. Cunningham's sister moved in. She was Mrs. Ann Barnes, a widow in her late twenties, described as "a low-sized woman"—meaning short—who "looks like a servant girl in dress as in other things," but "not at all in any respect like Mrs. Cunningham." She walked with a limp, and it sounds to me as though she needed a home. Possibly also she was brought in to take care of the boys.

The two hearings continued. Connery's lawyer "admitted that the Coroner had used the phrase, 'You carry your tail behind you,' to witness Mary Donaho," but not "out of disrespect . . . nor from levity. It was used as a compliment to her integrity—she being an Irish girl and familiar with the story of the Irishman who lost his cow, and who could only say, in describing her, that she was a very honest cow and carried her tail behind her. On that story some doggerel had been written that was well known all over Ireland. One verse was:

> " 'Teddy Brady lost his cow,
> He didn't know where to find her,

And the only mark he had on her, was
She carried her tail behind her.' "

If Henry Clinton had a rebuttal to this defense, it wasn't reported;
and a day or so later when Mary Donaho was on the stand, and was asked
about the coroner's infamous remark, she said she hadn't even heard him
make it.

The hearing ended, and Governor King announced that the evidence
against Connery was insufficient; as for his "imprisonment" of Mrs. Cunningham and John Eckel, the governor thought "even more stringent
deprivation of their liberty would have been beneficial to the ends of
justice."

So Coroner Connery was exonerated, but I don't think Henry Clinton cared: I think he'd scored points with at least some of the twelve men
somewhere in the city who would soon be trying his clients. Nor did he
push for a decision at the surrogate's hearing on whether Emma Cunningham's supposed marriage to Dr. Burdell had really happened or not. In
fact, Clinton often delayed this hearing deliberately, getting frequent post-
ponements, some for as long as a week, some even longer. I think he didn't
want a decision before the trial, for if the surrogate decided the marriage
was false, it could convict his clients.

I also believe Henry Clinton thought Emma Cunningham was innocent; that she'd convinced him, if nobody else. Because years later, in the
late nineties, he published his memoirs, including a long account of this
case, still insisting, in a way that makes me think he believed it, that Emma
Cunningham had been innocent. And now, in the days left before the
district attorney would try to hang her, Clinton continued to work hard:
industriously contriving defenses for the evidence against her, and he
developed some ingenious ones. A good lawyer, a little humorless I suspect after reading his memoirs, but Mrs. Cunningham hadn't hired him
for laughs.

As the town waited, almost holding its collective breath, for what
would be its most sensational trial in many years, other trials took place
almost unnoticed—most of them not five minutes long. In the Court of
General Sessions James Brady was tried for pocket-picking, and almost
instantly found guilty. He was "about 12 years old," and his "guilt was
fully proved," said the brief newspaper account. "The Recorder inquired
whether the prisoner had ever before been arrested. One of the attendants
answered that he had, and for a similar offense. The lad cried bitterly, and
declared the attendant mistaken. His mother and sister stood beside the
little 'knuck' at the bar, and begged that he might be forgiven, saying that
it was not he but his brother, who had been arrested once before. After

receiving a solemn promise from the mother to take better care of her precocious child in the future, the Recorder suspended judgment, and Master Brady was permitted to depart.

"Mary Riley was arraigned for an assault and battery on Mary McDay. The complainant's eyes were black and her face much swollen. She swore the injuries were inflicted upon her by the prisoner without any just cause or provocation. She told the circumstances of the case very fully. Mrs. Riley made her own defense, but it was not a satisfactory one, and she was sentenced to thirty days' imprisonment in the Penitentiary."

"A man named Johnson pleaded guilty to stealing a package of tea worth $3 and was sentenced to the Penitentiary for three months.

"A man giving his name as Thomas Little, a cooper, from Boston, was then put at the bar on a charge of stealing an iron wrench from a bar room up town, into which he went for a drink. He said he didn't mean to steal the wrench, he only had it to assist the landlady in tapping a barrel of beer, and that while working about he put it in his pocket. He said he had no friends in the City, was a stranger, and came here in search of work. The Recorder said the story was a 'made-up' one—30 days in the Penitentiary.

"John Tappan, a miserable-looking old man, then hobbled up to the bar. His neck was twisted to one side, and he was otherwise maimed. He came to answer to the charge of stealing a wood engraving worth 25 cents. He did not deny the charge, but dwelt emphatically on the fact of his having been 'an old soldier,' and of having been 'in this country more than 28 years.' His mother (who looked much younger than himself) came forward and begged that he might be forgiven. 'Sure, there isn't much harm in the poor fellow, any how,' she said, and upon her promise to take him home with her the Court suspended judgment.

"Mary A. Livingston was tried and convicted of stealing a table-cloth from Eunis McGowan. Four months in the Penitentiary.

"John Mullens was arraigned for an assault and battery on his wife, Ellen. Mrs. Mullens was put upon the stand, but was very reluctant to press the charge which she had already made before one of the Police Justices. Her head was bound up, and she trembled violently. 'In the name of God, Judge, let my husband go this time,' she implored. The Recorder said he had no disposition to be lenient with brutes who so maltreated their wives. He would give the full extent of the law—six months in the Penitentiary. When Mrs. Mullens saw that her entreaty for her husband's pardon was of no avail, she cried loudly, and pointing to a pretty little girl of about six years, that sat on one of the benches, said 'What will now become of my darling little girl? Oh, God! Oh, God!'

" 'You will be better off away from your brute of a husband,' said the Recorder.

" 'But he is our support, and we'll starve,' she answered.

" 'The City authorities will support you if you cannot get along in any other way—I will assist you myself—call at my office.'

"But Mrs. Mullens could not be consoled, and when her husband was being escorted out of the Court, she turned toward him and screamed, 'Good bye, Mullens,' whereupon many present laughed loudly.

"Mr. Beale's agent for the Prison Association interposed himself in behalf of Mr. and Mrs. Mullens, and finally succeeded in effecting the release of Mullens on his promising never to get drunk again. . . ."

11

The trial of Emma Cunningham was also quick, comparatively speaking; and by our customs a strange one. They held it here in the new courthouse at City Hall Park, in the Court of Oyer and Terminer, and

these were its principal figures. On the bench, presiding over the trial:
Judge Henry E. Davies. This man, S. B. Cushing, assisted—a little—in the

prosecution, as attorney general of the state. But this is A. Oakey Hall,
district attorney, and he was the
actual prosecutor. He's an
interesting man, reminding me of
Jimmy Walker, the dashing mayor
of New York in the twenties.
When Hall later became mayor
and part of the infamous Tweed
Ring, he was labeled by Thomas
Nast, the great political cartoonist,
"O.K. Haul," for marking crooked
bills "O.K." for payment. Albert
Bigelow Paine said Oakey Hall was
"a frequenter of clubs, a beau of
fashion, a wit, a writer of clever
tales, a punster, a versatile
mountebank, a lover of social

distinction and applause." You wonder how he seemed, formidable or

140

only a dilettante, to the defense attorneys, who *were* a pretty formidable pair. They are Henry L. Clinton, here, and his associate, Judge Dean. Just

look at Clinton's face; this is from a Mathew Brady ambrotype: I'd want him on my side, not against me. Dean, too—also from a Brady ambrotype —looks tough.

And here, of course, is Emma Cunningham—drawn directly from a Meade ambrotype, "as she appears in court," said the picture caption. Wearing full widow's weeds, she is now literally to be tried for her life. Yet in the bizarre mind just behind those eyes she is already (this became known in time) looking far beyond this trial. As though the trial were already behind her, she is still thinking and planning you know what: how to get everything the Doctor owned.

The trial opened here on May 4 with a panel of four hundred jurors

sitting or standing wherever they could find places. The panel contained no women because, of course, they were not fully reasoning beings. An adjoining room, the Marine Court, its folding doors opened, was filled with spectators, and to their disappointment Mrs. Cunningham sat with her mourning veil lowered at first. Helen and Augusta sat with her. George and Willie had been sent off to boarding school. John Eckel, whose trial had been separated from Mrs. Cunningham's, sat with his counsel wearing "a particularly fine-looking auburn wig, and were it not for an

142

occasional glance of his eyes that seemed rather apprehensive, he would have seemed in high spirits."

It was hot and the "breathing of the fetid exhalations of 1,500 lawyers and rowdies, confined in the ill-ventilated rooms of City Hall," said the *Tribune* man crankily, "is enough to try an ordinary constitution severely."

Two hours of hearing excuses from prospective jurors, then at one o'clock A. Oakey Hall stood to say, ". . . I call up from the calendar of the Court the indictment against Mrs. Cunningham, charging her with murder. We are ready to proceed. . . ."

"The prisoner is ready," said Dean.

"Bring the prisoner to the bar," Judge Davies replied.

"Mrs. Cunningham was conducted by an officer to a seat beside her counsel," the *Times* continued, "and removed her veil. Her face was much flushed, and she trembled slightly. . . .

"Mr. Clinton arose and said, 'We waive the reading of the indictment, and would put in a plea of *Not guilty.*' "

But real trials have no sense of drama; now they began questioning members of the jury panel, and it went on for hours. The first few were excused, and then—this is one thing I meant by saying aspects of this trial were strange to our custom—panelist Gilbert Oakley said that while he had no prejudice against her, "he had an impression as to who committed the murder, and suspected that Mrs. Cunningham might possibly know something about it, as it occurred in her house." If I can judge from my own experiences as a juror, both sides today would join in throwing Oakley out; instead they swore him in.

Another had read all the inquest testimony, and had known Harvey Burdell as a passing acquaintance, but he was sworn in, too. At four in the afternoon they took a break, then back at it in the hot smelly room: "A fan fluttered under Helen's veil, Augusta sat motionless, her eyes fixed on the jurors."

Nathaniel Chater "had formed no opinion" but thought Farrell's testimony important, and had an opinion as to its truth. If true, he thought it would implicate Mrs. Cunningham, as an inmate of the house. He had an "impression concerning her guilt or knowledge of the murder, unfavorable to her." But he was nevertheless quite competent to serve on the jury, Judge Davies ruled, and the defense had to use a peremptory challenge to keep him off it. And so in only this one day they picked a full jury, adjourned, and were ready to begin trial in the morning.

143

This is the room next morning: jury at the right, Mrs. Cunningham

up front just beyond the standing man, Helen beside her, Augusta not here. The rest are reporters and spectators, crowding in wherever they can. As the trial begins, Mrs. Cunningham has already discussed or is about to—she was in the Tombs when she did this—what is going to happen as soon as the trial is over and she is free again. She had had this discussion, or is about to have it, with Dr. Samuel Catlin, her old family physician when she lived in Brooklyn; and whom, as she later said, she has "in her power."

But now the trial is just beginning: with A. Oakey Hall standing, facing the jury, and demanding Emma Cunningham's life in a speech that would be better illustrated than presented in words. If I could, I'd imitate cartoonist Saul Steinberg, and show the D.A.'s address as a huge speech balloon filling the courtroom above everyone's head, and packed with a montage of ornate curlicues, skyrockets, fancy border designs from a nineteenth-century printer's type book, and samples of Palmer penmanship.

He started out fairly simply with a statement of what he said he would prove by witnesses, including that this murder "was the deed of a woman . . . a deed planned and contemplated from a different stand-point from which men of the world contemplate crime, perpetrated to a great extent with the ignorance of human nature which, compared with men of the world, women at all times . . . have possessed. . . ."

But trying a woman had its problems, A. Oakey Hall told the jury; because "she sits there, a veiled picture of sorrow . . . by her looks demanding a sympathy which belongs not to a murderess but to a woman. . . . Oh!" he said, the verbal fireworks suddenly igniting. "It is no wonder that all these holy associations that cluster around the name of woman should force themselves into the jury-box. . . . When we remember the wife of our life until death, when we remember the children who are to be the future women of the world, that sit upon our knee, and we feel as we look upon young girlhood and growing maidenhood, we say, can it ever be that this being, upon whom God Almighty has put His own seal of purity, should ever live to be the . . . midnight assassin. . . .

"And yet, when we open the book of history, we are forced to come to the conviction that crime knows no sex. In . . . Romish history we read of her who, having murdered her husband, the servant of Imperial Rome, drove her chariot over the dead body of her father. And . . . Fulvia, when the head of Cicero was brought to her, spat upon it, and drew from her bosom, which had nourished children, a deadly bodkin, and thrust it again and again through the tongue of that gaping corpse. The same great dramatist who spoke to you of the wife of William Tell narrates how Agnes, Queen of Hungary, bathed her feet in the blood of sixty-three knights, exclaiming as she did, 'It seems as if I were wading in the May dew.' . . . Throughout the life of Dr. Burdell the prisoner pursued him with a fiendish hate, jealousy and revenge until the knife held by this woman fiend had found a repose in his heart. . . ."

The D.A. reviewed the history of the relationship between Mrs. Cunningham and Harvey Burdell, and said that, through witnesses: "We will take the roof off [31 Bond], and allow you to gaze into that depth of moral degradation which in that family clustered around that woman." He talked of the persecution of "this hunted, haunted man by this fiend in woman's shape," of how "with the sly cunning of her sex" she spied on him, and said that when Eckel arrived, "the greedy and lascivious eyes of this woman . . . fastened upon him."

He offered his theory of why the murder was committed and how; hinted that Eckel and the daughters had helped; referred to the slyness of Snodgrass. He fitted facts to his theory, referring to the sending of the servants to bed; the burning, he said, of the bloody clothes in which the murder had been done; and all the other damning things his witnesses would testify to. These things, he said, would prove that Emma Cunningham, "woman though she is, was guilty of the crime." (He added that Daniel Ullman was "a highly honorable man who had no part or parcel in that household.")

And then in only the next two days, D.A. Hall presented all of his witnesses. Old Dr. Francis once again sat describing the wounds he'd found in the body he'd examined on the morning it was found. Hannah Conlon told her familiar story of the Thanksgiving Day miscarriage; of the many quarrels at 31; of Mrs. Cunningham's overheard threats; of being sent to bed early on the night of the murder. . . .

On cross-examination the defense asked Hannah if Mary Donaho hadn't been fired for drunkenness, but Judge Davies wouldn't allow "any statements in regard to her character no matter how humble she may be." When they asked if Hannah herself hadn't been "in the habit of getting drunk a good deal," she said, "I could always take my share, but never so much as not to be able to work. I never saw anyone throw it over their shoulders, whether they were rich or poor."

Catherine Stansbury . . . John Burchell . . . Mary Donaho . . . On cross-exam the defense again suggested that Mary was a drunk; had, in fact, been fired by Mrs. Cunningham for drunkenness. She denied it, but in doing so revealed a flash of hostility: "I was never in the beastly state of intoxication that I have seen Mrs. Cunningham in," Mary retorted, and the crowd laughed, the judge rapping his gavel.

When Dr. Stephen Maine was on the stand, the D.A. interrupted: he had commissioned the building of a model of the house at 31 Bond, it had just arrived, and: "A large and perfect model of Dr. Burdell's house, exhibiting every story separate, with stairs, windows, and furniture was now brought in and shown to the Jury, who rose from their seats and gave it a minute examination." Also brought in, courtesy of the D.A., were four paintings showing the four sides of the murder room; and someday, somewhere, I'm going to discover and recognize that miniature house on sale at a junk shop, and buy it; at any price. When I get it home the four paintings will be stuck away inside it. Dr. Maine used both the little house and the paintings in finishing his testimony.

The cross-exam was effective. Yes, said Maine, he had once lived at 29 Bond right beside number 31. It was a "stereotype" of number 31, in fact; they were both "pattern" houses, exactly alike. And yes, they were "very firmly built, and the walls were thick and solid."

"When you were in an upper room, could you hear a person moving in the story below you?"

"No, you could not do so in any of those houses unless the doors were open." So now there existed for the jury a possible innocent explanation

146

of why no one in the house had heard any sound of murder on the floor below them.

Daniel Ullman . . . DeWitt Baldwin . . . the cops who'd heard Dr. Burdell charge Mrs. Cunningham with stealing papers from his safe . . . Samuel Parmly, whose dog had stood on the steps of 31 the night of the murder; and who had seen mysterious lights in an attic room, and smelled the stink of burning leather and wool . . . a lockmaker . . . doctors who'd done the postmortem . . . witnesses who'd heard quarrels and sinister remarks.

Then came Mrs. Frederika Schwartzaelder, who now lived at 29 Bond, next door to 31. Her bedroom was beside the room in which the Doctor had been murdered, and she'd been in her bedroom before eleven that night, but heard no sound.

I don't know why the prosecution called her, but the defense was ready. On cross-examination she said four men had recently come to her house, including two she now recognized here in the courtroom. One was an assistant defense attorney, the other Dr. David Uhl, who had been a witness at the inquest, and who was also Emma Cunningham's doctor. The men had asked permission to come into her house, and conduct an experiment. And then, with Mrs. Schwartzaelder, they all stood in her bedroom while people next door in the murder room yelled, "Murder!" And, said Mrs. Schwartzaelder, they could all plainly hear those shrieks coming through the walls.

But on the night of the murder she'd heard nothing, so the jury now had something else to consider. The cries of *murder* heard by passersby that night might have come not from the house but from the street, from playful "rowdies," and the people in the house at 31 who said they'd heard nothing that night could have been telling the truth.

A couple of prison matrons from the Tombs said Emma Cunningham was left-handed; they'd watched her embroidering. But the prosecution couldn't get Dr. Woodward to say the murderer had been left-handed; you couldn't tell that from the wounds, he said.

And then David Uhl, Emma Cunningham's doctor, helped her a lot. The dagger found in her possession, he testified for one thing, could not possibly have made the deep wounds in Dr. Burdell's body. "Would you expect to find marks of violence upon the person who committed the act?"

"I should undoubtedly."

"Did you look particularly at Mrs. Burdell that day [of the discovery of the murder] to see if she had any marks of violence upon her?"

He had. ". . . when I left the room I shook hands with her on purpose to get very near her person. I did not discover any marks of violence upon

147

her. She had a fur cape which dropped off her shoulders."

"Were her shoulders bare so that you could see?"

"Yes, Sir."

"Did you look at her neck and hands . . . ?"

He had, and saw no marks. And were the wounds on the corpse made by a left- or right-handed person? No telling, said Dr. Uhl, and then he gave the listening room an explicit and detailed description of every place blood had been found in the house. It was Dr. David Uhl, in fact, who had directed the artist in making the four paintings being used here in the courtroom to show where blood was found in the murder room. As for other places, Dr. Uhl described bloody marks found out in the hall and on down the staircase, some of these being "on the right-hand side of the wall," where, presumably, a left-handed Emma Cunningham would not have put them.

"Would it be a place where a person going downstairs would naturally put his hands on the wall, if going down in the dark?"

"Yes, Sir." And, said Uhl, there was blood "on the door at the foot of the basement stairs . . . on the basement front door there was a finger mark in blood on the hinge side, very much like a spot which one would have made feeling for the knob of the door with his fingers. . . ."

When Dr. David Uhl had finished, the possibility of, not resident John Eckel, but some outsider feeling his way out of a dark and unfamiliar house, finally reaching the front door and escaping into the night, seemed real. When Uhl stepped down from the witness stand to walk out past Emma Cunningham and her counsel, he had helped her very much, and if she now thought of him, her family physician for the past year and a half, as also being a loyal and trustworthy friend—and later evidence shows she did think this—it is understandable.

A cousin of Harvey Burdell's, Benjamin Maguire, was put on to examine various documents found in Emma Cunningham's possession, and say which were in the Doctor's handwriting. And then—on cross-examination again—the defense brought out from Maguire that quite a few of Dr. Burdell's relatives had been on bad terms with him. And now the jury had to consider the possibility that someone besides Emma Cunningham might have had reason to want Harvey Burdell dead; someone else who might inherit.

Surprisingly and suddenly, the prosecution rested. That was all; that was their case against Mrs. Cunningham. Why Farrell wasn't called—the man who said he'd sat down on the steps of 31 Bond the night of the murder, and seen Eckel peer out the front door—I don't know. There had been hints in the paper that possibly he was a drunk. Maybe the prosecution had learned that he was, and that the defense was primed for him, though that's unsupported guesswork. Of course, Farrell's story was remarkable: that he'd come along at just the moment Harvey Burdell had come home . . . had sat there evidently listening to the actual sounds and cries of the murder . . . and then that John Eckel had opened the door to look out at him. Too good to be true? I never found anyone suggesting that a man opening the door as Farrell sat on the steps might have been, not Eckel who lived there, but the murderer about to escape the house. And who sees Farrell sitting there, orders him away, and a few minutes later does flee the house. But to me that's more likely than Eckel, having done the job, opening the front door. Why would he? The explanation by the *Tribune* that it was to make sure no one was there is silly. But those are only my speculations; no one mentioned these possibilities. We know only that Farrell simply wasn't called.

Nor were others you might have expected. The *Times* published a letter saying: "In common with the whole community . . . I have shared the general conviction that the parties in the house *must,* in the nature of the case, have known something about that awful deed.

"At the Coroner's inquest . . . the evidence of Dr. Blaisdell made upon my mind an indelible impression. . . . It tended far more than anything else . . . to fasten my suspicions upon Mrs. Cunningham. . . . It was to him that Burdell made those repeated declarations of his hatred and fear of Mrs. Cunningham . . . of the apprehensions which haunted him. . . . And it was to Blaisdell . . . that Burdell stated that he had made a will—a fact which, taken in connection with the non-appearance of any such instrument, went far to fasten suspicion on the woman who stands indicted for his murder.

"With these impressions . . . I looked forward to the trial as certain to clear up the mystery. And when I read Mr. District-Attorney Hall's opening speech, much as I disliked the unwarrantable, repulsive, and utterly savage tone in which he speaks of a woman whose position should have shielded her from abuse as unprofessional as it was needless and ungentlemanly, I certainly expected that he would leave nothing undone which could tend to clear up the question of her guilt.

"But I see from this evening's papers that the prosecution has closed; and *yet Dr. Blaisdell has not been called to the witness' stand at all.* What does this mean? Is the public to be amused with a *sham* trial? Is Mr. Hall merely going through the *forms* of law, and purposely excluding all the really pertinent and important testimony . . . ?

149

"Not a word has been said of the sham marriage. . . . Only one of the inmates of the house,—neither Snodgrass, Eckel, nor either of the daughters—has been examined. . . ."

This was signed "JUSTICE," and the *Times* said: "We publish the above, although it conflicts with our purpose not to enter upon any discussion of the case while the trial is ending. The question which it asks is certainly one which the public will echo. But it is quite fair to presume that the District-Attorney is the best judge of his duty. . . ."

The prosecution abruptly rested, but Judge Davies didn't adjourn. There were some hours left of the day, so he simply directed the defense to begin—immediately. And Henry Clinton stood up, walked to the jury  box, and began: "May it please the Court. Gentlemen of the Jury: Although not altogether unaccustomed to address Juries in capital cases, I have never done so under the circumstances which surround the present case. I have never before arisen to address a Jury where the prosecution, after closing their evidence, had so utterly failed to point even the finger of well-grounded suspicion toward the prisoner at the bar, as in the present instance. . . ."

I think Clinton might very effectively have stopped right there, but of course he didn't. Orations were de rigueur, possibly the jury might have felt cheated, and Clinton went on, did a good job of denouncing the D.A.'s denunciation, and then rivaled him in oratory: ". . . the anguish which wrung her soul when scarce three short years ago the husband of her youth was entombed beneath the sod . . . when she lay stretched upon the bed of sickness herself, as she supposed, about to be drifted into the oceans of eternity . . ." (During this part "Mrs. Cunningham was in tears, and the Jury listened with much interest and attention.") "Suddenly there shone out from the horizon, not that star of Bethlehem, whose serene and hallowed light had pierced the darkness of her affliction, as the grave . . . had closed over the lifeless form of her husband and her earthly hopes, which were all entombed—but the baneful star of her destiny—her ill-fated union with Dr. Harvey Burdell. . . ." Etc.

But there wasn't too much of that; just enough. Clinton then summed up the prosecution's evidence, in his client's favor; pointed out its clear deficiencies by referring to witnesses who hadn't been called; and said he'd call some of them himself for the defense.

Among his witnesses was a professor of surgery at New York Medical College who said the Doctor's wounds were made by a person with both anatomical knowledge and great strength. Why great strength? Be-

150

cause the professor had propped up a naked corpse in sitting position, and then had a couple of students (who surely got A's) stab the dead body in various places. This didn't take much force, but then they dressed the corpse in underclothes, shirt, and heavy outer clothing, the students went at it again, and this time it took a lot of force to plunge those daggers in; sometimes a dagger actually recoiled.

Dr. Walter B. Roberts talked about the good relations he'd often seen between Emma Cunningham and Harvey Burdell. Ten-year-old Georgie Cunningham gave a very persuasive child's-eye picture of a calm domestic evening before the murder, spent in preparing sister Helen to go off to boarding school in the morning. (Incidentally, when George undressed that night in this pre-petroleum age, nearly all of America's oil still lying untouched belowground, his room was lighted with "a sperm candle" made from whale oil.) Reading George's testimony, trying to hear it, it isn't easy to reconcile the evening this boy thought he saw with that of a family planning murder.

The Reverend Snodgrass, George Snodgrass's father, had seen nothing amiss at 31 Bond when he and his wife visited Mrs. Cunningham there. Dr. Samuel Catlin (with whom Mrs. Cunningham had already discussed her secret plans once this trial was out of the way) was very helpful. He had been her family doctor when she lived in Brooklyn, and said that ". . . three years ago she was attacked with inflammatory rheumatism, which affected [her] shoulders. . . ." This enlarged the joints, Catlin said, and: "The strength of the parts affected would naturally be very much diminished." So she could hardly have struck the blows—through all those layers of clothing—that killed the Doctor, if you believed Catlin.

George Snodgrass told his familiar story: of a household in which, yes, there'd been quarrels but nothing compatible with murder. And then the defense brought on a new and powerful witness, Daniel D. Smith, doctor of medicine, who lived at number 35 Bond Street. This was only two doors from 31, easily available to the coroner, the newspaper reporters, or anyone else. But it was the defense who found him.

Dr. Smith sat down, and told the jury that he and his son had been conducting experiments on the night of the murder, ". . . testing the power of the electric current on various articles, such as alcohol, phosphorus, &c. He had occasion, in these experiments, to use pieces of leather, and shellac, for joining tubes, and scraps of woolen rags, for cleaning instruments. The woolen and leather so used, became saturated or impregnated with chemical fluids. When a quantity of leather or rags accumulated, it was his custom to burn them up. On the afternoon of Friday, January

151

30th, intending to spend the night out of town, he gathered a heap of woolen rags and pieces of leather, and threw it upon the remains of an anthracite coal fire, opened the window of the room wide, locked the door, went off and took the cars. The room in which he burnt these rags was the front room third story. . . . On his return to the house, the next morning, he found that the smell of the smouldering rags and leather pervaded the whole premises, and so strong and unpleasant was it, in the room in which they had been consumed, that he had to fumigate it. It was a mixed smell of burning leather and woolen, saturated with chemicals."

I think Smith's testimony has the sound of simple truth, a disinterested witness without reason to lie; and A. Oakey Hall hardly bothered to cross-examine, asking only what time Smith had left his house, and the condition of the fire when he returned. When Dr. Smith left the stand, an important part of the case against Emma Cunningham left with him—good-bye bloody clothes burned in a midnight fire. However bright the light in the attic had seemed to Dr. Parmly that night, it appears to have been only the candle or candles of some of the half-dozen people who went to bed in the attic.

Smith's son, Fernando, corroborated his father's testimony, and added that he had come home to number 35 between ten and eleven on the night of the murder wearing a large gray shawl and cap. The possibility that it was he whom witnesses had seen in Bond Street that night, and not Harvey Burdell, was real, adding more confusion and doubt to the case.

Then a cousin of Dr. Burdell's, Mrs. Catherine Dennison, said that relations between the Doctor and Mrs. Cunningham had always seemed friendly to her. Helen Cunningham took the stand "a little confused on first entering the witnessbox, owing to some difficulty in extricating herself from her veil which had inconveniently wrapped itself around her. She smiled and blushed several times and nodded her head to someone in the Court-room, apparently to Snodgrass, or to a lady beside him." Then Helen once more described a quiet domestic evening before the murder as she prepared herself with the others' help to leave for school in the morning. Smith Ely, Jr., told the jury that he'd sent the note asking Eckel to meet him in the morning the murder was discovered, as it happened; and now again Eckel's mysterious early departure that morning turned commonplace. Augusta described the same evening as Helen had; confirmed that lights had been used in the attic that evening; that they often lighted a fire in the unused attic room and dressed there on cold mornings, and had done this a day or so before the murder, which was

152

why ashes were found in the grate. In response to the questions of her mother's attorney, she said 31 Bond was easily accessible from the rear, the back door being fastened only by an ordinary lock. A desultory cross-exam changed nothing.

A man named Henry Smith was sent, apparently by the court, to inspect "the rear of the premises No. 31 Bond Street. He returned now, was sworn, and testified that "there was a shed covering the piazza im-

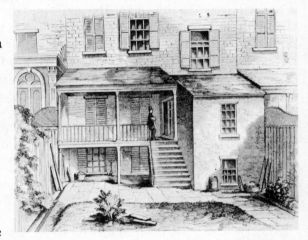

mediately under the window of Dr. Burdell's room . . ." and "a fence which ran up to within four feet of the top of this shed. . . ." And, Smith said, "the door of the stable in the rear of the house No. 31 was fastened by three or four nails on the inside," and finally that he had also "noticed a ladder in the rear of the premises." It could hardly have been clearer that on the night Harvey Burdell was murdered or any other night, probably, his house and room might have been entered from the backyard without much difficulty.

It's said that no one ever knows what a jury will think or do, but when the defense rested, as now it did, there didn't seem to be much actual evidence against the prisoner. To give Oakey Hall the benefit of any possible doubt, the suspicions that had seemed so powerful at the inquest may have been recognized by an experienced D.A. preparing for trial as without much substance: suspicions but not evidence. And yet Emily Sallenbach, the corset-maker's daughter, had sworn she recognized John Eckel as the man who came to her apartment to meet Emma Cunningham on the night of the wedding: I don't understand why she wasn't called. Or Alvah Blaisdell, who could have told this jury who Harvey Burdell was scared to death of. Or why the Cunningham girls weren't relentlessly cross-examined to show this jury the contradictions and memory lapses they'd demonstrated at the inquest. But these wonderings aren't to imply anything, not at this distance; I just don't know. Even the newspapers of the time apparently didn't know; they had the same puzzled questions. The prosecution seemed strangely weak; without heart.

When former Judge Dean stood up to address the jury now, the entire Cunningham family—the mother with her daughters and two small sons home from boarding school —sat together: at Henry Clinton's suggestion? And they listened to Dean ask the jury to acquit without leaving the jury box. Why had Emma Cunningham even been indicted, he asked them, any more than anyone else of the five million people who lived in the area? "He contrasted the position assumed by the District Attorney in his opening, with those which had been sustained by the proof. . . . Why had they not called Mrs. Demis Hubbard—Dr. Burdell's mistress—Dr. Alvah Blaisdell, Farrell, and so on? . . . Such omissions were singular, to say the least." He made fun of Dr. Parmly and his dog, and spoke for about two and a half hours. "During some of the most eloquent passages, several of the jurors were tearful. Mrs. Cunningham was apparently much affected, and the young ladies sobbed violently."

A. Oakey Hall summed up for the prosecution, speaking of quarrels and threats, and of how Harvey Burdell's words and actions seemed to repudiate his having married Emma Cunningham. He told the jury that Mrs. Cunningham had asked for counsel before testifying at the inquest, which suggested guilt, he said. At one point, more prophetic than he could know, he said, ". . . property, property, property, was the burden of her thoughts. She MUST own 31 Bond Street. . . ." He finished by assuring the jury that if they should "give immunity to crime, by acquittal, when circumstances were damning, there will come into the world and be inaugurated that millennial triumph of the powers of darkness of which we have all read in holy writ."

A recess, for which everyone must have been grateful, then Henry Clinton spoke for an hour and a half of the weakness of the case against his client. No evidence of the famous abortion, for example, except from "the slanderous lips of a woman who was drugged with liquor," and who had been bullied into so testifying by the notorious coroner. "But God in His wisdom supplied the antidote to the poison she sought to instil in the jury-box—the face of this drunken cook bore the index of inebriation; it looked, indeed, as if she were seething in bad liquors." So much for Hannah Conlon—who'd been locked up for weeks now: in the precinct jail; in Captain Dilk's house; and in the Tombs; and who hadn't even been paid for her work at 31. At times Hannah may have wondered if the job there had been entirely worth having.

154

Lots of speeches: Attorney General Cushing was next man up, and began, for the prosecution, "quite forcibly," the *Tribune* thought, "but soon fell into the stump-speech style of oratory, and made points at some of which a portion of the audience took to laughing. We did not notice a smile on a juryman's or upon the Judge's face."

It was a curious talk. He said he'd "rejoice to see her acquitted if she were not guilty, but there was no sympathy due her merely because she was a woman." The evidence was "composed of a chain of circumstances . . . which taken separately would seem to be of little importance." But they mounted up.

He defended Hannah. "It would not do to say that because she was an Irish cook she was not to be believed. The girl who earns her livelihood by the sweat of her brow is as much entitled to respect as the one dressed in gaudy colors, who lived in the Fifth Avenue."

He thought a loving wife hearing of her husband's violent death couldn't have been stopped from "rushing downstairs, and throwing herself by the side of the corpse. . . ."

But if what he had to say wasn't enough to hang Mrs. Cunningham, it almost sounded as though that would be all right with him, because he said: "The consequences of a conviction are awful. This whole family would be ruined. These young daughters lost forever. They must suffer beyond redemption. And these boys, too." But with that the jury had nothing to do "except carefully examine the evidence." If they should convict, it must be "on evidence which was irresistible to their own mind and which carried deep conviction to their bosoms." Whatever was in Attorney General Cushing's mind, his talk was hardly a rabble-rousing call to a lynching.

Finally, Judge Davies charged the jury. "Above all, gentlemen, you must not forget that although you are sitting upon the life of one who belongs to that sex which instinctively appeals to you for your protection and support and sympathy, and which forms the tenderest ties and associations of life, and is always so promptly and willingly rendered, you are to shut your eyes and steel your hearts to these considerations."

He quoted the law on circumstantial evidence; told them what they must consider about the evidence they'd heard, and suggested what weight he thought it should be given. ". . . you will bear in mind whether her conduct that morning, in dressing herself, in going down stairs, taking her breakfast with her daughters and the rest of the family . . . returning to her room in the third story, engaging in domestic avocations—if the witnesses are to be believed—whether it is consistent with guilt or innocence"; and whether or not "a strong, stout, active healthy man, as this deceased is proven to have been, in the prime and vigor of life, could have been murdered . . . by a woman"; and if so, "without leaving upon her person some marks or evidence. . . . You remember the evidence of the physician, of such marks remaining upon a female longer than upon a male . . . no such marks were proven. . . ."

Furthermore, the testimony strongly suggested, said Judge Davies, that whoever did the murder would have been covered with blood, but there was "no evidence of garments in the house thus defiled or stained." They were also to consider "the testimony of Dr. Catlin, in reference to the alleged disability of the prisoner, by reason of the rheumatic affection with which she was afflicted three years since."

"During the delivery of the charge the most profound silence was observed throughout the vast assembly," and finally the judge concluded, ". . . I will quote an old and well-known authority: 'The case must . . . exclude to a moral certainty every other hypothesis but that of the guilt of the accused.' In cases of doubt," Davies instructed the twelve listening men, "it is safer to acquit than condemn." Then: "To your decision I now commit the fate of this unfortunate woman and the future of herself and her family. While you deal justly by her, it is your privilege also to deal mercifully; for as I have before remarked, if you have any reasonable doubt of her guilt, that doubt is to be cast into the scale in her favor, and entitles her to your verdict of acquittal. If, on the contrary . . . you deem the charge . . . proven, it is your duty to your country and your God to say so, though it be with anguish of heart, and may cause deep shame and sorrow to others. But if in this final reviewing you are not satisfied of her guilt, pronounce a verdict of acquittal, and let the accused go free."

Mrs. Cunningham had been "resting her head upon a chair in front of her, her daughters . . . still seated at her side, fanning themselves beneath their thick brown veils to partially escape the effects of the heated and unhealthy atmosphere which pervaded the room." The jury was sent out now, at precisely seven o'clock, said *Times* and *Tribune*. "Mrs. Cunningham, who had wept very much during the address of Mr. Clinton, the Attorney General's summing up, and the Judge's charge, and whose physical system appeared nearly prostrate, covered her face with her handkerchief, and seemed very nervous and agitated." "The counsel arose and began to indulge in familiar conversation, and the auditors began to speculate among themselves as to how many minutes

156

would pass before the Jury would return with a verdict of acquittal. . . ." And "nobody was surprised, when after having been out thirty-five minutes they returned. . . ."

The men took their seats; Mr. Vandervoort, the clerk, called the roll; then (a dramatist at heart must have devised this ritual) he said, "Gentlemen of the Jury, have you agreed upon a verdict?"

Playing his part, the foreman responded, "We have."

Mr. Bartolf, a court officer, "caused Mrs. Cunningham to stand up, and turn her unveiled face to the Jury-box." She did so, "evincing in the act a seeming unconsciousness of what was transpiring about her; she stood still and motionless until her eyes, without expression, turned toward the Jury."

Vandervoort, the clerk, then said, "Prisoner, look upon the Jurors; Jurors, look upon the prisoner. How say you, gentlemen—do you find Emma Augusta Cunningham, otherwise called Burdell, guilty or not guilty?"

And at last he was allowed to disclose the verdict. "Foreman—NOT GUILTY." *Times* and *Tribune* both quoted him in capitals, but there hadn't really been much suspense. The judge's charge, I think, had been virtually an instruction to acquit; and, I also think, properly. What else? There'd been no case made, that's all.

Not guilty, said the foreman, and Emma Cunningham "stooped down, and asked her counsel what the verdict was, and on being told," supplied a little drama herself, falling "back into the arms of her daughter, Helen."

". . . when she had sufficiently recovered," she was led with her family into an adjoining room "where she received the congratulations of her friends and the Jury. An hour later she and her daughters . . . were rolling in a carriage toward the house No. 31 Bond Street. . . ."

Home they all went to what had once been Harvey Burdell's house, and there "small knots of people gathered about the premises, with the expectation that Mrs. Cunningham might appear at the windows. . . . Occasionally they would raise a feeble cheer, with the intent to draw her forth. But she did not make herself visible—and before the dusk had darkened into night the last straggler had departed."

The drama, they may have thought, was finished at last, but instead the curtain had dropped only on Emma Cunningham's preparations for an astonishing final act. The cops gone, the three Cunningham women and Emma's lame sister, once the boys were in bed, had the house to themselves; and I wonder if the talk this evening didn't quickly turn from what had just happened to the future. For nothing had changed; it was a future

Emma Cunningham was as single-mindedly determined upon as ever. And now on this evening of the very day she'd escaped being sentenced to hang for murder, she was planning to bring that future about—with the most bizarre act of her life.

12

Emma Cunningham had a secret reason for believing she'd win the next big one: Surrogate Bradford's decision on whether she was really Harvey Burdell's widow; and, a free woman now, she began attending his hearings. How much of a secret it was I'm not sure because I don't know how she was dressed, though of course she'd have worn the many-layered garments of the day, but she'd already told her secret to at least two people. One was Dr. David Uhl, her physician here in Manhattan, and he'd guessed it long before.

". . . Shortly after Mrs. Cunningham was confined in the Tombs," he said later, "she sent me a note requesting my professional attendance." In her cell, David Uhl listened to her symptoms, then prescribed for her, because of course he recognized what those symptoms meant. They were "peculiar to persons who are *enceinte,* and during one of those visits, I asked her if she *was* in the family way. She said she'd hadn't told that to anybody, and wouldn't answer the question at that time. . . ."

But just before her trial began she told her attorney, Judge Dean, and, I would suppose, Henry Clinton. And apparently others guessed, because "shortly after the conclusion of the trial, a rumor prevailed that she was with child. . . ." And now she confirmed to Dr. Uhl that yes, she was seven months pregnant by Harvey Burdell.

As she sat listening to the testimony at the surrogate's hearing, however, Emma Cunningham said nothing about being pregnant, nor did Judge Dean, her attorney. Familiar figures took the stand once again: Hannah Conlon . . . Samuel Ashton . . . Dr. Cox . . . Mary Donaho. And there were new witnesses, and depositions from upstate, as the two sides tried to prove either that Dr. Burdell was in New York City on October 28, when Emma Cunningham said they'd been married, or that he was not; neither side ever quite succeeding. Sophronia and Cyrenius Stevens once again described the mysterious visit of lawyer "Van Dolan," sent by Mrs. Cunningham, and who Harvey Burdell had suspected was John Eckel in disguise; and whom Sophronia Stevens—her husband not quite sure—positively identified as Eckel.

This time the Stevenses got rough treatment from Mrs. Cunningham's lawyer. "What is the nature of your business?" Dean wanted to know of Sophronia.

"I decline to answer that. I don't think that is any business to you. (Laughter.)"

"Who has lived in the house with you? . . . Any ladies, young ladies?"

"No."

"Any females?" he persisted.

"My domestics."

"Do you keep an assignation house, then?"

"I don't choose to answer any such questions as that. . . ."

He was just as rough on Cyrenius. "I decline answering what has been my business for the last nine years," Cyrenius replied once; and to further questions: "I never was indicted in the United States Court in Philadelphia for passing counterfeit money in 1832. . . . No matter whether I knew Smith Davis, old Hayes' pimp. I had him arrested, and sent to State's Prison in spite of all the police. Smith Davis was called King of the Conakers. I did not turn State's witness. I knew of his tricks; we had to get an honest District Attorney and an honester Judge than Dickey Rickey before I could get him to the State Prison. . . . I followed the tanning and currying business 35 years ago; it is none of your business what I have done since."

160

"Have you been engaged for the last nine years in keeping houses of assignation?"

"I abide by the laws of my country and this State."

Personally, I was with the Stevenses all the way. I think they were a couple who'd seen worse times, all right, but were now just trying to get along, Dean raking over their past to discredit them here. No doubt he was only doing his duty, but that's what lawyers say when they get an ax murderer free on a technicality.

A dozen or so days of the hearing, and not till the final day did Judge Dean play Emma Cunningham's trump card; didn't actually play it, but just sort of flashed it.

"If it were true," he said to Surrogate Bradford—and the italics are *Times*'s and *Tribune*'s both—"that in the *ordinary gestation,* a child should be born to Harvey Burdell, then not only all the ties of blood and nature, but all the dictates of humanity, demand that the Court should lean in favor of that *innocent unborn child,* rather than in favor of those who have no direct *claim* upon the property. I will say nothing of the consequences of a decree of bastardy in advance. . . ."

The *Times* said, "This announcement was . . . received as authoritative that Mrs. Cunningham was *enceinte,* and as she soon after began to appear in public it was noticed that her form gave corroborating evidence. . . ."

When Bradford adjourned to think over his decision, I would imagine Mrs. Cunningham felt hopeful. Being pregnant by Harvey Burdell was no proof they were married, of course; but this was a practical world, and I assume that in reaching a decision Bradford would have to consider Mrs. Cunningham's pregnancy, and the consequences of a decision that would make Burdell's unborn child a bastard. But Mrs. Cunningham had a worry; while she felt sure she'd produce a baby all right when the time came, the possibility of a miscarriage troubled her, she said, since a stillborn child would not inherit. And it would also, I think, leave Bradford free to consider only the evidence of the hearing.

Dr. Uhl had worried all along. In the Tombs, when he'd first guessed Mrs. Cunningham was pregnant, "I told her that . . . she should be examined by physicians. And at another conversation she asked me how we found out when a person was in the family way." After this Mrs. Cunningham didn't seem to feel an examination was immediately necessary, according to Uhl, but when the trial was over she sent for Uhl, "and I attended her at No. 31 . . . and she frequently expressed anxiety of having a miscarriage, as she wanted to have a living child, so that she could have an heir to the Burdell estate. I pressed upon her on different occasions the

161

importance of having an examination by other physicians." She remained unwilling to do this, and "after I mentioned that subject," Uhl said, "she avoided me. . . ."

At home, Emma Cunningham seemed happy in her pregnancy. Her widowed sister, Ann Barnes, said, "She would often want little things, like women who are in that situation. She . . . talked with me frequently about it, and I would often joke her about her little heir, and she would laugh and say she wished it was here."

Mrs. Cunningham had friends named Wilt whom she'd known for twenty-two years. He was an unemployed butcher, they lived at 43 Second Avenue, and Mrs. Wilt's sister, Jane Bell, who was a nurse, lived with them. The Wilts and Mrs. Cunningham visited each other often, and she had confided in the Wilts and Jane Bell that she was pregnant, and expecting in August. .

She hadn't told daughter Helen in so many words, but of course Helen knew. "Other persons had spoken to me about it, and asked me when mother would be confined." And "I judged from her appearance." Mrs. Cunningham did tell Augusta, but Augusta said, "I told her I did not wish to hear it." It was news she just couldn't take: "my nervous system . . . had been so deranged that I was sick for three days after the conversation." Her mother was careful not to speak of it again, Augusta said, but nevertheless Augusta mended "the bottom on an infant's dress" in preparation.

Nurse Jane Bell also repaired some infant clothes, and her sister, Mrs. Wilt, had some baby clothes bleached for Mrs. Cunningham. The baby clothes, you wonder, of some of the Cunningham children, saved through the years?

During this period, on July 23, Hannah Conlon filed suit against Mrs. Cunningham for back wages. Her complaint said that, at the rate of $7.00 a month pay, she was owed $34.50, plus interest. In addition, Hannah said that on January 1 she'd been given a dollar as "a New Year's gift," which Mrs. Cunningham took from her under pretense of keeping it for her. But she'd never given it back, and Hannah sued for this dollar, too: a total of $35.50, of which interest was due on $34.50. She signed her complaint with an *X*.

Dr. Uhl was trying to decide what he thought about Mrs. Cunningham and her pregnancy. Once before he'd vacillated in his feelings about her: on the morning Harvey Burdell's dead body was found, David Uhl had stood in her bedroom looking at the apparently distraught woman, and there had entered his mind, he had said, the thought that she was faking, and that she was the killer. He was wrong, he'd decided presently,

162

and had come to believe she was innocent: possibly her two best friends at the trial had been the doctors Uhl and Catlin. But now Dr. Uhl found himself doubting Emma Cunningham once again. She'd avoided him, he said, after he'd urged a medical examination, "and this gave me an indefinable suspicion that something was wrong. After frequent conversations on that subject I was assured by other persons that everything was all right, and that Dr. Catlin, of Brooklyn, her former family physician, and myself should make the proper examination, and attend her during the confinement." So once again it seemed that he had misjudged Emma Cunningham.

Then an odd thing happened: at Bellevue Hospital. During the hearings before the surrogate, Mrs. Cunningham had visited Bellevue several times—to visit Mary Donaho, who was sick there; this in spite of some of Mary's testimony. Presently a nurse of the lying-in ward, a Mrs. Avis, "received a note written in a charmingly delicate hand. The nurse was requested to furnish her with a new-born child, unwashed, and money would be no object. If the nurse assented, she was to address the initials 'L.B.' at the Broadway Post-Office." Mrs. Avis threw the note away.

One morning a few days after he'd agreed to attend Emma Cunningham at the birth of her new baby, Dr. Uhl went to 31 Bond to see his patient. She had a new and much larger bedroom now: Dr. Burdell's old bedroom, the one in which he'd been laid out in his coffin. It wasn't his bed, though, or furniture; that had been sold at the auction, and Mrs. Cunningham had had to buy new, making a down payment, the rest on time. Now in that bedroom David Uhl learned from Mrs. Cunningham the remarkable size of the fee she offered him for attending a simple confinement along with Dr. Catlin. It was to be a thousand dollars, an enormous fee; to be paid just as soon as the newborn heir and its widowed mother had Dr. Burdell's estate.

The fee wasn't too much, however, because "she told me then, very plainly," said Uhl, "that she was not in the family way, and that we would have to get hold of a child in some way or other. . . ."

Where had this weird idea of a fake baby come from? I don't know, but months ago at the inquest, an anonymous letter signed "Observer" had come to the coroner. He'd read it aloud, and the newspapers published it. "Observer" suggested that Emma Cunningham had gotten Eckel to impersonate Dr. Burdell at a fake wedding, and that then they'd murdered the Doctor. But he also suggested something no one else had thought of: suppose Emma Cunningham were to get herself pregnant? "If in the family way," he suggested cleverly, "the child would be supposed to be his, and she and it would get all the property." Now—wadding shoved deceptively up under the front of her dress—Emma Cunningham sat in the murdered man's bedroom offering David Uhl one thousand dollars to find her a newborn baby.

He wasn't that good a friend. "I did not give her any satisfaction, but the next day I called on . . . my lawyer, and told the whole case, and asked what course to pursue. He told me . . . to inform the District Attorney. . . . I did as he advised, and . . . called on Mr. Hall at his office in Broadway, and told him all I knew of the matter, and that I wished to have nothing more to do with it."

No such luck. If, as I do, you see A. Oakey Hall, in spite of his old-style glasses, as a man about town, then also, as I do, you may see him as rubbing his hands in anticipation of what may just have looked like fun, and grinning at this solemn David Uhl here. For the worried Dr. Uhl,

wanting "nothing more to do with" this, said, "Mr. Hall thought . . . that I should assist him in detecting her, and prevent the consummation of the contemplated crime." And so, in the iron-and-cobble clatter of Broadway just outside the windows, the two men sit in an antique office, wearing the loose dark clothes and huge neckties of the day: Hall is waiting, smiling perhaps; Uhl frowning. Then David Uhl tells Oakey Hall that he'll think it over; as he did for a couple of days.

For apparently Uhl was a conscientious man, and what he had to think over was the confidentiality of the doctor-patient relationship. Finally he decided that while this applied to what a patient told a doctor treating her, it did not apply to a healthy woman urging her doctor to join her in crime. And he went back to Hall's office, and said he'd do it.

"Almost every day" then, said Oakey Hall, "Dr. Uhl would come to see me at my house, generally late at night. Neither of us mentioned it to anybody else." Hall decided it was "advisable to have the confinement hurried; I had received an intimation that possibly the Surrogate might decide the case by the middle of August, and thought we had better have it through."

The two men worked out a scheme, then back went Dr. Uhl to 31, where his patient sometimes lay sick and nauseated as befitted her condition, and sometimes—feeling better—walked around the house, her dress shoved out in front a little more each few days.

I think her daughters believed she was pregnant. I feel sure Helen did, and I think Augusta did, too. Anyway, David Uhl told Emma Cunningham he'd help her, but what about Dr. Catlin, who was to assist in the fake delivery? He wasn't to worry, Mrs. Cunningham told him. "She stated that [Dr. Catlin] could be trusted in this matter, for she had him so completely in her power, that he did not dare disclose anything connected with it, that he had adhered to her interests during all her troubles with her first husband, and she could rely upon him."

So Uhl and Emma Cunningham began working out details. "Dr. Uhl asked her when it would be most convenient for her to become a mother. Thursday, July 28, was the shortest possible time for the 'ordinary gestation' (as spoken of by Judge Dean), under the theory of the marriage before the Surrogate, and so the first week in August became the settled upon time." Uhl told her he'd see what he could do about lining up a baby, and returned to Oakey Hall to ask what next.

Hall talked to a member of the Committee of Bellevue, who spoke to the warden of Bellevue, Timothy Daly, who said no problem: he'd produce a new baby from the lying-in ward whenever they needed one; and Hall passed the good word on to Uhl. But Uhl was worried. Mrs. Cunningham, he warned Hall, "was a very shrewd plotting woman, . . . and he was afraid the plan might not work. . . ." If a new baby seemed too easily produced, she'd be suspicious, he thought, so A. Oakey Hall figured out a story.

Uhl was to go back and tell Emma Cunningham that he'd found "a California widow" who'd be giving birth in the first couple of days of August, and who was ready and anxious to be rid of the new baby just as fast as possible afterward because she was sailing to California to rejoin her husband.

It was a believable story, and clever of Hall: because "California widow" meant a woman whose husband was long gone to the far-off gold fields; and more than one such woman had found herself pregnant too many months after her husband had left her. It was well known that such babies were often wonderfully easy to adopt without fussy legalities or questions; and just as quickly and secretly as could be managed.

The new baby was to be born in Elm Street, Oakey Hall also decided, because Elm (since renamed Elk Street) was a street full of apartments for rent, and not far from Bond. Uhl passed on that news to Mrs. Cunningham along with the "California widow" story.

Dr. Uhl's lawyers had advised him to have nothing to do with Dr. Catlin. "But one day as I was going up Broadway," said Dr. Uhl—over and again we see that Broadway was the true center of town: the theaters, big hotels, the fashionable restaurants and saloons, prosperous offices, all the action, seemed to be here—he ran into Dr. Catlin.

There was no avoiding it: Catlin "stopped me in the street," said Uhl —this is Catlin—"and insisted upon conversing with me on the subject.

I told him I supposed we understood each other; there was no necessity for any conferences. . . . He said no; we must arrange things together. I did not say much. During the conversation he said he had devised this plan while he was in the Tombs [visiting Emma Cunningham]. It was a mere matter of justice to her, for she had been a very much abused woman, but that they had made up their minds that they must have another Doctor, they could not get on without one, and certain parties had been applied to to get me to enter the plot. I told him I was in a hurry, and if he wished to see me he must call at my office. I then got into a stage, and went up town. He never called."

Up in his patient's bedroom again, Uhl told Mrs. Cunningham that the California widow's baby was due Monday or Tuesday, August 3 or 4, and now things began to move. It had occurred to Oakey Hall that whoever was to be hustling a new baby around the city probably ought to be a doctor, so he got in touch with his brother-in-law, personal physician, and "classmate," Dr. John De La Montagnie, who lived at Fishkill Landing in Dutchess County. De La Montagnie said he'd be glad to come to New York and lend a hand in this, as who wouldn't.

He arrived Monday morning, went to the D.A.'s Broadway office, and was introduced to Dr. Uhl. Then the two men went over to Elm Street to find an apartment, but had trouble. It had to be here on Elm because that's what they'd told Mrs. Cunningham; and it had to be secluded enough so that whoever came for the baby wouldn't be too worried about being seen. Not till afternoon did they find, at 190 Elm, a parlor and bedroom both available and secluded enough; and it still had its problems. For one thing, it was unfurnished, and the owner, a German immigrant named William Vieser, lived in the building and ran a little business here besides: a "lager-bier cellar" where he also sold wine.

They took it anyway—it was late—paying a month's rent in advance, and while Dr. De La Montagnie went up to Bellevue, the D.A. himself sent over a load of his own household furnishings: a sofa-bedstead, round table, rocking chair, roll of carpeting, five plain chairs, looking glass, candle, matches, nursing bottle, a trunkful of bedding and pillows; he thought of everything.

In the Bellevue lying-in ward lay two new babies, and when Dr. De La Montagnie arrived, Warden "Daly told me that I might make my own selection," but Daly was wrong. De La Montagnie picked one of the infants, but its mother refused to let him borrow it; just didn't feel like loaning out her brand-new baby, even for a worthy cause. So he turned to the only other choice, "a pretty, blue-eyed little girl," he said, "which was born on Saturday, and the mother consented. . . ."

I wonder, though, how much choice she was really given. She was Elizabeth Ann Anderson, drawn here from life, at Bellevue, and "but 27

years of age, though from her appearance she might easily be mistaken for a woman of 40. Something is to be allowed for the prostration incident to childbirth, but her features plainly exhibit traces of care and suffering. Her hair has turned prematurely gray, her cheeks are sunken, and her eyes hollow. . . ." Her husband, "by occupation a physiognomist," and who "she reluctantly confesses to be very intemperate, deserted her, and she then supported herself . . . by plain sewing. She made up aprons and sacks, sun-bonnets, &c., and then sold them personally at Washington Market. On Saturday last, being conscious of the symptoms of confinement, she . . . procured a permit to enter [Bellevue]—as many indigent women do in such cases—and rode up in a Third-avenue car to Twenty-Seventh-street, from which point she undertook to walk to the Hospital, situated at the foot of that street. When near the corner of Twenty-Sixth-street and Second-avenue, she began to be seized with labor pains, and seeing a yard gate open, staggered in and sat down on the steps. An Irish domestic found her in that condition, but declined to take her in the house, as her mistress, she said, was not at home. The most she did was to send to the Hospital, not far distant, for medical assistance. A physician soon came and found Mrs. Anderson in a rear house in the yard, having just given birth to a female child. From thence she was immediately conveyed to the Hospital. . . ." And now: a charity patient at Bellevue; in 1857; with no money, husband, or shred of power; the warden of the hospital standing at her bedside explaining why she ought to cooperate; Elizabeth Anderson said yes, they could take her baby.

"About noon on Monday, Captains Speight, Dilk and myself," said Captain Hopkins of the Twenty-third Precinct, "were standing in Broadway, conversing. Mr. Hall [the D.A.] came along at the moment. . . ." Captain Hopkins's description of what Hall then said to the three of them is in the grand police tradition of unlikely speech: ". . . addressing us, [Hall] said, 'Gentlemen, I am glad to meet you. I want you on very important business, very important business indeed. You are aware that . . . Captains or Inspectors of Police [now have the] power to enter at any hour any dwelling in which they have reason to believe a felony is being or about to be committed. I shall want some of you gentlemen to act in accordance with the section of the law to which I allude, this evening. . . . Meet me at 7½ o'clock this evening, at the Fifteenth Police Precinct Station-house, without fail. Say not a word about what I have spoken to you, to anyone. Seven and a half, remember!—good bye."

In the early afternoon Dr. Uhl arrived at 31 Bond, went up to the bedroom, and told Emma Cunningham that it looked as though the baby would be born tonight. She thought about that, then told Uhl that if the baby was born in the early part of the evening, a lady would come for it, and bring it back here to number 31 tonight. But if the baby was born late in the evening, the lady would wait all night at 190 Elm, and then bring the baby back to 31 Bond in the very early morning. But of course it was impossible to allow anyone from here to wait around 190 Elm all night; and then Mrs. Cunningham had still another frightening idea: she said she thought she'd send a lady around to 190 Elm this very afternoon just to look the place over in advance.

Uhl got out, hurried over to Elm, and told the D.A.—who was there, fortunately—that not only did the baby have to be born early this evening, but someone would be along any minute to inspect the place. It was panicky news: what if the lady decided to actually come inside? The furniture wasn't even in place, *and what about a mother?* Well, they didn't have a mother yet, and no time to get one. So, shoving the furniture into place as fast as they could heave it around, they also sent someone for "a friend of Dr. Uhl's," said Oakey Hall, "Dr. William N. Gilchrest, a druggist, at No. 62½ Spring Street, near by. . . ." He came right over, and they told him what he had to do: "put on a night-cap and lie in bed and moan as if in all the agonies of afterbirth."

The druggist got into bed, and pulled on the nightcap. "I had an old fishing basket, one of my own," Oakey Hall continued, "with a small pillow in it, ready to put the child in to be given to the messenger." They were ready now with everything but the baby, Uhl sitting on the sill of the front window watching the street, ready to signal for moans from Gilchrest, the druggist.

At 31 Bond the action had also begun. Georgiana was home from Beecher's Saratoga boarding school, and I suppose she believed her mother was pregnant, as I think Helen and Augusta did. Because now Mrs. Cunningham put on what seems to have been a sham for their benefit. Helen said, ". . . My mother had not been well for the past week. She was taken with a violent pain on Monday [afternoon]. I ran upstairs and got some brandy and peppermint, and she took it . . . felt much better, and went upstairs. . . ." I make the guess that this may have been the excuse and the time for Mrs. Cunningham to sneak out of her bedroom and the house to go inspect 190 Elm.

For no more than fifteen minutes, Dr. Uhl thought, he sat on the front window sill at 190, the furniture in place, Gilchrest waiting in bed in his nightcap. Then "I saw Mrs. Cunningham pass the house," Uhl said, "and look at it closely." He watched her, ready to call for moans, but: "She stopped and looked" at the house, he said, then turned away.

Minutes later—and fortunately not meeting Mrs. Cunningham there on the sidewalk—Dr. De La Montagnie arrived with the baby. He handed it over to Uhl, and then it suddenly occurred to him that they needed more than just a baby for a convincing birth; they had to have a placenta, too. "For this purpose," said De La Montagnie, "I took a carriage, and drove straightaway to Bellevue Hospital again, leaving Dr. Uhl . . . to take care of the baby."

Back home at 31 Bond, Mrs. Cunningham got into bed again, and resumed crying out with simulated labor pains. After a while Augusta had all she could take of that, and simply walked out of the house, and over to an aunt's, a Mrs. Simonson who lived on Lexington between Twenty-fifth and Twenty-sixth, and there Augusta stayed. Mrs. Cunningham sent word to her friend Catherine Wilt to hurry over; her labor was beginning.

Mrs. Wilt arrived, and stayed for twenty minutes of watching her friend tossing and crying out. She was sent back home around seven with a message for her husband, George. He hadn't worked for four years, was available for errands, and was to hurry over to Brooklyn in the ferry now, and fetch Dr. Catlin.

At seven-thirty, as requested, Captains Dilk, Speight, and Hopkins met A. Oakey Hall at his office in Broadway, where, said Hopkins in splendid police-ese, "he imparted the nature of the business which he desired us to aid him in."

"At the Hospital at 8 o'clock," said Dr. De La Montagnie, "I got possession of the afterbirth of another child, rolled up in a piece of silk oil-cloth, and also obtained the services of an intelligent Irish girl named Mary Regan to personate the nurse of the California widow and the baby. . . . With my load I drove as fast as possible to Elm Street, fearing the woman might get there before me." (Another fine moment for time travel: to stand watching that carriage speed through the Manhattan dusk bearing its silk-wrapped placenta.) "We stopped the carriage at the corner of Broome and Elm Streets," De La Montagnie continued, and he and the nurse walked to 190 Elm.

"Just after dusk," said Captain Hopkins, at about eight-thirty, the three police captains and a few ordinary cops took the stations to which Oakey Hall sent them. Hall put cops everywhere: one at each end of Bond Street, one in the shadows directly across from 31, one in the alley behind the house, of which we have this picture. And still another across the street from 190 Elm.

At about the same time the cops were taking their positions, Dr. De La Montagnie was busy doing something I feel must have been the D.A.'s idea: because who else would be thinking just now in terms of courtroom evidence? Oakey Hall seems

already to be hearing a defense attorney demanding: *How can you prove it was the same baby you got from Bellevue?* Well, a New York D.A. would have prosecuted more than one crook caught with paper money secretly marked beforehand. And now, up in a bedroom of 190 Elm Street, Dr. De La Montagnie pulled down the hospital gown of Elizabeth Anderson's about-to-be-born-again baby, and dabbed it "with lunar caustic behind its

left ear and under each arm." "Lunar caustic" is silver nitrate, which left no visible marks now, but in a day or so the marks would turn black, identifying Baby Anderson like a marked bill. And just to make absolutely sure of a positive identification later, Dr. De La Montagnie pulled out his pocket handkerchief, tore off a thin strip along its colored border, and tied this onto the stump of the baby's umbilical cord. Nurse Mary Regan then tucked baby back into the D.A.'s fishing basket,

and Dr. De La Montagnie —having a wonderful time, I suspect—went out and across the street, where he joined Patrolman Walsh in watching the house.

Somewhere around the time all this was happening, "between eight and nine o'clock," said Dr.

Uhl, "I called on Mrs. Cunningham again, and was shown upstairs to the second story. The room was very dark indeed. There was no light. I walked into the front room where Mrs. Burdell was pretending to have labor pains. She said she would call the lady who was to go, and whose name she would not tell. She called her to her bedside, and I recognized the person who calls herself Mrs. Burdell's sister. . . . Mrs. Burdell asked her if she was ready to go. She said yes, and asked where the black dress was, and then it was arranged between us that the lady would follow me [he means she would come along a little later] to No. 190 Elm-street, that I should wait in the front door for her, and that the lady should hold in her hand a white handkerchief, that I should recognize her."

"After Dr. Uhl had left," Dr. Catlin arrived at No. 31, said Helen

172

Cunningham, and she let him in. "He went into mother's room, and I went into the back room. I asked the Doctor if mother was dangerous, and he said it was nothing but a cramp or colic. He did not say anything more in reference to her condition. After that, Mrs. Barnes called him in the room, and I went in after him. Mother appeared to be in great pain, when I went up to her and asked her if I could do anything for her. She said, 'No, daughter.' I then asked Dr. Catlin if he would stay all night. He said, 'I'll see whether I will or not.' I then left the room, and went down to the kitchen. I called my sister Georgiana . . . to go with me. I got some cheese, preserves, and bread and butter, with some ice and ice water. I put them on a tray, and took them upstairs to the back room, and placed them on a table. . . . I saw Mrs. Barnes' son come in with a bundle, and take it to the third story."

George Wilt came to the house after having gone to Brooklyn for Dr. Catlin, arriving after Catlin because he'd "stopped in the Third Avenue awhile." I don't know where; a saloon, maybe. But George Wilt was a butcher, and someone that night obtained a bucket of animal blood and brought it to 31 Bond. Though it could have been "Mrs. Barnes' son come in with a bundle. . . ."

Dr. Catlin sent George Wilt up to Dr. Uhl's on Twentieth Street to fetch him here. Across the street, concealed in the darkness, Captain Speight watched Wilt leave. "I went to Dr. Uhl's," said Wilt, "and left a message on the slate, the Doctor not being at home."

Wilt came back to 31 Bond, lay down on the front-parlor sofa, "heard groans which appeared to come from the room of Mrs. Cunningham," and fell asleep. He didn't wake up, he said, till eleven o'clock.

Helen had done all she could think of for her mother, and now she asked Georgiana "to come see mother, but she refused, as she was unwell, and did not wish to see mother suffer so. I then told mother I was going to bed, and that she was to call me if she grew worse. . . . Dr. Catlin was standing at the bedside. . . ." And now, with Helen and Georgiana upstairs getting ready for bed, the boys staying elsewhere, Augusta out of the house, and George Wilt asleep downstairs, Emma Cunningham was alone with Dr. Catlin and her sister.

Quickly she got dressed in dark concealing garments, including a coal-scuttle bonnet with veil, concealing her face; and then this steel-nerved, ever-bungling woman sneaked out of number 31, and began a stealthy walk, nearly every step of which was as well documented as Macy's Thanksgiving Day Parade.

From across the street Captain Speight "saw a woman closely veiled, and having a black skirt and a gray mixed duster, come from the premises No. 31 Bond-street, and proceed up Bond. . . ." He followed her "to the corner of the Bowery," where they both stood waiting "a few minutes for a car. . . ."

One came along, and even before it stopped rolling, the conductor's attention was drawn to the waiting woman because "she was much muffled-up, and seemed disguised. . . ." The car stopped, the muffled-up lady got on at the back platform, and Captain Speight at the front, where he stayed. Said Conductor James Carrol, "From the fact of the locality and the disguise, I received the impression that it was Mrs. Cunningham."

Conductor Carrol walked on through the car to the front platform, where he recognized Captain Speight. "I took him by the arm, and said, 'Is not that Mrs. Cunningham?'

"He caught me by the arm, and said, 'Say not a word.'

"I returned through the car, and took the lady's fare. I tried to see her face, but from the manner in which her head was enveloped I could not get a view of her features. We had passed along a few blocks, when Captain Speight came through to the back platform and asked me the time of night. I looked at my watch, and said, 'It is just five minutes past nine o'clock.'

"I talked to the Captain until we reached the corner of Centre and Broome streets, when I felt something at my back like a person behind me. On turning round I found the lady standing at the door in the act, as I thought, of running away, or in the act of getting off without stopping the car. I then took her by the arm and pulled the bell, saying, 'Madam, you must not get off till the car stops.' The car stopped immediately and the lady got off. She never turned her head until she reached the sidewalk. She then turned her head, apparently scrutinized us both and passed down towards Elm-street."

Speight rode on for half a block, then hopped off, and—the hooded lady still in sight—followed her as she walked down Broome Street toward Elm. She walked on past Elm, Speight said, then "turned suddenly and went up Elm-street on the west side." Speight stood watching from the Elm Street corner until the woman "disappeared in a house." Others, he knew, were stationed to watch that house, so Speight turned away, and went on back to his Bond Street post.

Dr. Uhl stood waiting at the front door of 190 Elm, as he had been for some time now. He wore "a white hat and white pants, and a dark coat," De La Montagnie had noticed. Said Uhl, ". . . Finally the lady came, dressed in black, having a black hood over her head, partially disguising her features. I asked her if she was the person that came after the basket. She made no reply, but merely shook her handkerchief, and walked upstairs with me to the room." This was an outer room, in which Nurse Regan waited with Baby. In an adjoining connecting room lay mother Gilchrest in his nightcap, in case the visitor decided to walk in; and, said Oakey Hall: "The apothecary groaned satisfactorily." I assume in falsetto.

"The light burnt dimly on the centre table" of the outer room, and "the door which opened into the adjoining room displayed the foot of a cot on which the sick mother was supposed to be prostrate. Mrs. Cunningham only glanced in, but a glance must have satisfied her all was right; the nurse, Mary Regan, sat with the child in her lap, the basket at her feet.

As Mrs. Cunningham presented herself she was asked if she came for the child, as agreed upon, she shook her handkerchief in reply, the next instant the 'little thing' was placed in the basket and handed through the partially opened door. . . ."

The lady in black just as quickly took the basketed baby, and, said Dr. Uhl, "went off with it. I was led to believe from her general appearance that it was Mrs. Burdell herself who came after the child. The child and afterbirth were in the basket. I saw her go off with it."

Across the street stood Patrolman Walsh and Dr. De La Montagnie, but: "The street is narrow," as the D.A. said later, "was rather dark in the moonlight, and Walsh and Dr. De La Montagnie, in their anxiety, did not see her come out, but they were soon satisfied, by the lights in No. 190 being put out and by preparations made to shift the scene, that she had gone."

The realization must have come quickly because Walsh and the doctor now hurried through Prince Street to the Bowery, and there "on the block between Bleecker and Bond-street, coming up towards Bond-street," De La Montagnie said he "saw coming in the distance a great basket, borne by a woman with dark clothes, a very peculiar dress like that

of a nun." He "passed very near to her, but could not see her face." However, he "recognized the basket distinctly as one which [he] had that afternoon procured from the house of the District Attorney, and which [he] had last seen twenty minutes previously in premises No. 190 Elm-street." The doctor "followed on the other side of Bond Street . . . ," saw the woman with the basket turn into 31 Bond, and then encountered Captain Speight, back at his post across the street from 31. The captain, too, "saw the same person, having on the same dress, who had previously left the house, return with a basket . . . and go down the area of the premises No. 31 Bond Street." And now with Mrs. Cunningham back

home, Speight hurried toward Broadway to let our old friend Captain Dilk know what was happening. Dilk's post was in front of Burton's Theater on Broadway, where he could look straight down Bond Street. Captain Hopkins had just joined him, having seen nothing in the alley behind 31, and: "We had been there but a moment," said Hopkins, "and were preparing to return to the station-house, when Captain Speight approached almost out of breath. He told us that he had 'piped' a woman from 31 Bond," followed her to Elm, and now she'd come back with a basket.

"On hearing this, said Hopkins, "I went back with Captain Speight. We stood nearly opposite No. 31 Bond-street, and watched to see who should go in or out." At some point Dr. De La Montagnie left to go join D.A. Oakey Hall, I don't know where. (I see De La Montagnie as the excited amateur so revved up by what he was in on tonight that he couldn't stay in one place.)

The two police captains stood across the street watching 31, and presently, Hopkins said, they "saw a little man go in." This was Dr. Catlin; he'd left the house to go get a prescription, possibly when Speight had left his post to follow Mrs. Cunningham.

Dr. Uhl had gone home after the hooded lady left 190 Elm with the baby. There he found the message George Wilt had left on his slate. Now the police captains watched Dr. Uhl walk up the steps of 31, and pull the bell.

The bell woke George Wilt, he said, asleep in the front parlor. He got up, and let Uhl in, and Uhl felt impelled to explain that he'd been out of town, and had just come back. "I went upstairs to Mrs. Burdell's room," Uhl said, "and saw Mrs. Burdell lying on her bed. Her sister and Dr. Catlin were in the room, and the child was lying in one corner of the room. Mrs. Burdell pretended to have all the symptoms of severe labor." Since she couldn't have been trying to fool anybody in the room, I suppose she meant to be heard elsewhere in the house. "Dr. Catlin brought out a tin pail containing a quantity of blood," said Uhl, "which he mixed with water and spread over some sheets. He bloodied his hands with it. . . ."

Little Ann Barnes, Emma Cunningham's sister, was now sent downstairs—not easy with her lameness—to ask George Wilt to go get his sister-in-law, Jane Bell, the nurse. "They pretended she was not in the secret," said Uhl. Across the street the police noted the departure of George Wilt, Hopkins's report said, and Captain Speight followed, and "piped" him as far as Second Avenue, and then returned.

It seems to me that Dr. Uhl was mistaken in thinking Jane Bell was in on the plot; because if she was, then who was it they were trying to fool with the bloody sheets? Not Catlin and not Uhl, and hardly sister Ann Barnes. And the Cunningham girls were upstairs asleep. I think the whole setup may have been for the benefit of Jane Bell, a nurse, who would then swear, if the need arose, that she had arrived to see every evidence that a child had just been born.

And as they waited for nurse Bell, they seemed to prepare for exactly this. While Emma Cunningham got up out of bed, and went into the next-door room—in which Harvey Burdell had been knifed to death—and had herself some supper, the supper Helen had left there for her, I imagine, they got out the phony placenta, and left it where it could be seen; they took the half-empty bucket of blood and the baby's shabby Bellevue clothes, and locked them in a closet of the room where Emma Cunningham sat eating; and then Dr. Catlin sent Ann Barnes limping down the stairs again, to the kitchen, to carry up a washtub partly filled with water.

Wilt soon returned with Jane Bell, who was "a middleaged, plain looking woman," said the *Times,* "with nothing peculiarly striking in manners or address, for one of her avocation"—which seems an odd comment to me: maybe nurses will understand it. Apparently Wilt and Jane Bell had to ring the bell, because Dr. Uhl went down, "Let them in, and the nurse came upstairs just as Dr. Catlin was removing the bloody sheets from Mrs. Cunningham and her sister was washing the child"— I suppose in the washtub she'd just carried up here. To me the delay in washing the child and removing the wet bloody sheets from Mrs. Cunningham, while waiting for George Wilt to walk over to Second Avenue and come back with Jane Bell, again suggests that it was Jane Bell for whom the performance was staged.

Nurse Bell said that when she came into the room, "Mrs. Barnes . . . was in the room, also Dr. Uhl and Dr. Catlin. Mrs. Cunningham was in bed, and appeared to be very sick. I took the child, and finished dressing it." Who then looked just great in the refurbished layette they'd prepared for her. "I then fed it, and got it to sleep, and laid it in bed by Mrs. Cunningham." A *Leslie's Illustrated Newspaper* reporter quoted Emma Cunningham as saying at that moment that "she had put her trust in God, and in return He had been pleased to favor her" —a line meant, I also suppose, for Jane Bell.

Who noted all the props. "There was a wash

tub in the room containing water. I saw a towel stained with blood on the bed." The room was a stage, apparently, the set properly dressed, actors moving through their parts, speaking their lines. "I did not see any blood on the floor or elsewhere," Jane continued. "My attention was taken up with the baby. I was in the room about half an hour . . . Mrs. Cunningham, while I was there, spoke of having suffered great pain, and said she had a hard delivery. . . ." During her half hour up here, Uhl said Jane Bell "performed all the operations usually performed by a nurse." And at some point, George Wilt downstairs had "heard a child cry."

Mrs. Barnes sent Jane Bell downstairs to make some tea for Mrs. Cunningham. Catlin piled the bloody bedding and towels into the washtub, and Ann Barnes carried it back down to the kitchen, and left it there. And now, Baby in her new finery tucked in beside Emma Cunningham,

179

the false accouchement was completed.

Catlin told Uhl that he'd soon be going to a Bowery drugstore for something—which again suggests to me the preparation of independent testimony to confirm their story. Uhl "remained till after it was all concluded," he said, "and then I left the house, Dr. Catlin closing the door after me." Uhl walked west along the midnight street, and, Oakey Hall said, he "joined us on the corner of Broadway. He said that Catlin would be out shortly."

Emma Cunningham got her tea. Downstairs, George Wilt told Ann Barnes that he thought he'd go home now. "As I was about leaving she said, 'Mrs. Burdell has got a fine child.'" Catlin left for the drugstore.

The house quiet now; Emma Cunningham's new baby asleep beside her; two doctors and a nurse, she believed, prepared to swear she'd delivered it: this woman of unending determination must have believed that she'd finally pulled it off; that this house and at least two thirds of Harvey Burdell's estate would at last become hers. But outside on the streets, just as Dr. Catlin turned off Bond onto the Bowery, two cops stepped forward, and grabbed him. "He was pinioned," Oakey Hall said, "as we were informed that he had pistols." He was taken to the Fifteenth Precinct station house.

The two captains across the street left their post about twelve, and walked over to Broadway. "Here we were met," said Hopkins, "by District-Attorney Hall, Capt. Dilk, Dr. Montagnie, Dr. Griswold (I believe) and Officers Smith, Wilson and Walsh." No mention of Dr. Uhl; I suppose he'd gone home, and glad to.

The cluster of half a dozen cops, two doctors, and the D.A. stood there on the Broadway corner, "A conversation was had," said Hopkins, "and it was resolved to proceed at once into the house and make the necessary arrests." Back to 31 they walked, eighteen boots and shoes sounding on the late-at-night Bond Street. Then "Capt. Dilk and Dr. Montagnie went forward and rang the bell" of No. 31.

Do you wonder, like me, what Emma Cunningham thought at that unexpected ring? "There was no answer," De La Montagnie said. "I then rang violently"—he was pulling the bell by hand, of course—"when the door was soon opened by two women, who objected to our coming in and asked what we wanted at this late hour. Inspector Dilk and I excused ourselves for the hour, and stated that we had intercepted a Doctor, who had stated there had been a delivery at the house and Inspector Dilk said he had come to see if it was all right." This sounds like one of the flimsiest excuses of all time, and the women wouldn't buy it. "One of the women said Mrs. Burdell was sick and couldn't be seen." But Captain Dilk said they insisted "to see her," and came in (shoving their way, I would bet). It was important that they see Mrs. Cunningham, they told Jane Bell in the hallway. " 'You can't see her until I ask her,' " Bell replied, according to Captain Dilk, "and as she proceeded upstairs I with the Doctor followed her . . . ," and it's nice to know that with cops, even in 1857, people didn't walk but "proceeded."

Upstairs, said De La Montagnie, one of the two women "looked into the large front room and said, 'There are two gentlemen who wish to come in.' A voice said from within, 'Lock the door—they must not come—I tell you to lock that door.' We then went [shoved?] into the room, and apologized to a lady in bed, whom I . . . believe to be Mrs. Cunningham . . . and the . . . lady said, 'Why do you disturb me? I am very sick.' "

Questions and answers: " 'It is my lawful legitimate child.' " The men wanted to get hold of the baby, of course, before saying why they were here. "I wished Dr. De La Montagnie to look at the child," said the Captain, "when Mrs. Cunningham and the nurse, Jane Bell, both refused." The men didn't seem to know what to do; they had to get the baby but were afraid Emma Cunningham would kill it, they said, if they tried to take it from her. Which is puzzling, but maybe they meant only that in a tug-of-war a new baby might accidentally be killed.

They needed help, the Captain now decided, and announced that he was leaving. Ann Barnes walked downstairs with him toward the front door—on the other side of which five more cops, the D.A., and a spare doctor stood silently waiting.

Still in the room with Emma Cunningham, Dr. De La Montagnie stood assembling courtroom evidence, I think; possibly under Oakey Hall's instructions. " 'Do you claim this child as the child of Harvey Burdell?' " he says he asked her, "and she said, 'of course—whose else should it be?' "

Down in the front hall, Ann Barnes opened the front door, and seven men shoved their way in. The D.A. stayed downstairs while the others, said Dilk, "proceeded to the room of Mrs. Cunningham, when she was informed she was under arrest. . . ." Still gathering formal evidence, I think, Dr. De La Montagnie then "demanded in the presence of the officers to see the umbilical cord. Mrs. Cunningham and the nurse objected. After some persuasion they consented."

Some persuasion is right: what happened was that Dilk and another cop suddenly grabbed Emma Cunningham's arms like this, while a third

cop rushed over, and snatched the baby. " 'Don't take my dear baby from
me!' " De La Montagnie said she cried out.

But they had it now, and De La Montagnie undid its new finery—
What was the *effect* of that fantastic afternoon and long evening on that
child? Did Baby Anderson grow up into a neurotic wreck?—then he
checked out the lunar caustic markings and the umbilical stump. He "saw
the piece of pocket-handkerchief on the cord . . . but the [lunar caustic]
marks were not as yet visible, and would not be until the following day."

De La Montagnie then "proceeded in a carriage in company with
the District Attorney to Bellevue Hospital, taking the said infant, and
about half-past one o'clock on Tuesday morning restored it to the
mother . . . ," who was "delighted to find," said D.A. Hall, "that it had
such handsome clothing." And then I hope, she rocked it, and crooned,
and breast-fed it, for the rest of that nutty night.

At 31 the cops searched the place, though they didn't go up where
Helen and Georgiana lay, asleep or awake. They found the locked closet,
Captain Dilk brought out "a bunch of keys, belonging to the Station-
house," Hopkins said; one key worked, and they discovered the bucket of
blood and the discarded Bellevue baby clothes, and Hopkins found the
placenta, which he "wrapped in a napkin, which I found at the dressing-
table." They found the remains of Emma Cunningham's supper in the
repainted room where Harvey Burdell had died. And the tub full of bloody
bedding.

"We left the house about three o'clock in the morning," said Hopkins, "Captain Dilk taking with him to the Station-house Mrs. Bell, the nurse," who I suspect was the one innocent of the bunch. He also took along all the bloody evidence, and that poor old placenta. "Mrs. Cunningham"—lucky again—and her sister "were permitted to remain, under arrest," the house being left in charge of Roundsman William Dilk and Officers Wilson and Williams.

Then: "We all retired," said Captain Hopkins, "jaded by our most singular night's work.

"About 3 o'clock, when most of us had gone, one of the daughters, I learned, came part way downstairs."

13

In the morning crowds once again stood on the street and walks before number 31 Bond to watch the door and windows behind which Emma Cunningham was once more held under arrest. Six cops again guarded the place, under the command, naturally, of Captain Dilk.

No newspapers were allowed to enter the house, and—unable to believe that Dr. Uhl might have betrayed her or simply stonewalling from instinct—Emma Cunningham hung on to her pretense. Remaining in bed, she pleaded, said the *Times,* "that her 'dear baby,' 'her legal baby,' 'her poor murdered Doctor's baby' might be brought to her. 'Why have they taken my baby from me,' she demanded. . . ."

Dr. Catlin sat in a cell, held as a witness.

Georgiana was reported "very sick," and so was Augusta, who said she would never again set foot in 31 Bond. Helen took care of her mother.

Within a few days the Burdell relatives flatly insisted that this time the house at 31 be cleared of Cunninghams; and ten days after the appearance of the bogus baby, as the newspapers were calling it, there happened at last what Harvey Burdell had so longed for. Her unpaid-for furniture repossessed, Emma Cunningham—never giving up—was forcibly carried from the house on a mattress, by cops. She was taken back to her old cell at the Tombs, the daughters moved to their aunt's where Augusta was, and number 31 Bond Street stood empty at last, and desolate, the crowd outside dwindling to occasional passersby glancing up at it curiously; and then, in time, dropping out of public consciousness; and finally out of all human memory.

On August 24 at noon, Surrogate Bradford announced a decision that could have surprised no one. In "54 closely written folio pages" he explained why "Emma Augusta Cunningham is not the widow of decedent. . . ." The *Times* thought this long, reasoned decision—filling nine of its columns—"has many of the elements which make fiction so attractive. It would not be easy for the most ingenious novelist to invent a more strange and curious plot than that which the Surrogate's decision seems to unravel. A false marriage,—a real murder and a simulated birth are the three grand incidents of this singular drama." And the *Times* wondered "Whether a still more startling climax is still to come. . . ."

But none was; finally it had all ended. Charges against John Eckel had long since been dropped; no point in trying him after a jury let Emma Cunningham go. For a time bail was refused to Emma Cunningham, but when more time had passed she was allowed it; and she moved in with her daughters on Lexington Avenue. After still more time—she was always lucky—the case against Mrs. Cunningham was dropped. The reason, or excuse, was that no crime had quite been committed. No law against saying a baby was yours when it wasn't; and she'd never actually reached the point of formally claiming Harvey Burdell's estate for the baby. Well, maybe. It sounds a little thin to me, and I wonder if the truth isn't that the D.A. and New York City had finally just gotten tired of Emma Cunningham.

Popular novels of the nineteenth century sometimes gave readers an afterword: the story over, you then learned what had finally happened to all the people you'd come to know. Who lived on to old age? Who died, and of what? Who married whom? Sometimes you were even told their children's names. I like this vanished practice because I always want to know. And I've advocated a return to the custom by today's novelists. With no luck so far. So I'm sorry I can't tell you what happened to these people. George Snodgrass would have been twenty-two when the Civil War began; and before it ended, the two Cunningham boys would have been just old enough to join it. Even John Eckel, at forty, could have been in it. But I've been unable to find anything to tell me they were.

As for Emma Cunningham herself, she was only thirty-six or thirty-seven, free as a bird, still "well preserved," and still, I assume, hungry for money. So who was next? And what happened to *him?* I don't know. A famous New York cop, Inspector Byrnes, published a book in the nineties, and in it he says Mrs. Cunningham went to California. Maybe she did; somewhere near where I live now. And maybe I'll find her diary on a dusty top shelf of that old-book shop. I'll let you know if I do. Meanwhile, I don't know what happened to her, or to the girls or boys either.

"Coroner Connery," the *Times* said, "smiles serenely . . . and says he will not have to wait for posterity [that's us] to do him justice. . . ." And we get one last glimpse of Baby Anderson. On August 12 she and her mother left Bellevue far more comfortably than they'd entered it: in a carriage, the *Times* said, and they were driven to Barnum's Museum, where, I am happy to tell you, they had a fine and successful run, Bar-

185

num's ad here appearing several times a week until September 16, mother

sitting with her celebrated daughter "on a raised platform, ready to answer (if able) all the curious questions that may be asked. . . ."

But not by us: even Baby Anderson would be well over 120 years old now. They're all gone: lost in vanished times. Except for one, of course. He lies today in the large, and still unmarked, family plot—four more

Burdells following him, the last in 1933—here where they laid his murdered body to rest on a snowy February day of 1857.

186

Intermission

It's been a while since I last saw a magazine cartoon of a helmeted explorer standing in an iron pot suspended over a fire as spear-carrying natives cavorted around him. But I and all of us have seen endless variations of it published over funny captions; and it could be that we haven't yet seen the last one.

I suspect that this overly familiar cartoon is a last flicker, a remote attenuated survivor, of certain real news stories that appeared regularly in the middle nineteenth century; often illustrated, as shown opposite. "Three Hundred Persons Butchered and Eaten by Cannibals" one such story was headlined. These were Chinese men, women, and children who sailed from Hong Kong for Sydney and the Australian gold fields. Unfortunately they were shipwrecked on the island of Rossel in the South Pacific, where cannibals ate them up a few at a time, except for the one survivor who told the story.

"At night," he said, "we were placed in the center of a clear piece of ground, and fires lit in several places, the natives keeping a regular watch over us, and during the day they would select four or five Chinese, and, after killing them, roast the flesh, and eat it. . . . Their mode of proceeding was as follows," and he gave the recipe, adding: "the fingers, toes and brains being eagerly sought after. . . ."

And: "In a book recently published by Mr. Baker, in London, [he gives] an account of his expedition to the sources of the Nile, [and] relates the following story of the Makkarikas, an African tribe, on the authority of a black named Ibrahimawa, who had been in Paris and London, and had an almost intuitive knowledge of geography. He had visited them with a trading party . . ." and said, " 'They are remarkably good people, but possessing a peculiar taste for dogs and human flesh.' " He, too, gives details, including some about a young girl victim who "was remarkably fat, and from the wound"—received as she tried to escape a slave master —"a large lump of yellow fat extruded . . . the Makkarikas rushed upon her . . . and seizing the fat, they tore it from the wounds in handfuls, the girl being still alive, while the crowd were quarreling for the disgusting prize. . . ." The paper that published that, and more, did add that: "We own to a lingering distrust" of the story.

But these stories were wonderfully horrifying, and in one of the best "a Prussian named Louis Bauer, a New Yorker, H. Homer by name, and a native boy called Charley, had proceeded in a small sloop to Waga (in the Fijis) to purchase oil and some provisions, taking with them trinkets, iron and other merchandise to barter. After making several purchases in a satisfactory manner," trouble began. The natives insisted on selling Homer some oil which he refused as overpriced. "An angry discussion ensued, which led to a scuffle, in which the oil was upset, and lost upon the sands. The rascal [who owned it] then swore he would be paid for it all the same, and upon Homer, Bauer and Charley retreating to their sloop, they were intercepted. Homer and Bauer seeing it was a struggle

189

for their lives, resolved to sell them as dearly as possible. Drawing their revolvers, and telling the boy to make his escape to the sloop, they faced the devils. . . ." Who rushed them. Three of the natives were shot down, but Charley and Bauer were killed, and Homer captured.

The savages "conveyed the murdered men to their village in the mountain . . . and the tribe assembled that evening to partake of their revolting banquet."

They had at least two recipes. In one, "the body is disembowelled, and washed with salt and water, the head is taken off, and then [the body is] placed in their oven, which is composed of smooth stones on all sides except the top; this is then made hot by burning furze and wood till it has the required heat. The ashes are then swept out, and green leaves are then placed at the sides," and "a stone that fits pretty tightly is then placed over the top, and it is left to undergo the regular time for baking."

They also used cooking pots and ate with forks, these illustrations

seem to show.

And they had a fast-food recipe, the bodies simply "trussed up like fowls and cooked over a roaring fire . . . which is their impromptu method. When it is sufficiently cooked a gong is sounded and the warrior masters who are invited hasten to their infernal meal." This is the method used with Bauer, Charley, and Homer. It is Homer—"a citizen of New York" says the caption—who is shown about to be dispatched in the illustration you've seen.

News of their fate spread through the Pacific islands and ports, and a "gallant Captain Sinclair, who commanded the Vandalia . . . resolved to punish these cannibal devils. . . . The Vandalia was lying at Levukin, about one hundred and thirty miles from Waga, where the outrage was committed. . . ." They reached the Fijis in three days; Lieutenant Caldwell selected forty seamen and ten marines for his landing party; and somewhere along the way they'd also picked up a volunteer. ". . . the appearance of these islands," he wrote after first seeing them, "is the most charming in the world. I hope to see the stars and stripes waving over them before long."

At a small village near Waga, the lieutenant found an interpreter, a "grim old chief, named Ravata . . . and another native to act as guide." Then on to Waga, where: "The whole scene was one of the wildest and most romantic I have ever beheld."

"Anchoring . . . Lieut. Caldwell despatched . . . Ravata to the village . . . demanding the murderers. . . . He also requested a visit from their chief, Dora Sivu." Ravata returned that afternoon with the chief, "who bore a mortal defiance . . . in these words:

" 'Do you suppose we killed the white men for nothing? No, we killed them, and we have eaten them. We are great warriors, and we delight in war. We have heard of the Papiliangi; we wish to meet them in battle. We are glad to see the little man-of-war; why did you not bring the large one? Come Papiliangi, our fires are lighted, our ovens are hot. . . .'

"This insolent bearing was doubtless owing to their strongly fortified position" on "the summit of a mountain nearly two thousand feet high." And: "Owing also to their prowess, and their numerous victories over their own countrymen, the three hundred warriors of Lomati deemed themselves invincible."

I don't know what happened to this chief; released, I suppose. Then Caldwell's party landed. They brought a mortar, which they tried, unsuccessfully, to drag up onto a hilltop, but had to abandon. They persevered, though. Dividing into two parties, "the Marines with Minie rifles in the advance," they climbed toward the mountain village, but "if these savages had practiced the tactics of our own Indians we never could have reached the town."

They did reach it, though, because Caldwell passed up the obvious easy route to the top, and instead chose a heavily wooded, extremely steep, and very unlikely route. "Our flank movement . . . completely disconcerted them; they thought, as a matter of course, we would approach by the paths . . . where they were posted in large numbers. . . . After gaining a position near the top, we took a long rest, a number of the men being almost exhausted. . . . When ready for the attack the divisions were reformed, and to remove any erroneous impressions the natives may have received of our determination, owing to our long halt, the favorite song of the 'Red, White and Blue' was sung in full chorus, three hearty cheers given, and the whole force rushed [the mountaintop]."

191

As they ran, the natives "To show their readiness to meet us and their contempt of death . . . were clothed in their funeral robes of white tappa cloth, with long scarfs sweeping over the ground, their hair combed to radiate from their heads, forming an immense bunch, or with wigs of enormous dimensions, some six feet in circumference, all enveloped in cloths of white tappa. However beautiful this adornment may have appeared in their own eyes, or however becoming to their notions of propriety the dress of the grave may have seemed to warriors preparing for battle . . . [it made them] conspicious objects to our marksmen as they glided among the thick foliage."

It was Minie rifles against arrows, and: "We took immediate possession [of the village], planted the American ensign in front of the chief's house, posted sentinels, and enjoyed a most welcome rest and refreshing breeze under the shade of the large trees that adorned the town. We found it to contain one hundred and twenty houses, of all sizes," and "the natives and our men keeping up a constant skirmishing," they "prepare[d] themselves with combustibles, and, under the direction of [Master's Mate] Bartlett, supported by the marines," they "fire[d] the town, commencing to leeward, and coming up to windward. This was speedily done and the town in flames, sending up an immense column of smoke visible for many miles around, [which was] distinctly seen by the tribes on the Ba coast thirty miles distant."

Now they headed back for the beach, and: "The 'tom-tom,' or native drum, commenced beating furiously, and the whole ravine through which we were obliged to pass appeared alive with warriors. Having concentrated in full force, they commenced a violent assault upon our front, flanks, and rear, with a tumult of yells and screams, a heavy discharge of fire-arms, stones thrown from slings, short heavy clubs hurled with great force, and a flight of arrows. They approached quite near us, moving with surprising agility, and making horrible grimaces, which their large mouths and white teeth enabled them to do after the most ferocious and disgusting manner. Our men returned the assault with a steady and rapid discharge of their rifles, and after a severe action of twenty or thirty minutes, repulsed them, with a heavy loss on their side in killed and wounded."

Making sudden unexpected changes in their route, they continued on down, but the natives, "availing themselves of their local knowledge of the passes, and the superior advantages they afforded them to harass us . . . endeavor[ed] to secure at least one body for their horrible feast, an end we were assured they would leave no effort untried to attain. Had they succeeded, it would have removed a part of their disgrace in losing their town and suffering defeat, and impaired the full measure of our success in the eyes of the natives."

Carrying their exhausted and wounded, the landing party reached the beach with no one killed. But in addition to the loss of their town, the cannibals "lost fourteen killed and sixteen . . . wounded. Doubtless others fell unobserved." The punitive expedition had been gone from the ship "ten and one-half [hours, and we] arrived on board, grateful to a merciful Providence for preserving us from all serious evil, 'though we walked through the valley of the shadow of death.' "

In 1876 a bill was introduced in Congress by Senator John Sherman (brother of the Civil War general, and author of the Sherman Antitrust Act), proposing that these wonderful coins be minted. There would be a ten-dollar gold piece and a silver half-dollar, their faces ordinary enough, but their reverse sides allowing them to be spent most anywhere. Since the important world currencies were solidly based on gold and silver, their relationships remained constant; and ten dollars in gold would always be 20.70 gulden in Germany, 51 francs and 81 centimes in France, 37.31 kronen in Sweden, and so on. Same with the silver half-dollar. And if other countries followed suit with their coinages, we'd approach a universal currency, saving all sorts of trouble. Unfortunately his bill got about as far as Esperanto; and we all know what's happened to the dollar since.

"The most interesting feature of the past week [in Washington]," the *Times* reported one morning during the administration of President Buchanan, "was the presentation, on Saturday last, of the Elk horn chair to the President by Mr. Seth Kinman, the California trapper. The ceremony took place . . . in the East room . . . where a large concourse of ladies and gentlemen had assembled to witness the ceremony. . . ."

The trapper walked in "dressed in his deer-skin hunting shirt and trowsers, with his rifle on his shoulder. He wore his hunting shirt open at the neck, exposing a red flannel waistcoat, and the legs of his boots outside his trowsers. He is about five feet eleven . . . spare but well made, and of great muscular power . . . sharp, keen blue eye, dark chestnut hair . . . full beard and mustache. . . ."

A little welcoming chatter, then: "The trapper . . . took his position . . . leaning upon his rifle" beside his creation, "made of the horns of the stag or elk . . . the antlers forming the back and arms," and James Buchanan came walking in.

Quite a lot of talk between them then, with appreciative laughter from the concourse of ladies and gentlemen. "I left . . . for the West" in 1830, said Seth Kinman, and "I return to the States for the first time with the only purpose of presenting to you, Sir, this chair. I killed the elks myself. . . ."

The President accepted the chair "with great pleasure. It will serve to remind me of the . . . Californians. They are a stamp of men that can be coaxed, but cannot be driven. . . . What do you call your gun?"

"Long Tom, and many a time has my life depended on her and a steady nerve. . . ."

The President tried the chair, liked it, and trapper Kinman pointed out "that one fork of the antlers at the foot of the chair will make a good boot jack . . . (Great merriment)." Presently: "The audience being over, the people, and the trapper and his friends, dispersed highly gratified with the interview."

So gratified, in fact, that eight years later trapper Kinman repeated the whole fine experience. This time he outdid himself, and

195

Leslie's had the story.

THE BEAR CHAIR.

MOST of our readers will remember the name of Seth Kinman, the California hunter, and the walkers upon the streets of the principal cities will recall the stalwart form, dressed in full backwoods toggery. He has just presented to President Johnson a chair, made by his own hands, from the furs of the bears killed by himself. The chair would appall almost any one with a less firm seat than Andrew Johnson, but, putting looks aside, will, without doubt, make a warm and comfortable seat in the coming cold weather.

It seemed to me almost impossible that the chair could really have looked like that, but I should have known *Leslie's* artists can be trusted. Because—I learned from the Library of Congress—this time around trapper Seth Kinman, seated in what is surely his masterpiece, had his picture taken. I suppose that's "Long Tom" there beside him, and maybe those

are the very knife and ax with which he battled those bears to the death, if Long Tom hadn't quite finished them off.

I wish I knew what happened to that chair; and the White House, whom I asked about it, says it wished it did, too. For the chair was kept and used. All I'd ever known about Andrew Johnson was that he was the only one of our Presidents to be (apparently unfairly) impeached. But I felt I knew a lot more about him when I learned that he kept and used the bear chair; and in no less a place of honor than the President's Library, as it was called then—or as we call it now, the Oval Room.

And I grew actually fond of Andrew Johnson when I learned, in addition, what he did with Jefferson Davis's coffee maker.

This marvelous locomotive-shaped coffee maker and accompanying brass tender illustrated a brief

news story of 1866. They'd been given to Jefferson Davis, it said, by friends in France (those are the Confederate battle flag and the ensign of France on the locomotive's front); then sold at an auction of some of Davis's possessions. They were bought by "a gentleman of taste" and given to President Johnson "as an ornament and not an article of use."

They were wrong about that, I'm happy to say. Andrew Johnson's great-granddaughter, Mrs. Margaret Johnson Patterson Bartlett, was interviewed by the author of *They Lived in the White House,* Frances Cavanah. Mrs. Bartlett's father, she told Frances Cavanah, had tea as a child with Grandfather Johnson in the White House, and it was made in Jefferson Davis's coffee maker. The boy and other children present watched as the boiler heated; heard the engine's steam whistle signal that the water was boiling; and finally, as they all sipped tea, listened to a music box hidden under the tender play "Dixie."

So Grandfather Andrew Johnson knew what to do with this wonderful toy. And he preserved it carefully, as has his great-granddaughter, who owns it now, and who has allowed the Smithsonian to exhibit it and me to show you this photograph of how it looks today. The music boxes under

the tender are rusted now, and no longer play, the park historian of the Andrew Johnson National Site, Hugh Lawing, tells me. And the little engineer and some of the accessories seem to be gone. But in the main Jefferson Davis's and Andrew Johnson's locomotive coffee maker and tender are wonderfully still with us yet. I wish the bear chair were, too.

"All of New York rejoiced" in 1875 "when the announcement was made that the Post Office was finished." It stood at the intersection of Broadway and Park Row, and in its newness was "at last . . . an edifice worthy of the Metropolis . . . ," for the old one had been in an abandoned church. "Looking down from what was formerly the gallery of the old church," says one account, "there appeared bands of Post Office employees working like gnomes by flickering gaslight in the cave-like body of the building. . . ."

Nevertheless, people grow fond of places in which they spend their days, and when finally it became time to leave: "The carriers' Department . . . the first to leave the old building," began to sing " 'Auld Lang Syne' [as] they filed out . . . while the remaining employees . . . and the crowd

which had gathered . . . cheered uproariously. The carriers, still singing, marched up Nassau Street, to the new Post Office. . . .

"At 10:30 o'clock, the distributing clerks . . . filed down the stairs from the gallery [10:30 at *night:* just after the final delivery of the day], and out of the building on the Liberty Street side, where they were met by a drum corps consisting of two fifes, four snare and one bass drum, and, forming in procession in the middle of the street, marched" to their new Post Office "to the tune of drums. Every man in the procession bore some trophy of his past labors and future intentions, in the form of a bottle of

ink, a high stool, a paper box, an article of clothing, or something which he had been in the habit of using in his daily duties in the old building, and which he was loath to part with, now that he was about to enter the new. At the head of the procession was carried the ensign of the squad, composed of a piece of white muslin . . . with the letters P.O. in black ink. The procession was received with loud cheers on its march. . . ."

1

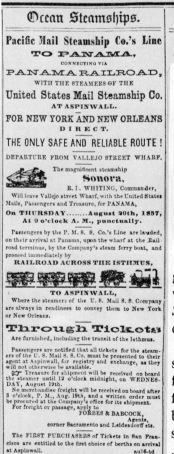

What was it like Thursday morning, August 20, 1857, as her San Francisco passengers walked out onto the wharf toward the docked *Sonora*—to begin a journey longer by many days than any we ever make?

She lay waiting, a splendid sight: single stack, and rigged for sailing if the engines failed. Possibly it was chilly, with some high fog, on an August morning in San Francisco, but still: "The day of departure of the mail steamer from San Francisco, or 'steamer day' . . . was a colorful event," says John Haskell Kemble, author of *The Panama Route*, "with crowds aboard and ashore calling to one another. . . ."

I'm sure of it, but under the excitement and behind the smiling nods to ships' officers as these people endlessly stepped down from gangplank to deck, I think there often lay a touch of dread. I think they felt as we do walking past the stewardess to find our seat on a jet. We'll get there all right ("Good flight?" "Oh, sure"). But the things can crash and we know it, and here in the middle of the nineteenth century these people know what can happen to ships.

The newspapers from which I am telling you their story are the papers they read, too; and in the California papers, in the New York *Times* and *Tribune,* all the many others, stories of disaster by shipwreck are absolutely commonplace. While in the illustrated weeklies like *Harper's,* the *Police Gazette,* and *Frank Leslie's Illustrated Newspaper,* our people regularly looked at pictures like these.

And so our people walk out onto the Vallejo Street wharf here (Angel Island there in the background)—the women in bonnets, shawls, and the long puffed-out skirts of their time, many of the men in narrow-brimmed stovepipe hats. And as they board they know they are taking their lives in hand. But just as we do, they hope for the best, and in their hearts expect it.

Many are carrying gold: strapped around their waists in "treasure belts" or in pockets and purses; pounds and pounds of it are coming aboard. More passengers arrive, stepping down out of hacks and carriages to turn onto the planking of the long wharf, and more gold comes with them, and still more in the trunks and carpetbags trundling beside them on porters' handcarts. One of these people later told a New York *Tribune* reporter "that there was seldom so large an amount of money owned by passengers" as these carried. "Many were persons of large means, and there were but very few whose immediate wealth did not amount to hundreds, while numbers reckoned their gold by the thousands of dollars. The greater portion of the passengers [are] returned miners. . . ."

They carry their money because this is mostly a cash-only world of few personal checks; and in California money is generally gold. Two of the women boarding this morning are carrying on $10,000 in twenty-dollar gold pieces; and the miners and gold-field entrepreneurs—the successful ones—are taking their gold back home in bullion, coins, and sometimes just as they found it, in nuggets or actual dust. William Chase is carrying gold. So is John Leonard, returning to Buffalo. A young man named McClough has $3,000 worth; another man has $20,000 in dust; S. C. Caldwell has a sackful of dust weighing twenty-one pounds; sea captain Thomas W. Badger, traveling as a passenger with his wife, Jane, has $20,000 in gold coins in his valise.

"Billy" Birch, a minstrel comedian, and his San Francisco wife, Virginia, two young and remarkable people, as they will demonstrate, come aboard, on their way to New York for their honeymoon. They, too, have a considerable amount of money with them. Billy has just finished a profitable engagement at Maguire's Opera House in San Francisco; and last Friday night at the Metropolitan Theatre on Montgomery Street, the *Daily Alta California* reported this morning, "that spacious edifice was jammed, the entertainment being given by the San Francisco Minstrels for the benefit of 'Billy' Birch, who goes hence on the steamer today, having brought his 'fun' to a good market, as he is said to have cleared some thousands of dollars."

They were married yesterday, and the bride, said an appreciative man who saw her, "is young, petite in form, and in personal appearance very attractive. Added to this, she is possessed of a lively vivacity which renders her interesting in conversation." As Virginia and Billy Birch climb the gangplank to the *Sonora*'s deck, she is carrying a cage housing her pet canary.

Quality people mostly, "amongst them . . . several prominent citizens," said the *Daily Alta California*. "Their absence, we are pleased to say, will be but temporary." John Haskell Kemble says the Panama Route

205

"was used almost exclusively by merchants, politicians, army and navy officers, and travelers of means. Persons of wealth and position accepted the Panama Route as the 'only' way to travel before the advent of the [transcontinental] railroad. It was so much more rapid, comfortable and reliable than the other routes that it was taken as a matter of course by those who could. . . ." The fare is huge, just under $400, says Joseph Henry Jackson; but there's a steerage, too.

At 8:30 A.M. the Atlantic mail closed, and 102 mail sacks were lowered into the *Sonora*'s hold: they contained 38,000 letters and the newspapers that would bring the last fortnight's West Coast news to the East. Also brought aboard was yet more gold, $1,595,497.13 worth, figured at $20 or less an ounce, I believe: a routine shipment in settlement of recent financial transactions between the coasts.

At ten minutes past nine, a little later than the advertised time of departure, U. S. Navy Commander R. J. (or R. L.) Whiting—by law, all ships carrying the mail had to be captained by a navy officer—ordered her cast loose, and she steamed out into the Bay, the helmsman swinging her prow toward the Golden Gate. They passed clumps of ships anchored out here by the dozens and scores: empty hulks, their rotten rigging black on the sky, deserted long since by their crews off to the gold fields. On past these the *Sonora* steamed with 494 passengers. Then on past the brown, empty hills of Marin County, hardly populated now, and out into the sea.

Nearly two weeks of only the first leg of the journey lay ahead; they'd find their cabins, unpack, explore the ship, begin getting acquainted. Can we see them? Yes, obliquely. Kemble quotes a man named John Peirce, who, traveling on another such ship, said, "We have no noise or boisterous mirth, each passing the time as best suits his taste & some coiled up over the [paddle] wheel taking the breeze, some leaning over the rails, others in chairs, or on seats under a large awning spread over the quarter deck, some reading, others smoking, others in little knots conversing, other little parties enjoying a bit of a sing . . . and all apparently good natured and happy. These are all cabin passengers.

"There are steerage passengers and crew forward. Hard sun brown men with Hoosier rig or a tan colored short frock [coat] with trows[ers], heavy soled boots or barefoot as the case may be, with the round top slouch hat California cut—all colors, white, red, green, brown, black & dun—some hitched up in the rigging, some seated on the rail, others coiled up on the hurricane deck along their trunks and baggage, others stretched out on casks, barrels or boxes in whatever position they happen to hit."

Our people learned one another's names and stories: Mrs. Eleanor

O'Conner was traveling with her eighteen-year-old son, Henry, but the small boy with her wasn't hers; she was to deliver him, in Albany, New York, to friends of his family . . . Mr. and Mrs. Swan came from Rough and Ready, the California gold-field town . . . Mrs. Eliza J. Caruthers was from Placer County, where a good deal of the gold aboard would have come from. (The land destroyed to get it lies ruined still.) Passenger Frank A. Jones was described by a newspaper as "a rich New-York socialite," and I wonder if he could have been related to a New York socialite-to-be, the as yet unborn Edith Jones who became Edith Wharton? Probably not. Jones was traveling with his "colored boy, servant," Charles Jones. A slave, possibly, taking his master's surname?

C. Samuel Shreve of San Francisco, a jeweler, told fellow passengers he was on his way to New York to be married. Rufus Lockwood, fifty, told people he was John C. Frémont's legal adviser. A. C. Munson, an elderly man from Sacramento, said he was a judge. A man named Dobbin allowed it to be known that he was brother to a late Secretary of the Navy. Marcellus Farmer, thirty-five, had been the first associate editor of the San Francisco *Chronicle* when the paper began. Charles McCarthy, a passenger now, was actually chief engineer of the steamer *Golden Gate*.

And so on. Her passengers conversing, sleeping, and watching the slow panorama of California's almost untouched shores, the *Sonora* steamed down the West Coast, passing a tiny Los Angeles; and finally, on September 2, reached New Granada, as Colombia and its province of Panama were attractively called. She dropped anchor at Panama City, and from her deck our people could see "the cathedral towers, the high tiled roofs, and dilapidated fortifications," as a writer for *Harper's Monthly* described the view in that same year.

They came ashore by ferry directly to this metal-roofed railway terminus at the water's edge, for rail was the new way to travel coast to coast; not for the last two years did you have to spend five to eight months sailing around South America. Seven thousand men had hacked and dug a path right across the Isthmus of Panama through nearly fifty miles

of jungle and mangrove swamps, dying of malaria by the thousands—so many, so much death and sickness, says Joseph Henry Jackson, that the project was nearly abandoned.

But there was too much money already invested to allow that to happen, and they finished at whatever the cost in lives: filling tropical swamps dense with malaria-carrying mosquitoes, building high wooden trestles, setting up great iron bridges, then spiking hollow steel rails imported from Belgium—to pine ties at first, but these had rotted right out, so they had the rails respiked to ties of lignum vitae so rock-hard and impervious to moisture that they were solid as ever when finally they were removed in the 1930s. All this to carry the rush of gold miners that began in the years just after 1849, and the commerce that followed them, saving the long, often terrible sea voyage around the Horn or, equally terrible, by foot, mule, and dugout canoe across the Isthmus jungle.

Our passengers climbed aboard a nice new train now, the varnished cars less than three years old. The *Sonora*'s cargo of baggage, mail, and freight came on; though not much freight because rates were high; heavy stuff still went around the Horn. The wood-burning engine whistled, I hope, and an extraordinarily scenic four-hour trip began.

Glimpses of the trip survive, from a man who also made it, sketching or photographing, woodcuts made later. Up from Pacific sea level, and then about a mile from the top, the train rolled around this cliff from which giant basalt crystals overhung the tracks, looking as though they just might topple. Then down the other side of the slope, and past native settlements like this.

Exactly every four miles the train reached a station like these, all identical,

like so many Taco Bells, where they picked up more wood. Then on to

a junction where several lines of the road met, and passengers were allowed to get off briefly at the village of Matachin here, shown as the man who sketched it saw it. "As there is usually a little delay on such occasions, the natives take advantage of it to traffic with the passengers," he wrote. "Almost every hut displayed something for sale. One had a couple of tiger-kittens tied to a stake near the entrance; another a sloth and a pair of anteaters; a third . . . a

pet crocodile; while monkeys, parrots, and parakeets, cakes, dulces, and a variety of tropical fruits were exposed for sale on every side. Nor was this all; near the track . . . was a little cottage, containing a Yankified combination of saloon, variety store, and dwelling, kept by a Frenchman. . . ."

Back aboard, they rolled on across rivers and ravines, passed remote

huts, always through lush tropical growth screaming with birds, and the engineer would hardly have been human if he didn't occasionally reach for his whistle cord and scream back. This wonderful train slipped through solid walls of tropical growth—the chuff-chuff of the engine

bouncing back at them— growth so thick it had constantly to be cut back from the tracks. Their train crossed a river in which alligators were supposed to live, and our people saw giant leeches clinging to trees or dangling from their branches.

Then presently they looked out at two cleared acres called Mount Hope, for some odd reason; here lay a good many of the men who had cut the forty-seven miles of jungle path along which they had just rolled so pleasantly.

Down to the new port of Aspinwall (now Colón), where: "The white houses with small windows and

210

green blinds," says Kemble, "lent an American aspect to the town . . . the shipping lying at anchor in the bay. . . . The Palm trees on shore gracefully waved their tall foliage in the . . . trade wind, and . . . green hills . . . on two sides, encircled the bay—in the glow of the tropical sun."

Waiting at these Aspinwall docks lay a steamer whose name had been changed—from the *George Law*—only a few weeks earlier. Now her name, still newly painted, and which the entire country would soon know, was the *Central America.*

As well as those from the *Sonora,* still other passengers boarded the *Central America* here; among them a new widow, young Ann Small, and her two-year-old daughter. They had arrived by train yesterday from Panama City, and now the American consul at Aspinwall came aboard to tell their story to Captain Herndon.

Six days ago Mrs. Small's sea captain husband had died. She had buried him in the Panama City cemetery, and was on her way home now. Captain Herndon listened; he was forty-three years old, "of slight figure, but of an intrepid spirit," said one newspaper. He'd sailed with Commodore Perry; had traveled the almost four-thousand-mile length of the Amazon in an open boat; now, a naval lieutenant, he was in command of the *Central America.* Could the consul place this bereaved young woman and her child under the captain's charge? Herndon replied that he would personally see Mrs. Small safely to New York.

211

<h1 style="text-align:center">2</h1>

"*The appearance of the 'Central America,' Capt. Wm. L. Herndon, U.S.N. . . . as she left the port of Aspinwall, on Sept. 3rd, 1857, bound for New York via Havana,*" said the caption under this newspaper cut. Her million-and-a-half-dollar shipment of gold has been stowed like ballast "along the keelsons of the ship," said passenger Frank Jones. And now the people who boarded her yesterday are comfortably settled. If you'd been among them, traveling first class, your cabin, most likely, would be in that long deckhouse, according to John Kemble. He said, "The passenger accommodations on the Panama steamers varied in detail . . . but in the main were the same." First-class cabins stood along both sides of the long deckhouse, each with a window, apparently—look at the picture again. Each cabin opened onto "the dining saloon and other public rooms which extended down the middle. . . ." The saloon was "furnished with long tables, at which passengers sat for meals and which could be used for reading and writing between meals. Long 'railroad seats,' with reversible backs were fixed along either side of the tables, with racks for glasses above them. . . ." It sounds nice.

And comfortable, if a bit crowded; cabins "usually contained three berths, one above another, together with a cushioned locker which could accommodate another passenger . . . each room had a mirror, toilet stand, washbowl, water bottles and glasses. The floors were covered with carpet, and the berths . . . screened with outer damask . . . and inner cambric curtains."

Officers had quarters in the same deckhouse, and sometimes the galley was there. On the deck below (the *Central America* had three decks), a similar arrangement containing both first- and second-class cabins, the second-class being smaller. Second-class "dined at the same tables and used the same decks as the first-class." Below all the others lay the steerage, with wooden bunks, "no private rooms, and (usually) no segregation of the sexes. . . ."

Four days now to Havana, including a stop at Belize, British Honduras. "The weather was . . . delightful, and the sea calm," said passenger Henry Childs. On Monday afternoon, September 7, they reached Havana, to remain overnight, and I suppose some of the passengers would have walked out, on that September evening, into a Spanish Havana that is now all but gone.

A few additional passengers came on here. Two were seamen shipwrecked on a voyage from New York, now sent home on the *Central America* by the American consul. And a Mr. Jacobs came aboard without a ticket, hoping to buy one, but the *Central America* was fully booked. He'd have to wait for another ship, they told the disappointed man, and he walked back down the gangplank; with a story, I would guess, that he told for years.

A new fireman joined the crew here: Alexander Grant, only twenty-six, but he'd been at sea for thirteen years, during which he'd been shipwrecked three times. I don't know whether or not he met an old shipmate aboard as a steerage passenger: George Dawson, a black man—called "mulatto" on the passenger list—returning home to Rochester, New York. If he did, it would have been a rather special reunion, because two years earlier, in December of 1855, Dawson and Grant had been shipwrecked together while serving on the *Crescent City*.

And now, at about 9:35 next morning, Tuesday, September 8, said Second Mate James Frazer, the *Central America* steamed out to sea from Havana with some five hundred passengers and a crew of around a hundred. This final leg of the journey started out well. "Fine weather, moderate sea breezes and head sea" all day, Frazer said. There'd been some seasickness, but most of the passengers had recovered, and: "The general anticipation," said Virginia Birch, the young bride, "was that the few days which remained would pass merrily by." I think the Birches were a lively, sociable couple, and that they made the most of the good weather. Because it's from Virginia Birch that we know such things as that Mr. Shreve, the San Francisco jeweler, was on his way to New York to be married. I don't know that comedian Billy Birch entertained their friends professionally, out on the sunny deck that day or in the saloon that night; but he did entertain later under terrible circumstances, and so may have done so now. In any case, there was sociability of course aboard this nice ship in this fine weather.

But now the first hint of trouble. On Wednesday the weather worsened a little; a fresh sea breeze and head sea, Second Mate Frazer noted when he came on watch early that morning. A lookout high on a mast reported Cape Florida 15 miles to the west; moving with the Gulf Stream, the *Central America* had traveled 286 miles in the first 26½ hours.

In that "breeze and head sea," the ship began to pitch and roll a little, and a seventeen-year-old passenger, Winifred Fallon, traveling with her father and little brother, James, sharing a stateroom with a Mrs. Redding, got up that morning, and went right back "to bed again," she said, "where I staid. . . ."

But Virginia Birch came out on deck with a group of ladies. As they walked, she said, "a squall came up, and the wind blew like a whirlwind. . . . We were forced to leave the deck, and the word brought into the cabin was that we must again expect rough weather." During the day wind and sea rose still further, and "with the increase of the gale sea sickness again seized the passengers. . . . We passed the night on the sofas in the cabin, the sea sickness rendering it impossible to occupy our staterooms. I lay down on a sofa with my clothes on, and passed a very uncomfortable time, the vessel careening fearfully."

214

A storm, "a genuine West India hurricane," said a passenger, had begun, which would move along up the coast from Cape Canaveral, Florida, to Cape Hatteras, North Carolina, but to the ship's officers it wasn't too bad. Even the next day, Thursday, steaming along the Florida coast well out to sea, when the weather worsened still more, the wind and head sea strengthening, Captain Herndon and his officers weren't alarmed; a rough sea, all right, but within normal bounds.

But to Virginia Birch, Thursday was "a fearful day, the vessel rocking and pitching violently. . . ." And by that night, she said, "the sea breaking over the steamer had dashed large quantities of water into the staterooms, and subsequently they were not used. . . ."

Second Mate James Frazer took the watch again at eight that evening, went off at twelve, and all he said of the weather was, "The wind continued to blow heavy all night." Virginia Birch said, ". . . At night the storm did not abate, but darkness added to our fears."

When Frazer came on again at 4 A.M. Friday, it was raining as well as rough, so I picture him as wearing rain gear as he walked out onto the deck. He said only that the sea was "running high," but however accustomed he was to all kinds of weather, it could hardly have been pleasant out there in the dark and rain, the ship lifting, dropping, rolling, as he checked their course, keeping the steamer headed into that sea. Chief Engineer George Ashby said, "The day commenced with the wind blowing a perfect hurricane," but then he wasn't a deck officer.

Still, it was a full-fledged gale now, and I can't believe that many passengers came out on deck Friday morning. But at least two of them did: Captain Thomas W. Badger, traveling as a passenger, and his wife, Jane. They got up about six, dressed, and came out to walk that careening deck. I wish we had a daguerreotype of Thomas Badger or even only a physical description, but we don't know what he looked like. It is a fact, though, that he was remarkably powerful, so I picture him as a man of medium height with massive shoulders and chest. And for even less reason —no reason—he walks through my mind bald and with a short black beard: I have got to have a mental picture of him, since we'll see this remarkable man in some remarkable action. Your own mental illustration of T. W. Badger may be different.

As he walked the slowly rocking deck with his wife, this experienced seaman checked things out: the wind, he noted, was "fresh and directly ahead, but the ship came up finely, and was not strained perceptibly by the wind or the roughness of the sea." From below he could hear the steady sound of the two steam engines turning the enormous paddle wheels past which the couple made their way from time to time, and

Captain Badger noted that they "were working regularly and slowly." He had made three previous voyages on the *Central America,* so he knew the ship, and all seemed well to him.

But not to one of the cabin passengers, a Mrs. Thayer. "I got up early on Friday morning," she said. "I could not sleep for the tossing of the ship. I could hardly keep in my berth. . . . Some of the other ladies were already up. . . . The steamer was plunging and careening, and I felt a continual anxiety, lest a timber should be strained so as to let the water in. I told the ladies that I meant to go and see the Captain, and to ask him if he thought the ship was safe. Two or three of them laughed at me, and said that they had been out in just such gales before, and that they had never fallen into danger. Besides, they said that the ship was very strong. But I was not easy in my mind, and every time a high sea struck her sides, feared a leak. . . ."

At eight o'clock Third Officer Charles Myers relieved James Frazer. Who noted, writing it in the log, I expect, that the rain had stopped, but it was "still blowing heavy." The *Central America* had passed Florida, and now stood, well out to sea, off the coast of Georgia.

The Badgers seem obviously not seasick because about half past eight they went to breakfast, and then he came out on deck once more. Now, Captain Badger doesn't say he was concerned, and I don't suppose he was. Yet he seems to have continually checked and rechecked the condition of the ship; looking down an open hatchway now—inside the deck cabin, I believe—he noted that there was no water to be seen in the hold.

Somewhere between nine and ten o'clock that morning, as he later remembered it, out on deck again or still, he met George Ashby, the chief engineer, on his way somewhere. Ashby figures very importantly in what later happened, and we know what he looked like to a *Tribune* reporter: ". . . a fine, stalwart man of about thirty, with a frank, seamanlike face and bearing, and certainly with nothing about him from which to surmise . . . defect of character. . . ." Captain Badger now remarked to Ashby that it was blowing hard, and would blow harder still before long. But Ashby answered that he didn't think the gale would get any worse, and added, as Badger recalled, " 'Let it blow—we are ready for it.' " So finally bull-chested, bald-headed, black-bearded Captain Badger went below, and stayed there for the rest of the morning; even for him a yowling gale would be no fun out on deck. Badger believed that Engineer Ashby "apprehended no special danger," and he noted that the ship was "at this time working easily, and was apparently staunch."

He was wrong: about ship and Ashby both. For the chief engineer had "discovered that the ship was making considerable water, more than

216

ordinarily results from the drippings of various parts of the machinery." Ashby ordered his assistant, John Tice, to stand by the pumps for bilge injection, then he went up "to Captain Herndon at once," he said, to report that the ship was making water. Possibly this was when he met Captain Badger on deck.

Ashby had another problem he hadn't mentioned to passenger Badger: he was running low on coal at the boilers. The coal bunkers lay fore and aft, and ordinarily coal was brought down passageways to the furnaces by wheelbarrows. But now the *Central America,* heading into the gale, lay tilted so far over to starboard—which is the right side, facing front—that the barrows couldn't be wheeled down the passageways, and Ashby had his crew passing coal along in buckets. But that wasn't fast enough, because this morning he needed even more steam than usual, for the pumps.

Captain Herndon listened to Ashby's report, and then—breakfast being over—he sent down some of the waiters to form another coal-passing brigade.

But now another problem. Ashby noticed that the water pouring out of the pumps was hot. He thought he understood why: with the ship tilted over so far, the water down here lay only along one side of the ship. The other side stood high and dry, the pumps over there idle since they had nothing to pump. With only half his pumps at work, the water leaking into the ship was gaining and had risen high enough to touch the steam boilers on the starboard side. This not only uselessly heated the bilge water but also tended to cool the boilers. And they *had* to stay hot—to make the steam that turned the paddles that kept the ship alive and maneuverable.

With crewmen and waiters passing coal along as fast as they could work, Ashby kept the boilers going. The bilge pumps "worked freely," he saw, and the paddle wheels continued to turn. But slowly, the steam not at full pressure, and the water continuing to gain.

Trouble up on deck now, too. The lightly loaded *Central America* stood high out of the water, and as the press of the still-rising gale felt for the ship's sides, Captain Herndon had greater and greater difficulty keeping his ship headed into the wind. Yet he could not allow it to fall off and lie helpless in the troughs of these enormous waves. So about ten o'clock he ordered Third Officer Myers, still on watch, to set a sail called a "storm spencer," meant to help keep the ship into the wind. As it did, briefly, then suddenly the raging wind ripped the canvas to fluttering tatters.

The gale increased, the shrill sound of it in the rigging rising higher. And the height and stupendous power of the waves grew with it. More sail was set out to substitute for the shredded spencer, but still the high-

217

out-of-the-water ship fought them, kept turning its prow aside, wanting to lie sideways and helpless. That must not happen, for it would allow the entire towering tonnage of the gigantic waves to crash onto the full length of the ship. And so above deck and below, with canvas and rudder and with faltering engines, they fought the terrible wind and sea.

At noon Second Mate James Frazer took the watch, relieving Myers; but now First Mate Charles Van Rensellaer and Captain Herndon stayed on deck with him. As always, when he came on, Frazer noted the weather: the gale continued, but he thought the waves had abated a little.

In the saloon of the long deck cabin, those waiters who were left tried to follow routine, and set the table for lunch. But no one could sit at the sinking, rising, tilted-over tables; and dishes crashed onto the floor. So they simply passed out food to those passengers who even wanted it, to eat from their fingers as best they could.

Thomas Badger, experienced sea captain but with no authority here, again left his cabin, and headed for the hatchway down which, as I believe, he could look into the engine room. He doesn't say so, but apparently the hatchway lay on the raised side of the tilted ship, because looking down it, Badger still could see no water below. But he could see or hear the engines turning, and returned to his cabin. If he was dying to wander down into the engine room, he would have refrained, I think: George Ashby had been chief engineer on this ship for six years; this was the forty-fifth trip he'd made in her.

And the engines *were* turning, as Badger had noted, but ever more slowly as the water climbed higher up the boilers, cooling them still more, continuing to lower the pressure while it heated the bilge water. And now steam began rising from this heated water sloshing along the starboard side of the tipped ship. Then the water overflowed into the coal bunkers, steam filled the air there, it put out the lamps, and suddenly the men passing coal could no longer see.

Coal-passing stopped, and pressure in the boilers dropped. Ashby ordered an assistant to get up steam in the donkey engine boiler, which was smaller, and hurried up to the top deck and "reported to Captain Herndon the state of affairs in the engine room."

I see Herndon—young, not much past forty, and of "slight figure" —standing on that howling deck, his head averted from the wind, Ashby's mouth shouting at his ear. And then: you wonder what he felt at the order he now had to give: men passengers were to be organized into bailing gangs. And those of his crew he could spare, possibly the remaining waiters, were sent down to steerage with axes to chop up the wooden bunks for fuel. And you wonder what the passengers felt as the captain's

218

boy, Garrison, now walked the length of the deck cabin saloon crying out, as one passenger remembered it, " 'All hands down below to bail.' " The ship lay careened on her side, and the passengers knew she was in trouble —Virginia Birch spoke of the awful "crackings of the timbers"—but until this moment they hadn't known the ship was leaking. Mrs. Thayer, who'd been frightened earlier by the "plunging and careening" of the ship, said that now: ". . . My fears were painfully verified." All my quotations, incidentally, are from news publications of the time.

But: "After the first excitement caused by the news that the steamer had sprung a leak," said Mrs. Frederick S. (Adie) Hawley, a passenger, "the women were very calm. . . . I saw no weeping. . . ." Mrs. Hawley had been terribly seasick for the past few days, like many others, but she was up now; had to be, I suppose, in this storm, for the Hawleys' children were with them: William, only two years old, and DeForest, a five-month-old infant. Now, in the saloon, Adie Hawley watched one passenger, she said, rather dramatically pull off his coat, and leave to go help bail, walking as best he could in the tilted ship. The other men were leaving, too, including her husband, Frederick.

"Rich New-York socialite" Frank A. Jones was a friend of Captain Herndon's, and as Jones remembered it, Herndon now said to him, " 'You must take off your broadcloth, and go to work!' " I don't know whether Jones thought his good clothes still mattered, or whether he was just making a lark of this, but he immediately went belowdecks, and "borrowed a pair of sailor's pantaloons, red shirt and coarse boots, and with the glazed cover of a cloth cap on his head reported himself in working costume."

I suppose there is always an officious take-charge man around, if the crowd is large enough. And one showed up now. "The people were pretty quiet and orderly," said passenger John Taylor, but "one man . . . named Miller, a passenger, took a position at the top of the steps leading to the steerage; he drew his revolver, and threatened to shoot down any one who refused to work at the pumps and attempted to get upon deck. I saw him strike one person a smart blow in the face; that was all the fighting and disturbance that I noticed. After a time any man that wanted to come up was not prevented."

The women sat waiting in the long deck cabin. "The sea broke over [the ship] in avalanches," said Virginia Birch, "completely swamping the cabin and staterooms, and the vessel would be so completely buried that it was as dark as Erebus."

On deck, Frazer said to the captain that they ought to get the ship headed into the wind, but Herndon replied that he'd been trying just that all morning, and couldn't. "I then proposed to keep off before the wind," Frazer said—which I think meant keeping the ship as close into the wind as possible—"and he told me to do what I could. . . ."

Even though no longer fully headed into the wind, they were able to keep on course, but the gale continued to increase, and finally the *Central America* was forced off course to the southeast. Up to then Frazer thought "the ship behaved well," but now, listing heavily to starboard, her great paddle wheels barely turning with the last of the steam, the *Central America* at last fell off into the trough of the sea, and the tremendous waves began crashing onto the entire length of the deck.

First Mate Van Rensellaer ordered Frazer to "rig the bilge pumps" —deck pumps, I think, which worked by hand. "The lee pumps worked well and discharged water abundantly," Frazer said, but here on deck, like Ashby below, they could use only half the pumps. Those on the high side of the tilted ship "did not work, there not being water enough to supply them."

In his cabin Captain Badger felt the ship lurch, as it fell off into the trough, I expect, and another passenger, eighteen-year-old Henry O'Conner, was thrown right out of his bunk. Captain Badger immediately went out to look down his hatchway again. He "saw the engines moving very slowly indeed," and then, even as he stood looking at them, they stopped.

Still: he couldn't see any water, and on this ship he was no officer, so Badger turned away, but as he turned he saw Ashby standing down there listening to something one of his men was saying. Lamps had been relighted, I suppose, and possibly something done about the flooded floors of the coal bunkers. Because Badger overheard Ashby reply, he said, " 'Then call the stewards, and get buckets and set them to work passing coal.' "

Passenger or not, when Badger heard that, he went down and into the engine room, and now he could see the water flooding the starboard side of the ship. Badger walked into the chief engineer's office in time, he said, to hear Ashby call out, " 'Hurry up, boys, and pass that coal along, or we shall have to set a gang of men bailing.' "

"For God's sake, Mr. Ashby," said Badger, as he later recalled it, "don't wait until the ship is full of water—set the men to work bailing now." The ship "lay at the mercy of the waves," Badger said, and he went out into a gangway, and found the men passengers Captain Herndon had ordered rounded up, waiting there.

Badger simply took over. Buckets were "procured from the lower hold," he said, the grating over a forward hatchway in the saloon was taken off, and water-filled buckets passed along until under the open hatchway. Then they were lifted into the saloon, and passed along like this

out to the open deck to be dumped overboard. "Capt. Badger giving the orders," said a passenger who was there, "at 2 o'clock all hands commenced bailing." They formed two brigades, about fifty men in each line; and then presently three lines. "One string of pails went to

the steerage," said one of the bailing passengers, "one to the cabin, and one to the engine-room. I had charge of the one going to the steerage."

At first the leak didn't seem too bad; the bailing men down below could see pig-iron ballast just under the surface of the water into which they stood dipping. And up in the saloon passenger Frank A. Jones, in his borrowed red shirt, noted that as he and the others passed their buckets, "the ladies sat very composedly and many encouraged the men in their exertions." Mrs. Amanda Marvin of Sacramento even offered to help.

Another gang of stewards, waiters, seamen—and of passengers, too, now— were at work passing coal to the engine room, the engineers there struggling to work up steam.

Having organized the bailing, Captain Badger came back to the engine room. There he saw that in spite of the bailing the water level "had very sensibly increased." It was up to the ashpan of the lee furnace now, and Frederick Hawley, one of the bucket brigade down here, later told his wife that pretty soon the water came up to their knees. Badger looked around for the source of the leak, and saw it—seawater pouring in "very rapidly at a large leak around the shaft." This was the shaft from engine to starboard

221

paddle wheel; with the ship so steeply tilted, the outside shaft opening lay under the water, thus the leak. Authority or not, Captain Badger said to Ashby—shouted?—that he'd better have that leak "attended to," and Ashby said he already had six men working on it and had sent for blankets to stuff around the leak. Badger left, and—possibly—prowled the ship, because now he found that still more water, a good deal of it, was coming in through the deadlights of an after cabin. Deadlights are covers fitted over portholes and other openings to keep out water, but for some reason these couldn't be closed, and now Badger headed for the deck.

In the saloon and in their cabins, women and children sat watching crewmen hurry from cabin to cabin gathering up blankets. Below, the engineers were getting some steam, "but, having only the port fires to depend on," said Ashby, "it wasn't enough" and "the steam was soon used up." Broken-up bunks began arriving from steerage, so: "We . . . commenced firing up with wood. . . ."

Out on deck, with the paddle wheels motionless, they simply *had* to get the wallowing ship headed back into the wind. "The fore staysail was set," Mate Frazer said, then they turned the helm "hard to port," trying to make the wind itself pull the ship around. But almost instantly the staysail was "blown to pieces. There was still a very heavy sea, the gale continuing unabated. An attempt was then made"—Captain Herndon, I suppose, shouting the orders in the scream of the wind—"to hoist the foreyard . . . but before the yard was raised three feet from the deck the sail blew into fragments."

Herndon ordered a drag prepared. This was a sail tied over a large wooden framework to make a kind of kite-shaped object, and its name was its purpose. Tied to a long rope and thrown over the side, the drag would be pushed back behind the ship by the waves until the line went taut. Then the dragging effect would tend to pull the ship into alignment with the direction of waves and wind, helping to force the prow back into the gale.

Thomas W. Badger reached the deck. And "at my suggestion," he said, before throwing over the drag, Herndon ordered the foremast chopped down, and thrown over to lighten ship. It was five-thirty in the afternoon, "the ship listed over to the leeward so that people could not walk the deck," said Frazer. "I may say that she was almost on her beam ends," which means almost completely on her side.

If you have ever so much as even helped to cut down a big tree with axes, you know it's a job standing on solid ground. Now three men went at the tree-thick base of the mast with axes: Mate James Frazer, Boatswain John Black, and Captain Herndon. And with the deck on which they stood tilted so far a man couldn't walk it, and pitching and rolling besides, they nevertheless chopped their way through the mast, the fallen chips flooding away like children's gutter boats. The chunk of an ax blade into

222

wood is a land sound, and surely it sounded strange to the frightened passengers hearing it through the howling horror of the gale.

The mast chopped through, it still hung partly upright and sagging in the rigging. Then the three men cut through the ropes, and "let the foremast go over the side," said Frazer. "In going over, the rigging caught foul of the cathead and anchor"—the cathead is a projecting piece of timber near the bow on which the anchor rests—"which caused the foremast to shoot under the ship's bottom, she was injured by it, and probably the leak increased thereby. I don't know such to be the fact, but she thumped there for some time," still another awful sound for the passengers to wonder about.

Nothing worked. "After the foremast was cut away," said Frazer, "we paid out the hawser that was attached to the drag to about ninety fathoms in all, giving it a turn about the stump of the foremast." It "had no effect in bringing the ship's head up, and that was the last effort towards that objective which was in our power to make."

Tons of water repeatedly crashing onto the helpless ship, they did what they could: worked to keep the deck pumps going. Below, they had got up steam in the donkey boiler, possibly with the broken-up bunks, and: "The Worthington Pumps, which had previously worked by steam from the main boilers," said George Ashby, "were then worked by the donkey boilers, and continued to work till about 8 o'clock, with several stoppages of a few minutes each, which were made necessary to free the feed-pipe of the boiler from obstructions. When the donkey engine finally stopped, the feed-pipe had become so choked up that it was necessary to cut and repair it."

Captain Badger had a different story. He said Second Assistant Engineer Henry Keeler told him they'd "neglected to turn a cock, which was down in the lee bilge, until the water over it became so high and so hot that it could not be reached. No further attempt was made to raise steam to work the pumps, or to repair the pumps. . . ." But the blankets they'd gathered were now stuffed into the leak around the starboard shaft. And they'd gotten a sail wrapped around the shaft end in the wheel outside. So the leak was slowed. All they could do now was bail and hope.

The men "worked like horses" at bailing, said Mrs. Isaac McKim Bowley, a passenger. The work was endless and terribly hard, passing sloshing buckets hand to hand over and again, and: "Some of the men," Mrs. Bowley said, "became so exhausted that they dropped down in their places as if they were dead."

"But the leak continued," said Mrs. Thayer, "and the water gained in depth in spite of the exertions made to keep it out. There was then no more doubt as to the peril that we were in, and everybody began to look forward with great anxiety to the fate which awaited us."

At eleven that night the long hawser holding the drag far behind the ship—endlessly chafed by the railing over which it lay stretched—parted, and they lost the drag.

At midnight the chamber of one of the deck pumps burst. Boatswain John Black stayed out on the dark deck, working to keep the remaining pumps going. James Frazer "visited almost all parts of the ship," he said, "lending assistance wherever [I] could be useful . . ." and so did Captain Herndon. One of the bailing men said, "During the whole time I was on board . . . the Captain's conduct was truly noble. His example was a splendid one. He omitted no exertion to save the ship or the passengers. While the men were at work he came, every now and then, to cheer them on. 'Work on, my boys,' he said, 'we have hopes yet.' Then he would ask us if we wanted any fresh water, and whenever we did he had it brought to us. He was very active all the time. He told us to 'relieve each other like men, and not to suffer any one of us to drop while another man stood idle.' "

The observant Amanda Marvin, who had offered to help bail, also liked the captain; everyone seemed to. In contrast to the profane way she had sometimes heard George Ashby talk, Mrs. Marvin thought the captain "particularly mild and respectful in the presence of ladies," but she also thought Herndon "appeared . . . altogether too easy, and wanting in that stern energy and fearlessness so indispensable in an emergency like the present."

During the night more blankets were collected to shove into the leak around the shaft. Seventeen-year-old Winifred Fallon had been lying seasick in her bunk for "four days without tasting a morsel of food. . . . My father was with me most of the time through the gale. When we saw any of the [crew] men, we asked them, and they told us always that there was no danger." Now they knew better. For on "Friday night a man came down and picked up every blanket and counterpane and mattress to stop the leaks," and Winifred had to lie on the bare wood of her bunk.

At some time during this night James Frazer went out onto the dark wind- and wave-battered deck with a metal saw, and tried to cut through the chain of the starboard bow anchor to let it fall and lighten the ship. But in that gale, on the heaving tilted surface, he could not do it. The wind, he noted, was from "the northwest," and "blowing heavily."

All through the night men kept bailing, said Captain Badger, who was one of them, of course, the men "being changed as often as they became exhausted." And women stood by encouraging them. A man from Rough and Ready, California, traveling with his wife and an infant child, had been seasick for days, but he kept on bailing. Passenger Thomas McNeich said, "I was at work at the pumps all the time," which I believe meant the deck pumps. "The crew and passengers behaved nobly. I never saw men with more determination, and under better discipline. . . ."

But other men gave out, leaving to go to their cabins, lock the door, and drop onto the bed. Others got drunk. The only food served now was hard bread and water, handed out to those who wanted it. But many of the women, "intently watching the efforts of the officers . . . and the [men] passengers to save the vessel," didn't bother with food, said Ann Small, the new widow from Panama. And: "Owing to the scarcity of food, and the exhaustion consequent on the work of bailing," said Virginia Birch, "liquor was freely supplied to all who wanted it, and of course some took too much. . . ." Mrs. Hawley said that, in fact, some men drank "until stupefied, and all care for life vanished."

At some time during that terrible night the captain told his steward, Garrison, as Garrison later told Ann Small, that he knew what his mind was: if the ship sank, he would not leave it.

Toward morning the strength of the men who were still bailing began to give out, too, and inside the ship the water rose ever higher. "On Saturday," said the still-seasick Winifred Fallon, "the stateroom that Mrs. Redding and I occupied had three feet of water in it." Captains Herndon and Badger tried to encourage the exhausted men, "assuring them," Badger said, "that the ship could still hold out. Every passenger remained cool, and seemed to forget his danger in the united efforts to save the vessel. There was no weeping or exhibition of despair, even on the part of the females." One passenger remembered the women repeatedly saying to the exhausted men, " 'It's only another hour to sunrise.' "

As the chance of saving the ship became clearly smaller and smaller, people seemed to go silent. "When the prospect of the salvation of the ship began to grow darker," Ann Small said, "the conduct of the passengers, officers and crew was so quiet, orderly and considerate as to [leave] a deep impression on the minds of [those who saw it]."

At 4 A.M. Saturday morning the gale slacked off a little, but only a little, with "a heavy sea running," said Thomas Badger; and at first light Captain Herndon sent a seaman up to the lurching tip of the highest of their remaining two masts, where he tied on a signal of distress.

Some men kept bailing, and as soon as there was daylight to see, crewmen rigged great empty beef and pork barrels, and milk cans, tying on lines and lowering them down into the holds to be filled with water. These were then hoisted out with rope and tackle by gangs of fifty men each, and in this way they began emptying out 400 gallons a minute, George Ashby said. Frazer went out with his saw again, and this time, able to see, he managed to cut through the heavy chain, the anchor dropping to vanish instantly in the turbulent sea, lightening the ship a little. "The Captain all this time," said Frazer, "using untiring exertions and cheering the people to their work, we continued on bailing and pumping."

225

A passenger friend of George Ashby's, Charles McCarthy, chief engineer of the steamer *Golden Gate,* was down in the engine room helping. And they once again got up steam enough in the donkey engine boiler to work the pumps. But nevertheless the water continued to rise, presently submerging the pumps, which stopped. The boiler still had steam, and someone suggested boxing in the pumps, but they couldn't find the carpenters, couldn't find tools, and then the water burst through the blankets stuffed around the leaking shaft, and the water rose faster than ever and put out the boiler fire.

"About 10 o'clock on Saturday," said teenager Winifred Fallon, still lying on her blanketless bunk, her room awash, "a gentleman came down and took us up to the saloon; my father was with us; he handed me his money and told me to keep it—perhaps I might be saved and he not."

In the engine room the water, George Ashby thought, stood nine or ten feet deep, and he gave up all further attempt at raising steam, and left to report to Captain Herndon.

Badger was there before him. He "went to Captain Herndon's room and said to him that the storm was abating, but the water in the ship was gaining upon them rapidly, and the vessel must go down. Captain Herndon said he believed she must; that he had made up his mind to that; that it was very hard to leave his family thus, but it could not be helped. Mr. Ashby came into the room at this time, and [I] said to him, 'The ship will sink.' He seemed startled at the remark, and replied with earnestness, 'She shan't sink; I'll be d——d if she shall. We must all go to work and bail her out.' [I] replied that [I] wished talking in that style would do it, but [I] and all the rest on board had been very hard at work all night bailing, without avail. Captain Herndon seemed dejected and perfectly resigned, and laid [no blame] to Mr. Ashby."

No radio in this world: news came to shore only by ship. And on this day, Saturday, September 12, the only word of the *Central America* to reach the mainland came to New Orleans by a steamer from Havana. New Orleans routinely passed it on to the New York papers by telegraph: "The steamship *Central America,* from Aspinwall . . . and The *Empire City,* from New Orleans, left Havana at 9 AM on the 8th inst., for New-York."

But out on the Atlantic that Saturday morning the *Central America* was lying well over on her side, "with her portholes in the water," said socialite passenger Frank Jones. "By this time the water was up to the second cabin floors. We all knew our danger." They were bailing for their lives, each emptied bucket and barrel now only a few seconds' postponement during which the signal of distress, standing stiff in the still-terrible wind, might yet be seen. And so the morning passed, water endlessly dumped over the side, but endlessly coming in faster still, the ship steadily lowering into the sea.

226

3

In the early afternoon the lookout saw a distant white speck. He called down the news, and out on the awash and tilted deck men suddenly went motionless; staring over miles of tumbling ocean to see whether the speck swelled or shrank to nothingness. Herndon ordered the ship's signal gun fired, but the distant vessel—it *was* a ship—did not hear the explosive bark over the howl of the storm.

The eye of her captain, however, was caught by a tiny spark: the muzzle flash of the gun. He stared, saw something, and ordered his ship swung toward it. And on the deck of the *Central America* moments later, our people saw the far-off white speck grow just slightly clearer, barely larger, and then they knew: it was a ship and might have seen them. The news, the hope, shot through the *Central America,* people hurrying out to join the others on deck, or to portholes and windows to stand staring.

I don't think imagination can often tell us, with anything we ought to feel certain about, what long-ago people once thought or felt; we can be wrong enough about people we've lived with for years. And when someone tells me in print what Alexander Hamilton felt upon waking the morning of the duel, I put the book down and pick up the comic section. Once in a while, though, we *do* know what people felt because a mistake isn't possible. In your mind put yourself out on that wet and slanted deck, or peer through a glass pane, trying to wipe it clearer . . . and then, across a fast-moving expanse of gray ocean, suddenly glimpse that remote white flash. Watch it, forgetting to breathe, and then—*yes,* see it grow! And you know what our people on the *Central America* felt: not the intensity of it, but at least a pale tincture of their ecstasy of relief.

Inside the long deck cabin "when the cry of 'Sail, ho!' was heard," said Mrs. Frederick Hawley, "our feelings of joy at the prospect of deliverance then overcame us, and many wept, but they were tears of joy." And —don't we know also?—some embraced, some grinned crazily, some babbled while others went silent, unable to talk, and some would have spoken only a wordless cry. While others would have suddenly covered their faces, unable to look any longer at that steadily swelling expanse of sail. ". . . we all thought that we would be saved," said Mrs. Hawley, and she went to her husband.

Frederick Hawley, a man of about thirty-five, an original forty-niner, was one of the men still down below bailing, and there Adie Hawley asked if he wasn't tired. She said he replied, " 'Yes, I am tired, but I can work forty-eight hours in the same way, if necessary. I am working for your life, for you and my children,' " and I'm willing to believe that those are Hawley's actual words or close to them, come down to us over a century and more; that that is how people felt then, and was the way he phrased it.

Up on deck the experienced sea eyes of Herndon, Frazer, the other ship's officers, and Captain Badger could now pick out the thin stroke of black against the storm sky that was the single mast of the approaching ship, and make out the shape of her sail. Then her hull, then it was most clearly a ship, and after that it was *here,* and every staring person aboard the *Central America* could see that this ship, too, had experienced the awful gale. One of its two masts had snapped off in the storm, and she sailed toward them now, downwind, with only the canvas of her remaining foremast.

She was the brig *Marine,* so close now they could read her name; a tiny ship. Then she passed across the stern of the *Central America* not a hundred feet away, her captain estimated. Our people could see the faces of her crew, and for a moment the two ships were so close "a cracker could have been thrown from our vessel to her," passenger Frank A. Jones thought, standing watching in his borrowed red shirt and pantaloons.

Herndon spoke his order, and James Frazer drew in breath to shout across the gap: They were in a sinking condition. Would the other ship stand by, and take off their passengers?

Yes, he would, shouted Hiram Burt, the *Marine*'s captain, and "the passengers on the *Central America* cheered," said one newspaper's account, "believing that they were now all safe."

But not all of them thought so. Although the "weather had moderated," James Frazer said, "the wind southeast," the waves were still enormous, the ship's lifeboats small, and they'd be loaded to capacity: the truth was, said Frank Jones, "we did not think that [the lifeboats] could live."

It was their only chance, though, and: "The captain came down," said Mrs. Bowley, "and told us that the ladies would be saved first." Then, in their cabins, women strapped life preservers on their children and themselves. These were mostly of tin but some were cork, and those who understood, or whose husbands did, chose cork if they could, because the tin ones dented easily, and then leaked. Speaking to their children and their husbands, the women got ready . . . and now a curious thing happened.

The women knew or were now told that in transferring from ship to lifeboat to ship again in this dangerous sea, they might be dropped into the water; and of course the men didn't know what was in store for them at all. So now many passengers, men and women both, seem to have decided that they could not weigh themselves down with gold, heavy as lead. And yet . . . if you've ever held pure gold in your hand you know that it looks and feels like nothing else; has the look and feel of *value* like no other substance. And even in these life-and-death moments, many of these people simply could not just walk away from their gold.

"Treasure belts were opened, and gold was scattered on the cabin floors, lest a few ounces or pounds of weight should decide their desperate contest with the waves. Full purses, containing in some instances $2,000, were lying untouched on sofas. Carpetbags were opened by men, and the shining metal poured out onto the floor and spurned in contempt. One of the passengers . . . opened a bag and dashed about the cabin $20,000 in gold dust, telling all who wanted to gratify their greed for gold to take it. But it was passed by untouched. Two ladies brought out $10,000 in twenty-dollar gold pieces, and threw them down in the cabin, but no one wanted them. None of the ladies took more than two $20 pieces with them; as they prepared to leave the steamer, many relieved themselves of their weighty garments, except their outside dress."

Amanda Marvin and her husband left $18,000 in gold. Jane Badger told the captain she wanted to take their one thousand twenty-dollar gold pieces with her in a valise, but it would have weighed sixty pounds, I believe, and he said no, the gold "would have to take its chances with him." Mr. McClough took his $3,000 in gold out on deck, found Alice Lockwood, with whom he'd become acquainted, and asked her to take it to his mother. Although it was nine more pounds to weigh her down, she said she would. "Old Aunt Lucy," a black stewardess, took her money with her, whether in gold or paper I don't know.

Not everyone bothered with gold, or had it. Mrs. Mary Swan, of Rough and Ready, California, stood in her cabin preparing her baby to leave the ship. Her husband had left the pumps to be with her now. And Mary Swan said "he took me aside and bade me 'Good bye.' He said, 'I don't know that I shall ever see you again.' He was very glad to think that

I could be taken off. He wanted me to go, and said that he did not care about himself, if it were possible that I could be saved, and the little child. He told me that he would try to save himself if an honorable opportunity should present itself after all the women were taken off." Then the Swan family left for the deck. They were alive once, the Swans, and that is what happened; that's the way she remembered their last conversation down in their cabin on a sinking ship.

Also in her cabin, preparing her two children, Adie Hawley spoke to her husband; he, too, had left his bailing long enough to see his family clear. She'd been seasick for days, she said to him now; she had to have his help with the children; she wanted him with her in the lifeboat. "He went and took his money out of the trunk," Mrs. Hawley said, "but made no reply as to whether he would accompany me. My husband took the infant, and Mr. Bobke the oldest child, and we went on deck."

A young bride, Mrs. McNeil, had apparently told someone she would refuse to leave her cabin unless her husband left the ship with her. Now: "He came into her cabin," said one account, "to persuade her to go without him, but finding her resolute in her determination," he left. Back he came "shortly afterwards, and said that he would go with her."

A Frenchwoman, Mme. Pahud, had three children to prepare for the lifeboats, and apparently her cabin door stood open, for "many what I knew," a reporter later quoted her, "told me to write to their family and tell them they would not live. . . ."

Billy Birch had been on deck when the announcement was made, and his wife, Virginia, said that "my husband came to the cabin and asked me to prepare myself to go. . . ." He brought along a life preserver for her, "which I put on. I went into my stateroom for a cloak, followed by Mr. Birch, and I saw my canary-bird in its cage. It was singing as merrily as it ever did. On the spur of the moment I took the little thing from its prison and placed it in the bosom of my dress. . . ."

"Captain Herndon ordered the boats lowered as soon as the *Marine* hove to," said Engineer Ashby. In this huge sea each lifeboat would be rowed by four crewmen, a fifth commanding and steering. Boatswain John Black's boat and Quartermaster Finley Frazier's were lowered safely, and "several men stepped forward to get into them," said passenger Frank Jones. "Captain Herndon ordered them to step back, and allow the women and children to enter them. His orders were obeyed with the greatest readiness. . . ."

Women and children began appearing in their life preservers, the two crews in the water below them fighting to keep their boats from being smashed against the ship's side. As the women stood waiting their turns to be lowered over the side, men offered them gold they'd picked up in the empty cabins below. Fourteen women and children in this first lot,

Frank Jones said, Mrs. Frederick Hawley among them, and she knew half the others: Mrs. Badger, Mrs. Thayer and her nurse, Susan; the seasick Winifred Fallon, and her small brother, James, I'm sure; and two of the brides: Addie M. Easton and Mrs. McNeil, whose young husband stood with her, having promised to go along.

The women were lowered by ropes toward Finley Frazier's waiting boat one by one, Herndon and the purser giving directions. Some of the younger women put a foot into a loop, and held on above their heads, ready to step off into the boat as they reached it. Others had to be lowered sitting, and Adie Hawley said, "it was with the greatest difficulty we could be placed in the boat . . . we sat in the noose, and held on by our hands."

Mrs. McNeil's bridegroom husband told her to go first so that he could assist "at lowering her into the boat," but she had trouble. "Mrs. Badger, Mrs. Thayer, and Mrs. McNeil could not reach the boat at the proper instant," Mrs. Hawley said, "and were immersed in the sea, but they were soon hauled on board the boat. They were much frightened, but remained very calm.

"The little children were passed down, the officers lowering them by their arms, until the boat swung underneath, and they could be caught hold of by the boatmen. It was frightening to see these helpless little ones, held by their tiny arms above the waves. My baby was nearly smothered by the flying spray, as they were obliged to hold him a long time before he could be reached by the boatmen; but when I pressed him once more to my bosom, and covered him with my shawl, he soon fell asleep. The children did not cry, except when the salt water came over us and flew in their faces. We were all without clothing or bonnets, except the thin dresses we had on. I took nothing with me, except a heavy shawl and my watch. Some of the children were without clothing or shoes and stockings . . . when our boat was full I heard Mr. Hull give the order . . . to shove off. . . ."

As Frazier's crew dug in their oars, young Mrs. McNeil sat staring up at her bridegroom husband still standing on the deck of the *Central America.* He "bade her good-bye, and said that he could not follow her . . . it was the last time she saw or heard of him. . . ."

231

"I looked to see where the vessel was we were going to," Mrs. Hawley

continues, "and she seemed to be about a mile and a half away." For the *Marine* was drifting, the once narrow gap between the two ships widening fast; with only the sail on his foremast, Captain Hiram Burt couldn't fully control her. "The last I saw of my husband," Mrs. Hawley said, "he stood on the wheel house and kissed his hand to me as the boat pulled away from the ship."

Now women and children were being lowered into John Black's boat. "My husband left his place at the pumps," said Mary Swan, "to assist me into the lifeboat. My babe was put into the boat before I was, the rope was put around my waist . . . and I was lowered without accident. . . ." Mrs. O'Conner, knowing that she had to leave Henry, her eighteen-year-old son, behind, left the sinking ship with the child she had promised to deliver to his family's friends in Albany. Other women followed, then John Black yelled his order and the boat pulled away. "The last I saw of my poor husband," Mrs. Swan said, "was when he helped me into the boat," and she heard afterward, she said, that he had returned to the pumps.

A third boat had been lowered but was stove in by the heavy sea. The fourth boat was lowered safely, and put in charge of Quartermaster David Raymond. Ashby launched their fifth and last boat at Herndon's request, and bad luck came Ashby's way once again. A heavy sea, he said, "carried the boat under the lee guard"—the protective structure, I think, covering one of the paddle wheels—"and it was stove in and swamped, carrying me down with it. In a short time I regained the ship's deck."

The afternoon was wearing on, darkness approaching; they had only the three lifeboats now; and the *Marine* continued to drift farther and farther away. Each successive trip between the two ships would clearly take longer than the previous one; and it became obvious, presently, that at best there would be time to take off only the women and children.

So men began prowling the ship for life preservers. Eighteen-year-old Henry O'Conner found a tin one, buckled it on, and then, he said, Engineer George Ashby appeared—I don't know where they were—and threatened to take it. To cut the straps, and pull it off him. Just then, said O'Conner, another passenger came along, and stopped him.

"The *Marine* had drifted far from us," said Mrs. Hawley in the first lifeboat, "and we were half an hour in getting to her. [The *Marine*] was very deeply loaded, and rolled badly. Her bulwarks were nearly level with [our lifeboat] when it was lifted by the sea, and great care was necessary in going alongside, to keep the [life]boat from being swamped."

The *Marine* was small; even in calm weather her deck stood only seven feet above the water, and: "Consequently, when the boats from the *Central America* came alongside . . . the sea was so high that the [life]boat, when it crested the waves, rose absolutely higher than the deck of the *Marine*. Captain Burt took advantage of this, and stationed himself on the deck, close to the railing, and told the women one at a time to hold out their hands when he directed. This being understood, two sailors stood by to keep the boat from being precipitated on the deck of the *Marine;* when the boat rose, Captain Burt stood ready, and, at the agreed signal seized one woman and hauled her on to the deck; in this perilous way every one was taken on board. . . ."

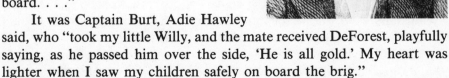

It was Captain Burt, Adie Hawley said, who "took my little Willy, and the mate received DeForest, playfully saying, as he passed him over the side, 'He is all gold.' My heart was lighter when I saw my children safely on board the brig."

With his boatload on the *Marine,* Finley Frazier headed his crew back for the *Central America.* John Black's boat was still on her way to the *Marine,* but—the *Marine* steadily drifting—it was a longer trip.

Widow Ann Small stood on the slanted deck of the *Central America* with her two-year-old daughter, waiting to enter the third boat. In her pocket she'd put her "port-monnaie," she said, and "saved it, together with some bills of my husband's ship, but they were all." Captain Herndon, First Mate Charles Van Rensellaer, and James Frazer superintended

233

the lowering of the women over the side, then her turn came, and "Captain Herndon came up and spoke to me. He appeared sad but very firm. 'Mrs. Small,' said he, 'this is sad;—I am sorry not to get you home safely.' " Mrs. Small was to be lowered into the boat before her daughter, and Herndon "stood by me and fixed my shawl and told me that my little one should be lowered down immediately. . . ." They lowered Mrs. Small, but a receding wave drew the boat out from under her, and she was dropped into the sea. They lifted her, tried again, and again she went under, and was yanked out. The third time they got her into the boat, and it immediately shoved off, oars digging in, Mrs. Small's two-year-old daughter left behind on the sinking ship.

The *Marine* was now, "I think, some two or three miles distant," George Ashby said, and as David Raymond's boat crawled across the sea toward it, Captain Herndon took Ashby into his room. "He inquired of me if I was armed?" Ashby said. "I answered that the only weapon I had was a knife which had been given to me by a passenger in the morning. He then said he would try and borrow for me a pair of pistols, and"— the two having again gone out on deck, I assume—"asked Mr. Payne, a passenger, for the loan of his, and would have got them but for the fact that they were in his trunk, and that was under water. The Captain then asked me to assist in transferring the passengers to the brig, and directed me not to let a single man get into one of the boats till after all of the women and children were saved."

Twelve miles across the sea, too small to be seen by the *Central America*, a little two-hundred-ton schooner fought the subsiding but still-powerful storm. "At 4 o'clock P.M. . . . blowing heavy, with high sea," said her captain, Samuel D. Stone, "faintly descried, with my glass, a vessel, but could not, at the time, make out her character; she was on my weather bow. As I kept on, in about half an hour I saw that she was a steamer, with all her colors set as signals of distress. As soon as I saw this I hauled my wind, and shaped my course for the distressed vessel; I could see that she was disabled, and was deep in the water."

But like every other ship caught out in that awful hurricane, the *El Dorado* had suffered. Her "foregaff was carried away, her foresail split to rags, her bulwarks stove. . . . She sprung her bowsprit so badly . . . that she leaked. . . ." She was "loaded down to her chains, and the peculiarly shaped barnacles of Matagorda . . . [covered] her hull, almost up to the chains." Nevertheless the *El Dorado* began laboring across the miles between the two ships.

With lifeboats returning to the *Central America*, Virginia Birch stood with other women, and children, waiting, her worst fear during the storm —that the ship might sink—now being realized. But Billy Birch stood with her, and she felt optimistic: "When on deck I gave my husband a good bye, fully believing that soon he would be with me on the brig." A lifeboat reached the ship, once again her crew fought the little battle to keep from being smashed against the wall of the ship's side, and "Chief Engineer Ashby superintended getting the passengers into the boats," Virginia Birch said. She was lowered in her turn "but was completely saturated by the waves," and several of the women were dipped under. Then, sitting in the lifeboat, drenched, Virginia Birch watched as the children were lowered over the side, and for some reason: "The lowering of the children recalled to my mind my bird, and my first thought was that it had been crushed by the rope about my waist, or else drowned by the waves which broke over us. . . . I looked and found the little fellow lying quietly under the edge of my dress, unhurt."

One of the children lowered into the lifeboat was Ann Small's little daughter, sent by Herndon in the care of a Mrs. Kitteridge. Still waiting on deck stood Mrs. Isaac McKim Bowley with her two-year-old, Charles, and one-year-old Isabella, and "I must confess that, being sick and weak, and with these two helpless little ones clinging to me," she said, "I became somewhat discouraged and disheartened. The sea was very violent, and the prospect of out-riding it in such a little frail craft was terrible . . . neither the lifeboat nor the life preserver [she wore] seemed like safety, for it is impossible to describe the roughness of the waves, and the brig was a great way off. . . ."

She watched as women were lowered, missed the boat, and went under, to come up gasping, coughing; watched as the elderly black stewardess, Aunt Lucy, went under three times, and then "was pinched between the boat and the side of the steamer. . . ."

Then it was her turn, and: "The rope noose was tied around me, and swung out over the water into the boat." She made it on the first try, but: "After I got safely into the little boat, and my baby with me, I had but little hope of getting to the brig. The peril then seemed to be greater than ever, but as the ship was in sinking condition, the only hope seemed to be in attempting even this dangerous escape from her."

All these women and children now in the boat, one of the stewards, said Virginia Birch, "got in, as he said, to help row the boat." Then Ashby "allowed some men to come in. Judge Munson, of Sacramento, and a Mr. Paine were among them." Not unreasonably, Mrs. Birch now "asked Mr. Ashby to let my husband come to me, but he refused, using insulting language." Also in this boat, "I believe," said Mrs. Hawley, was "the colored boy Garrison, the Captain's servant. I was told that Captain Herndon when he saw him going away in the boat, upbraided him sharply for deserting his post. . . ."

George Ashby said two "men attempted to get into [the] boat. They were both waiters, one colored and the other white. I ordered them away, (perhaps I drew my knife at the same time—I think I might have done so,) and they left."

Sitting at the tiller of the lifeboat watching and judging the action of the waves, the helmsman gave his order, the crew dug in hard, and once more they headed out for the ever more distant *Marine*. "As we left the steamer," said Virginia Birch, "I heard Captain Herndon tell the boatswain to ask the Captain of the brig to lay close by him all night for God's sake, as he was in a sinking state, and had five hundred souls on board, besides a million and a half of dollars."

At somewhere around this time, Adie Hawley, safe aboard the *Marine* with her two children, looked across the water to where she had left her husband, and, she said: "We saw the steamer very distinctly against the sunset clouds. She looked beautiful, and did not seem like a sinking ship."

In Virginia Birch's lifeboat they now discovered that the steward who'd jumped in to help row "did not understand the work, and the sailors made him lie in the bottom of the boat. . . ." During the long and fearful trip, said Mrs. Bowley: "The water dashed into the boat and we had to keep dipping it out all the time. Two high waves passed entirely over us, so that it seemed as if we were swamped and sunk. . . . [The helmsman] encouraged the sailors . . . and told them it would require the exercise of all their skill and courage to reach the brig. . . .

"It was fully two and a half hours before we got to the *Marine*, and then . . . the boat was tossed about so violently that the only way of getting out of her was to watch a fortunate opportunity and seize hold of the brig's . . . ropes on the side. I caught hold with one hand and hung for some minutes . . . [before] the men on deck caught hold of me and pulled me in." But when it came the turn of the elderly stewardess, Aunt Lucy, who had already been squeezed against the side of the *Central America*, "a heavy wave dashed the boat against the ship," said Mrs. Bowley, "and struck the poor woman a severe blow." Finally they got her on board. Got them all, and, said Ann Small, "Mrs. Kitteridge . . . handed [my] child to me. . . . I shall ever think of [Captain Herndon] with gratitude. . . ."

The other two lifeboats had returned to the *Central America*, and the last of the women and children waiting on her wallowing deck were lowered into them. "The moment the last lady and child were lowered," said Frank A. Jones, "a tremendous rush was made by the [men] passengers, and as many as could threw themselves into the boats and water. . . ." All discipline suddenly ended, and: "It was every man for himself . . . men would throw themselves overboard like sheep, filling [the

236

lifeboats] in an instant. . . . I succeeded," said Jones, "in getting into Frazier's boat." He added that the Chilean consul also made it, the only other passenger in that boat, the rest being crew. Jones didn't mention his "colored boy, servant," Charles.

At the sudden rush of men: "The boats shoved off immediately to keep themselves from sinking, and those who remained in the water, were drawn into the sinking steamer by means of ropes . . . at the time I left, those on board were occupied in ripping up the hurricane deck for the purpose of constructing rafts." Other men, said Jones, stood throwing gold into the sea.

Again the hundreds of men left aboard the *Central America* waited for another of her boats to return, a longer wait than ever this time. During this, Captain Herndon and a passenger friend named Theodore Payne stood talking, and "he asked me what I thought of affairs," said Payne. "I said, 'Thank God, the women and children are off, and we are strong.' He replied, 'Yes, thank God,' and added, 'You take the next boat.' " Then "he requested me to go into his office and get his gold watch and chain, and if saved to carry them to his wife. Said he, 'Tell her—!' but his utterance was choked by deep emotion, and he said no more on that subject. . . ." Herndon managed to speak of other things, Payne said, then "he walked away a few steps, and sat down on a bench, with his head in his hands in that position a few moments. . . ."

Finally a lifeboat returned: John Black's, back for the third time. I assume from what happened that this time men were prevented from throwing themselves into the waiting boat. For word had come to the captain that somehow three women were still aboard, down in steerage, and he sent Theodore Payne to bring them up on deck; meanwhile the waiting lifeboat, I believe, was loaded with men but with places apparently saved for Payne and the women.

And now George Ashby did something startling, seen in different ways by different people, discussed and debated for a long time after. Ashby said this is what happened: "Captain Herndon and myself were on the upper deck. I said to him that if I could be of any service in any manner, I was at his disposal." Herndon replied, Ashby said, by asking "me to go in [John Black's] boat, to the brig, and do all in my power to induce the Captain to bring his vessel nearer to the steamer."

Theodore Payne came out on deck again, with the three women from steerage, and, he said: "They were placed in the boat by Mr. Ashby." Payne got in, too, and "the boat shoved off." Now, if Payne was remembering accurately and the lifeboat had already shoved off with Ashby still on deck, Ashby does not seem to be obeying the order he said Herndon gave him to go along. Payne continues that "before [the lifeboat] could clear the stern a steerage passenger sprang from the deck of the ship into the boat, a distance of twenty-five feet. The Chief Engineer then hastily lowered himself into the boat," but only, it seemed to Payne, "to prevent [other passengers] from crowding in and swamping it. He had scarcely got into the boat before another steerage passenger jumped from the deck and fell upon the Engineer's back. [Ashby] seized him by the throat and drew a dirk knife, not, in my opinion, for the intention of using it upon the passenger, but for the purpose of deterring others who crowded the decks from following his example."

Ashby described the order of events differently: ". . . I got in with them, and asked Mr. McCarthy"—the passenger who was a fellow engineer from another ship—"to go along and assist me. He did so, and I think after the boat had received her full complement, two other passengers jumped on board just as we were shoving off from the steamer. . . ."

Another passenger, watching from the deck, was Robert Hutchinson. He said, "The Chief Engineer went to the boat into which the last three ladies were being passed, and after they were passed, he threw the rope around his waist and asked one of the men to lower him down. The Captain called out and asked him where he was going. He said he was going to try to get another boat from the brig. The Captain told him that he would not come back, but charged him solemnly to do so. He replied that the Captain might depend on him, that he would come back." Hutchinson added that after Ashby got into the lifeboat, "one of the steerage passengers caught hold of the rope and slid down after him. The Engineer, as soon as the man got into the boat, drew his knife and threatened to throw him overboard if he did not get out. The Captain shouted at him, 'Don't do that!' and a number of voices beside."

Young Henry O'Conner also stood watching the same incident, wearing the tin life preserver he said Ashby had tried to steal from him. "The Chief Engineer," O'Conner said, "stood by as the . . . boat was being filled; there were two seats vacant, and a person jumped into one of them: at this instant Ashby, who was overseeing the transshipment of the women . . . drew his bowie knife, and raising it as if to strike the man, commanded him to get out; his arm was arrested by a person near him, and the man retained his place; as the boat pushed off Ashby jumped in. A general murmur arose and a cry was heard, 'Shoot him.' Whether anyone seriously thought of doing so or not, the fear of hitting innocent parties in the boat deterred them from the act.

"Captain Herndon told him to come back, but Ashby said he would go to the brig and send her boats back as well as the steamer's. If this was the real motive of the Engineer, it was an extenuation of the act in the minds of the passengers. . . ."

238

Passenger R. T. Brown thought Ashby "jumped into the boat and pushed off in a cowardly manner. Among [other] passengers there is but one opinion, and that is that [the *Central America* disaster] is to be attributed to him in letting the fires go out."

John George, a thirty-year-old Englishman who'd been in California seven years, said he "was an eye-witness to [Ashby's] cowardice." He said it was Ashby's negligence that caused the leak; and was one of the few, though not the only one, critical of Captain Herndon, who "had very little command over his crew." George thought "Capt. Herndon, although personally brave . . . was too mild and easy a man for the position he occupied . . . ineffective. . . ." He also thought the crew "a miserable lazy bunch," and didn't think the gale was all that bad either.

"We arrived safe on board the brig," said Ashby, "although the sea at the time making a clean sweep over her deck." And now, the last three women having arrived, every woman and child from the *Central America* was safe aboard the *Marine*. "Not a mistake was made" in lifting them from lifeboats to deck in the wild sea. "It seems almost miraculous," said Mrs. Bowley, "but not one was lost, not even a single child." There was barely room for them on the little ship. A few were crowded into the cabin

here, "scarcely larger than a stateroom," Virginia Birch said, its floor awash with several feet of water. The tiny room held four bunks, one given to the badly injured Aunt Lucy, and another to a Mrs. Ellis and her four small children: this bunk quickly became known as the "Birdsnest."

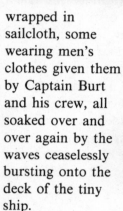

But there were over a hundred rescued, and most lay here on the open deck,

wrapped in sailcloth, some wearing men's clothes given them by Captain Burt and his crew, all soaked over and over again by the waves ceaselessly bursting onto the deck of the tiny ship.

George Ashby said, "I stated to Captain Burt the orders I had received. He said he would do all in his power to bring his vessel nearer to the steamer, but he was in a crippled condition, having lost his mainyard, maintopsail and jibboom, and could not work to windward. He said I could have a boat, but that it was only a yawl, and could not live in such a sea. While consulting with Captain Burt, the boat I came in left for the steamer in charge of the boatswain." This was John Black, who seems not to have known that George Ashby meant to return with him. Black's boat headed out again, on its fourth trip, and "I expressed my determination," said Ashby, "to return in the next boat. . . ."

The other boats had also returned to the *Central America,* and presently they, too, once more reached the *Marine* with their loads of rescued. "They put their passengers aboard the brig," said Ashby, but then the crews, he said, jumped on board themselves, "leaving only a quartermaster in each boat. . . . The boats thumped against the sides of the brig with every sea. I ordered the men into the boats to take me to the steamer, and save as many lives as possible, but they utterly refused. Captain Burt tried to make them return to their duty but without avail."

One of the passengers who had just arrived with these last two boats was Robert Hutchinson, who had seen Ashby leave the *Central America.*

Hutchinson said Ashby "did not offer to go back." But Theodore Payne was there, too, and he said that when the last two boats "came alongside, every man but one jumped out of [each] boat upon the brig, and refused to return. . . . The Chief Engineer, Mr. Ashby, implored them to return, but they steadily refused. He then tried to raise another crew, but did not succeed, and the boats were lashed to the bridge stern."

Mrs. Amanda Marvin's "opinion is that [Ashby] accompanied one of the boats to the brig in the absence of any other officer competent to take charge who could be spared, and with no view to desert his comrades in distress. After placing his precious load on board the *Marine*, Mrs. Marvin says he found one of the sailors willing to return to rescue more of the passengers. The other three flatly refused to again venture on the waves, and none of the passengers, (which is greatly to their discredit) would consent to take their places. Mr. Ashby entreated, saying, 'For God's sake come and help save some more of the poor men; if two men will go with me I will go back.' The steerage passengers when appealed to, declined risking their lives in trying to rescue others, saying they were as good as the cabin passengers. Under these circumstances Mr. Ashby was compelled to give over any attempt to save more of the people still on board the steamer. On the whole Mrs. Marvin thinks that Mr. Ashby was disposed to do his duty from first to last, and that the opinions already expressed as to his conduct have in most cases been too harsh and altogether undeserved."

Another passenger said that he gave "great credit to Capt. Herndon and all the officers except Chief-Engineer Ashby. They stood by their posts nobly and went down with the ship."

Passenger Frank A. Jones, safe on the *Marine,* though without his servant boy, Charles, "heard Mr. Ashby implore the men . . . most earnestly to return with him to the aid of the *Central America.* He offered them $100 a-piece to do so, and attempted to throw some of them by main force into [a] boat, but all to no purpose. With the exception of Mr. Raymond, they all absolutely refused to risk their lives by returning."

Ashby's assistant engineer said, "When [John Black's] boat shoved off I heard Captain Herndon reiterate his order to Mr. Ashby, to obtain the boats of the brig as soon as possible. I am certain that Mr. Ashby would have returned with assistance if it was possible."

A man in Panama who knew Ashby said, ". . . that he is a coward, or acted in a cowardly manner when danger surrounded him, no one on this Isthmus who knows him believes. . . . That Captain Herndon should have expressed the doubts he is said to have expressed, when Mr. Ashby took charge of the boat, about his coming back, is simply absurd. . . ."

Ashby himself said, "I was . . . left powerless, and was compelled to remain in the brig. . . ."

Whatever the reason, no other boat followed John Black's to the *Central America,* and: "It was a melancholy spectacle we were now compelled to witness," said Ann Small, on board the *Marine* with her little daughter. "Three staunch boats"—possibly she was including the brig's yawl—"floated uselessly upon the rough waves, while the wreck of the steamer, black with people, was visibly sinking before our eyes."

4

On the sinking wreck they seemed not to hope for the boats to return. "All hands . . . seized pieces of spars, chairs, and life-preservers, while others rushed below to secure their treasure," said one of the men. "The confusion now became very great, though all acted with coolness, each endeavoring to make the last effort for his own safety. . . . I . . . provided myself with a life-preserver and a piece of spar, and determined to go down with the vessel, with the great mass of passengers, all of whom stood about, bracing themselves up and securing those articles most available to buoy them up. . . ." Said another man, "There were a number of tin and cork life-preservers on board, with which each one helped himself, besides setting apart some portions of cabin furniture and deck materials."

Second Mate James Frazer said, "We . . . cut away the forward part of the hurricane deck"—a kind of promenade over the roof of the main cabin—"and made rafts." Fireman Alexander Grant was one of the crew hacking up the hurricane deck; shipwrecked three times, he now worked to save himself for the fourth time.

Herndon ordered parts of the upper works cut loose so that they'd float off when the ship went under, for the use of men struggling in the water, and "those on board," said a passenger, "commenced cutting away . . . cabin doors, state-room doors. . . . I wrenched a door from the wheel house. . . . When I saw there was no chance of escape, I . . . placed it on the deck, sat down on it, and remained in this way."

First assistant engineer John Tice "took himself to the deck, and looked about for the purpose of securing such means as would probably save his life. . . ." Tice was twenty-seven, "small, but well made, in stature," and with "an intelligent face and fine general appearance." He looked around, and: "Among the wrecks of the upper works which had been torn off . . . to make rafts, he found a plank ten feet long and about an inch and a half in thickness. . . ."

A gold miner went down to his cabin carrying two life preservers: he'd given five years of his life for the gold he had there, and wasn't leaving it behind. Now he put his gold either in his pockets or in a "treasure belt," I don't know which, then got both life preservers on. There wasn't much "terror" on board, he said, but "there was some praying, there was some swearing, and some fighting." Fighting? Yes, for "loose boards, tops of boxes and other light material." Others kept on bailing or working at the pumps, and "some deliberately turned in and went to bed, choosing . . . to meet their fate in this form." He thought "nearly all the passengers had been provided with life-preservers, but many of them had lost all hope and become discouraged . . . they lacked the energy to make any effort to save themselves, while others were affrighted out of all presence of mind, and lacked the judgment to convert to their use means which might have been rendered available. . . ."

A man stood in his cabin earnestly talking to his roommate: this was another gold miner returning home, an original forty-niner, in fact. But he had no gold, was coming home broke, and to a wife who had gone insane during his long absence. It was time to *move*, his roommate told him now, to get out of here and save themselves. But "when the critical

244

moment arrived," the man "refused to make any effort to escape, sitting down and calmly awaiting his fate."

In Captain Badger's cabin, said a passenger who was there with him apparently, the captain upended his valise containing one thousand twenty-dollar gold pieces, and "flung [them] onto the floor of the state-room. . . ." But the other man had twenty-one pounds of gold that he'd mined himself and he hung on to it; he was young, and thought he could save it.

And now once again—something after six o'clock, "about one hour before sunset," James Frazer said—someone on deck spotted a ship. They watched . . . then saw it was approaching. It was the little *El Dorado*, finally here. On her deck Captain Stone studied the *Central America:* "I could see that she was disabled, and deep in the water. I judged what he might want, and gave orders to stand by the main sheet, to heave our vessel to. The man at the wheel steered within fifty feet of the steamer . . ." and Stone "fully expected they would throw him a line to which he could make fast, but there was but a moment in which he was near enough for this. . . ."

Each captain, however—shouting to the other in the wind, unable to hear well or much—misread the other's mind: each assumed the other had boats. So "that precious moment," a reporter called it, when a line might have been tossed and the two ships possibly brought side by side, "was lost without any attempt made on board the steamer for this pur-pose. . . ." And that was too bad, because the *El Dorado,* "a vessel of two hundred and twelve tons," was large enough to have taken aboard every person still on the *Central America.*

Steering within fifty feet of the disabled ship, at 6:30 P.M., Captain Stone noted, he "hailed her in the following language: 'Can I render you any assistance.'

"The reply was: 'Lay by me until morning, for I am in a sinking condition.'

"Immediately I gave the order to put the wheel hard down and haul aft the main sheet, and hove to, directly under his lee, say about a gunshot distant; I warned him to commence at once putting his passengers on board, supposing that he had good boats. . . . During the time that I was talking with the captain I could hear the passengers crying and halloing, sounding like one simultaneous burst of shouting; one voice that I heard above the rest cried 'Send us your boat. . . .' " But "I had but one, a small jollyboat, which would not live in the high sea then running for a moment.

"He again said: 'Lay by me until morning.' I supposed his reason to be for thus delaying that he thought it advisable to await daylight, as he might, in making the attempt to transport them in the night, (it being then near dark,) lose more than he could save, while, by awaiting daylight, perhaps all might be saved.

"I then said: 'Set your lights.' By that time I had drifted out of hailing distance, and I ordered my lights set immediately." The *El Dorado,* prepared to wait until morning and then to receive the *Central America*'s nonexistent lifeboats, drifted away to leeward, keeping the lights of the *Central America* in sight.

I don't know why Captain Herndon shouted to Captain Stone, "Lay by me until morning," or if he did; perhaps Stone misheard him in that wind. For if there was any help to be had of the *El Dorado,* Herndon's sinking ship needed it now. And he ordered Second Mate James Frazer to send up a rocket, which apparently the *El Dorado* never saw, or if she did, was unable to approach again against the wind. Herndon ordered Frazer "to stop by the rocket box and send up a rocket every half hour. . . ." As Frazer fired the first rocket, he "at the same time saw a [small] boat on the starboard bow. We hailed the boat, and told them to come under our starboard quarter, but could not hear the answer. I suppose that he saw the ship settling down very fast, and kept away for safety."

It was boatswain John Black's lifeboat, returned once more. Black called to Captain Herndon, he said later, that his boat was "in a damaged condition," and he said Herndon shouted in reply "to keep off." Black did keep off, but remained near the ship. It was now "7:45 P.M., or there-abouts," Frazer said, and "the people still kept on bailing."

Across the long stretch of heavy sea, aboard the crowded *Marine,* Mrs. Mary Swan said she "looked out through a window about 8 o'clock, and saw the *Central America*'s lights burning. . . ." It was dark now. The sinking ship stood, far out to sea, due east of a point somewhere between Savannah and Jacksonville.

Aboard the ship whose lights Mary Swan saw, "the scene among the passengers on deck and throughout the vessel was one of the most indescribable confusion and alarm. The prayers of the pious and penitent, the curses of the maddened, and the groans and shrieks of the affrighted, were all commingled together, added to which were numerous angry contests between man and man, in many instances amounting to outright fight, for the possession of articles on which to keep themselves afloat. . . ."

Frazer said: "At about 8 P.M., or a few minutes after, the ship began to take water on the deck." Hundreds of men stood waiting: some with life preservers, some with planks or wooden fragments of the ship, hatch covers, or doors. Some had nothing. A dozen of the crew stood by one of the rafts they'd hacked out of the hurricane deck. A group of ship's butchers were still working on another raft at the forward part of the ship. Comedian Billy Birch came out on deck, saw the butchers, and walked toward them, hoping to join them, he said.

The Englishman, John George, stood near the wheelhouse beside Second Mate Frazer. Frazer, Captain Herndon, and First Officer Van Rensellaer were together, said a passenger who stood watching them. Countless men, in fact, stood or sat watching the group of ship's officers, among them the young Casey brothers, identical twins, who stood "within a few feet of Lieut. Herndon," and thought he "continued calm and self-possessed in his actions."

Eighteen-year-old Henry O'Conner also waited "for the fatal moment to arrive, determined to do his best to save his life"; and he *was* determined: besides the tin life preserver he wore, young Henry held two hatch covers he'd pulled off the skylight over the engineer's room.

Up in the rigging near the top of the only undamaged mast two men sat discussing which end of the ship each thought would go down first.

John Taylor stood wearing a life preserver, having "placed, as I thought securely," he said, "in my trowsers pocket all I had, about $300 in gold. . . ."

The man who had wrenched a door off its hinges continued to sit on it, both waiting and guarding it. Among the many men wearing life preservers stood George Dawson, the black man who'd been shipwrecked before. "Anticipating his danger," he had tried to secure a plank," but "it was claimed by another passenger."

John Tice waited with the ten-foot plank he'd found, wearing "thick cloth pantaloons, a stout peajacket, and a heavy cloth pilot overcoat."

"About 8 o'clock," said one of the miners, ". . . as we all stood forward, I said to the men, 'There will never be as many die as coolly. Boys,' " (he said that he said) " 'let us all die like true Californians.' "

Perhaps two hundred men waited out there on the deck, some of them estimated, but at least as many more were still down in the cabins and corridors or in the steerage: panicked, fighting, hunting for something to keep afloat with, still worrying about gold, or simply lying on their bunks. Naval officer Dobbin, brother of a late Secretary of the Navy, lay on his bunk exhausted, like many another of the bailers. Other men, "in my opinion," Virginia Birch said, "lay stupefied with drink in their staterooms."

Then: "Two heavy seas swept over the steamer," said Henry O'Conner, "the first carrying off a large number of persons, and the second filling the ship." Fireman Alexander Grant rushed up to the deck from below, saw the raft he'd helped make already shoved off the ship, men climbing onto it, and he jumped over the side and swam for it. An officer shouted at Grant to cut the raft loose, which he did. "The vessel gave three lurches, some of the passengers jumping off at each lurch. Those who jumped off at the first and second lurches swam off to some distance, but the great mass remained on deck. . . ."

". . . every remaining passenger and all the remaining crew resigned themselves to their fate," said James Frazer. "I looked over the side forward and aft; and saw the water spotted with people, jumping over to get clear of the ship before she was submerged. I saw a rocket go off to windward of the port paddle-box."

It was fired by Captain Herndon, said Thomas Badger: Herndon stood on the paddle box, so tipped by the tilted ship that the rocket's

mount fired it downward. He fired more, and a mile and a half away the steamer *Atalanta* saw them and knew—blue rockets fired in succession—that they were a signal of distress.

"Captain Herndon remained on the wheel up to the [last] moment, which was eight o'clock," said Badger. "I was standing on the quarter deck. Some jumped over, and put out from the now rapidly descending ship and seized on whatever they could. . . . Of those who remained on deck "no one shrieked or cried, but all stood calm.

The Captain behaved nobly, and said he would not leave the ship. I promised him I would remain with him, as also did the Second Officer Mr. Frazer. . . ."

"Just as she was about to go down, there came a flash of lightning which, for a moment, gave a full view of the entire deck . . . ," said a man aboard her. "Upon the wheelhouse stood Captain Herndon, with his hat in one hand and the other upon the iron rail, and with nothing to cling to when he went down. . . . In a moment the stern began rapidly to sink. . . ."

"All at once," said Badger, "the ship as if in an agony of death herself, made a plunge on an angle of 45 degrees. . . ." James Frazer "was lifted by the sea, and hove in amidships, and back to the starboard side. Then the ship sunk," he "came to the top of the water, [and] the only thing I saw was about ten feet of the ship's funnel. . . ." "With a shriek from the engulphed mass," said Captain Badger, though I doubt that he shrieked, "she disappeared." One man remembered that mass cry even as the suck of the sinking ship pulled him under with it: ". . . there arose a hoarse yell, as if coming from the bottom of the sea." Another man heard the *sound* of the sinking, "like . . . inserting a red-hot bar of iron into a tub of water—a moment's hissing and seething . . . ," and the young Englishman, who'd been standing beside James Frazer near the wheel-house, also heard "the seething rush and hiss of waters that closed above her" even as she pulled him under.

"She went down stern foremost," said Henry O'Conner, who was swept from her sinking deck, but—with life preserver and two hatch covers—he stayed floating on the surface, as did others who were either well prepared or lucky. But O'Conner saw countless men pulled "down in the vortex" of the sinking ship. "Many were sucked into the hatches and never came up."

Even men wearing life preservers were sucked under. Captain Herndon was one, and First Mate Charles Van Rensellaer, and engineer John Tice, who was "carried a good distance under water, a distance which seemed to him unfathomable, with such tremendous and irresistable force was he drawn underneath."

The Englishman George, "sucked in by the whirlpool caused by her swift descent," was carried "to a depth . . . and into a darkness that he never dreamed of . . . ," and the gold miner determined to die like a true Californian was carried down "fifteen or twenty feet—so far at least and so long that I had to breathe while under water. . . ." John Taylor, in life preserver and with $300 stowed in his "trowsers pocket," was washed clear of the ship, but his foot got snagged in the rigging of a submerged mast, and he was dragged down with it. So was George Dawson, who "caught hold of the gangway near the pilot-house" as the ship went under, "and the next instant found himself under water going down with his heels above his head. He let go his hold and came to the surface. . . ."

Watching at a distance, from his lifeboat, John Black saw the sinking, and "immediately afterwards," he later told a rescued passenger, saw "the

249

heads of the drowning passengers like blackbirds on the water." One of

those heads was that of Billy Birch, who never reached the butchers' raft he'd been walking toward across the deck. "Just as he got opposite the smoke stack, a tremendous sea struck the ship, and she went down." The butchers were never seen again, but Birch was left alive and floating.

Others, too, stayed on the surface. The young gold miner wearing two life preservers, his pockets stuffed with gold, floated clear. The man sitting on the door was swept off the deck, still sitting on it. Another man felt "the ship sink under my feet, and I was adrift in the sea. I saved myself by swimming." The hurricane-deck raft and its men seesawed in the waves, some of the men tied onto it with rope. But it was only inch-thick wood covered with oiled canvas, and only twelve feet square, so the weight of a dozen men submerged the raft and they lay underwater, heads awkwardly lifted to the air; Alexander Grant among them, shipwrecked now for the fourth time. Out in the darkness George Dawson, with whom Grant had once been shipwrecked, was still afloat even though a drowning man had grabbed him around the neck. But Dawson was "tall, well-built, muscular and young," and he broke free, "managed to get hold of three pieces of board, placed them together, and they assisted in keeping his body afloat."

Of those pulled under with the ship, a great many stayed under.

Others made it back to the surface. A passenger came up gasping, his life preserver and most of his clothes peeled right off him by the power of the suction that had dragged him under. All around him others were popping to the surface, too, and so was timber, pieces "breaking loose from the ship as she continued to descend." These "leaped to the surface, and fell back with a heavy splash," but other timbers and various wooden objects Herndon had ordered chopped loose came up directly under some of the men who'd just escaped drowning, and they were "killed, stunned and drowned."

One of the men who'd sat in the ship's rigging discussing which end of the ship would go under first made it up still alive, escaped the flying timber, saw a hatch cover, and climbed onto it. The other was never seen again.

The gold miner who had not, after all, died like a true Californian came to the surface, "found plenty of things to cling to, and got hold of a door, which I held onto. . . ." John Taylor, dragged under by the rigging, jerked and yanked his foot till it came loose, and his life preserver brought him to the top in time to draw breath again.

But some came up too late for that, and Taylor saw "a great many dead bodies floating about. I struck against many of them, they were all provided with life-preservers, yet dead, and with their heads down in the water. It was a horrible sight."

The man who'd been stripped of life preserver and most of his clothes swam aimlessly to keep afloat, then came to a friend who had two life preservers, and who gave him one. Then each found pieces of wreckage to hang on to. "An occasional flash of lightning, showed to each other a sea of struggling forms. Each strove to encourage his friend with hopes he scarce felt himself."

One of the men struck by wooden fragments bursting to the surface was Billy Birch, hit not once but several times. Now, with a few others, he lay on "a floating hatch window," painfully injured. Captain Herndon and First Mate Charles Van Rensellaer made it back to the surface alive. In their life preservers, they rose and fell with the waves, conversing with A. J. Easton, one of the ship's young bridegrooms. Van Rensellaer told Easton that "he was devoted to Herndon, rose with him"—in promotions, I think is meant—"and declared that he would not leave him."

Engineer John Tice "came up safe with his plank in his possession." He tried to pull off his water-heavy boots, couldn't, and lay hanging over his plank. The Englishman John George, "luckily escaping all injury from the timbers," came back to the surface, too. He wore a life preserver, but saw a couple of "strips of boards," and grabbed them. "The waves as they

251

rose and fell revealed a crowd of human heads," he said, and: "Those
. . . who had lost their life-preservers or planks while under water, owing
to the force of the whirlpool, were frantically snatching at . . . pieces of
the wreck. . . ."

Far across the wild night sea on the distant *Marine,* Mary Swan, who
had seen the *Central America*'s lights across the water, "looked out again
shortly afterwards. I saw no light. I then felt sick at heart, for I knew that
my husband must have perished in the meantime." Mrs. Bowley said,
"When it was known on board the brig that the ship had gone, there was
great wailing, for there were women there whose husbands had gone down
with the wreck."

The *El Dorado* "continued drifting," said her captain, "but was not
more than two miles distant when the lights of the steamer which up to
that time had been plainly visible . . . disappeared. . . ." They searched,
said Captain Stone, but could find no one. The *Atalanta,* which had seen
the blue bursts of the sinking ship's rockets, searched, too, but at night
and in that sea found no one either. But in their lifeboat John Black and
his crew sat watching the men afloat and struggling among the drifting
wreckage, but Black said that his crewmen "positively refused to venture
among them, afraid that the boat would be swamped by the multitudes
that would endeavor to scramble into it. . . ." Presently they rowed away
toward the far-off lights of the *Marine.*

By occasional flashes of lightning, Second Mate James Frazer saw
"over one hundred men and great quantities of driftwood," and others
made the same estimate of about a hundred men. From them "cries arose
that mingled into one inarticulate wail, then the lustier and less terrified
shouted for assistance to the *Marine,* which was far beyond hailing distance. . . . The swell of the sea was great, and successively the poor floaters,
holding onto their planks with the energy of despair, were riding on the
brink of a precipice and buried in a deep valley of water . . . respiration
was very difficult, owing to the masses of water which were constantly
dashed upon them as wave after wave rolled by." The man adrift on his
door had "great difficulty in holding on, on account of the roughness. . . ."
And the "true Californian," also afloat on a door, hung on to it for "about
fifteen minutes till three Irishmen grabbed it, when I left it, as I was
becoming so numb I was obliged to warm up by a little swimming exercise.
Though a large quantity of material was floating about, still there was a
good deal of desperate struggling and fighting to appropriate articles
promising the most security. I got hold of a trunk, but it soon fell to pieces.
But a flour barrel directly came in my way; in clinging to it I soon got
chilled and had occasionally to leave it and swim to get warm. But I did

252

not let it get far out of my way. I observed the Irishmen still fighting for the door the last I saw of them. . . . After a while I came across a board, concluded the board was better than the barrel, and so swapped. . . ."

". . . Speedily [the survivors] began to separate, and the last farewells were taken. One man called to another in [John] George's hearing, 'If you are saved, Frank, send my love to my dear wife,' but the friend appealed to answered only with a gurgle of the throat. He was washed off his plank, and perished as his companion spoke. Many were desirous of separating themselves as far as possible from the rest, being fearful lest some desperate struggler might seize hold of them, and draw them under. Others, afraid of their loneliness, called to their neighbors to keep together. Generally, they strove to cheer each other as long as they remained within hearing, and when the roar of the waves drowned all but the loudest shouting, the call of friendship or the cry of despair was heard in the distance. . . ."

". . . the full horror of [their] position," said the *Times,* is "not unparalleled indeed in the desolate annals of the ocean, but . . . no story so clear and so appalling has ever before been brought to the firesides of the land."

Gradually scattering across the nighttime sea, the survivors separated—Second Mate James Frazer by choice: "I hove off my overcoat and boots, and swam out from the crowd." Engineer John Tice, hanging on to his ten-foot plank, presently floated alone, and the man afloat on his door drifted so far that, looking back toward the place where he thought the ship had gone down, he could see no one else, and concluded that everyone but himself had drowned.

When John George, the Englishman, "had drifted so far from the companionship of any of his fellows in misfortune," he "began to realize his situation. Like many of the rest [he] was seized with the fear of sharks. The night was quite dark. Occasionally, as the driving clouds parted and gave a glimpse of the sky, a star or two would be visible, but this was very seldom and offered but the faintest gleam of hope. . . ." Another man, "floating in solitude, and terrified at his loneliness, after shouting himself hoarse to find a companion, saw at length a man with two life-preservers fastened about his body drifting toward him. His heart leaped with joy at the welcome sight, for the feeling of desolation which had overcome him was terrible to endure. He called to the other to join him if possible, and made every exertion to meet him halfway. There was no reply, but the other drifted nearer and nearer. A wave threw them together. They touched. The living man shrieked in the face of a corpse. . . ."

"I guess I had been about four hours in the water, and had floated

253

away from the rest," one man said, "when the waves ceased to make any noise, and I heard my mother say, 'Johnny, did you eat your sister's grapes?' I hadn't thought of it in twenty years at least. It had gone clean out of my mind. I had a sister that died of consumption more than thirty years ago, and when she was sick—I was a boy of eleven or so—a neighbor had sent her some early hot-house grapes. Well, those grapes were left in a room where I was, and—I ought to have been skinned alive for it . . . —I devoured them all. Mother came to me after I had gone to bed, when she couldn't find the fruit for sister to moisten her mouth with in the night, and said, 'Johnny, did you eat your sister's grapes?' I did not add to the meanness of my conduct by telling a lie. I owned up, and my mother went away in tears, but without flogging me. It occasioned me a qualm of conscience for many years after," but in time he no longer thought of it "till when I was floating about benumbed with cold I heard as plain as ever I heard her voice in my life, I heard my mother say, 'Johnny, did you eat your sister's grapes?' I don't know how to account for it. It did not scare me though. I thought it was a presage of death."

Henry O'Conner drifted alone . . . so did the man and the friend who'd given him a life preserver. Briefly they'd drifted with others, "but soon the waves separated us, and at each successive flash of lightning we discovered that we were being scattered over a wide area, and soon found ourselves apparently alone on the boundless ocean."

The man on the door drifted "for about two hours." Then "I was drifted near a larger raft, on which were five men. I then left my [door] and swam to them. The darkness was so great that I could not recognize any of them. We were frequently washed off by the force of the waves, and had to swim to reach the raft again. Soon I found one of our number was missing. The rest of us—there were now five—clung to the raft as best we could, at times being washed off, and then regaining the raft by swimming to it. . . ."

The men on the floating hatch window with the injured Billy Birch of the San Francisco Minstrels, "were all despondent at . . . the awful forebodings still overhanging their future. Birch, nevertheless, was as cool as a cucumber. To keep up their spirits he mimicked the sea monsters, told humorous stories, in his own peculiar way, and on that frail bark, stretched on his back, bleeding from wounds, at midnight, tossed to and fro upon the angry waves of mid-ocean, he not only showed himself a true philosopher, but inspired courage in others, nor did he cease his vivifying harangue until an overwhelming billow checked his utterance."

Aboard the *Marine,* Billy Birch's wife remembered the canary she'd tucked into the bosom of her dress. She looked to see if it was still alive

254

there, and it was. She lifted it out, it was unhurt, and when she set it down, she said, it began to sing.

At ten that night John Black and his men reached the *Marine*. Exhausted, I would suppose, after the many trips they had made, and possibly depressed and discouraged, Black didn't even bother tying up their boat. He and the crewmen stepped out of it onto the *Marine,* and let it drift off into the darkness.

There was no hope for any of these hundred-odd men adrift on the ocean except rescue by ship; they were too far from land to make it by swimming. And ships *were* moving through this part of the ocean, but of course it was dark: engineer John Tice saw the distant lights of one of them, and "made many efforts to reach it, but between nine and ten o'clock it disappeared below the horizon. . . ."

And William Osbourn, adrift on a hatch cover, also saw lights. He'd found and picked up a floating bunk slat, and now he used it to paddle toward the far-off light. Presently, in the darkness, he made out another man afloat on something, and the man hailed him: Did he want company? Osbourn called that he did, and the man paddled over. Now Osbourn could make out that the man was on a hatch cover, but it was too dark to see his face. Nevertheless they introduced themselves to each other; the other man was Julius Stetson. For an hour they drifted together, then Stetson spotted a light, and the two men began paddling toward it. Gradually their hatch covers moved apart, and presently Osbourn lost Stetson. For four hours he continued paddling toward the light, then it was gone.

Second Mate James Frazer, alone for a while, came upon two swimming men, and joined them. After a time "I discovered a light to the eastward," he said. (Even now Frazer noted that: "The wind was then about southwest.") With the other two men he "swam toward the light, but I found if I stopped with my companions I must sink, so I left them. I then came up with Dr. Harvey who was bound toward the same light I saw. . . ."

There were lights, there were ships, and men struggling toward them, but no one to see them or even guess they were out there. But one of these ships was the bark *Ellen* of Arusdah, Norway, en route from Belize, Honduras, almost empty of cargo, and taking the Gulf Stream to England. Johnson, her captain, had fought her through the storm, losing his foremast. His crew was exhausted, and now, something past midnight in the early morning of Sunday, September 13, he temporarily abandoned trying to hold his course. The wind was still powerful, and I suppose he was giving his worn-out men a rest from struggling against it. But as he allowed his ship to fall off, altering his course, a "bird flew across the ship

255

once or twice, then darted in his face. At first he took no notice of this circumstance, when the same thing occurred again, which caused him to regard the circumstance as something extraordinary, and while thinking in this way, the mysterious bird for the *third time appeared*, and went through the same extraordinary maneuvers. Upon this, said the captain, *'I was induced to alter my course into the original one which I had been steering. . . .'* "

This was "a superstition as old as the days of the Vikinger . . . ," said the *Times,* and because of it Captain Johnson now resumed his original course, and "a short time afterward, I heard strange noises. . . ."

Apparently not all the survivors of the wrecked ship had drifted apart; or each down among the huge waves thought himself more alone than he really was. For "on trying to discover from whence [the noises] proceeded," Johnson continued, "I found that I was in the midst of people who had been shipwrecked."

This was about one in the morning, and: "When, rising and falling with the swell of the waves, the lights of the *Ellen* were first discovered by the survivors in the water, the thrill of hope that at once filled every breast amounted, it may well be believed, to a perfect ecstasy. . . .

"The night was unusually dark, though the horizon was occasionally lit up with flashes of lightning, which served to discover fragments of a wreck floating about, to which human beings were discovered clinging. Captain Johnson immediately ordered his vessel hove to, and one of the four boats on board lowered to rescue the unfortunate seen and heard in every direction. But scarcely had the boat touched the water when some six of the unfortunate men seized hold of the gunwale and capsized her. . . ." It "was soon righted, and the men were taken on board. The work of rescuing the drowning men then proceeded with all possible dispatch; buoys were thrown overboard, ropes suspended from the sides of the ship, and lights hung out." The *Ellen*'s other boats "were not launched, partly on account of the darkness and the heavy sea, and partly because the crew of the *Ellen* were too much worn out to be able to manage them. A number of those floating on the water were picked up by Captain Johnson's men in the course of an hour or two, but the first ten or twelve were so exhausted as to be unable to give any account of themselves, or to state from what vessel they had been lost. . . ."

James Frazer was one. He and Dr. Harvey, swimming toward a distant light, presently "saw a bark hove to, and hailed her . . . ," Frazer said. It was the *Ellen,* who heard them, and when he was taken aboard, Frazer said the strength which had kept him going left him instantly. "I was perfectly unconscious, and I recollected nothing that transpired from that time until the morning after."

They picked up John Taylor, who "was quite exhausted when I was taken on board. . . . I could never have endured had not the sea become quieter. . . ." But now he knew he still had a life to live, and his hand went to the pocket where he'd put his $300 in gold: it was gone. "I had not secured it with a string as I ought, and the violence of the waves had reversed my pockets so I lost it all."

The *Ellen* continued picking up men, steering "in the direction whence the shouts for help came, but was too unmanageable to afford speedy assistance. . . .

"Two life-buoys on the *Ellen* were put to excellent use in cases where those saved were too weak to fasten about their bodies the ropes thrown to them. Occasionally a man would come floating across the bows of the bark, and the life-buoy having been cast into the water as near to him as possible, he would swim to it, and, clinging fast, would thus be drawn up in safety. Such as passed to the leeward were pulled up over the stern or side by ropes previously thrown within their reach."

"I never felt so thankful in my life," said the Englishman John George, when he saw the *Ellen*'s lights. "I never knew what gratitude was before. I do not know whether I cried or not, but I know that I was astonished to hear my own laughter ringing in my ears. I do not know why I laughed. That verse, 'God moves in a mysterious way' kept passing in and out of me—through me, rather, as if I had been the pipe of an organ. It did not come to me by my own volition, but somehow made me remember it. When the lights approached nearer a score of voices sprang up around me, crying, 'Ship ahoy!' 'Boat ahoy!' and then I began to shout too. And I never had any doubt that I should be saved. . . ." But he "saw the lights go by, about a half a mile from where I was, and recede in the distance. . . ." And so it was for others, some of whom undoubtedly never

257

saw them again.

Blind luck: a man floating on a spar lost it to another man who grabbed it, and he had to swim for two or three hours. But "during all that time I felt little or no fatigue. My strength was preserved to me in a wonderful manner." Then he "came up with a Cuban, who gave me a share of a long board he had. . . ." Presently "we fell in with . . . the bark *Ellen,* who threw us a rope. . . ." The *Ellen*'s crew dragged them out, and "as soon as I was rescued, I dropped away and was too weak almost to move."

Another hail, the man seen, a rope thrown, the man lifted to the deck: one of the identical-twin Casey brothers. But the other was not aboard.

Two men hanging to a pair of lashed-together doors hailed the *Ellen,* were seen, but they lay in the wrong direction. The damaged *Ellen* could not maneuver into the wind to reach them, and the two helplessly drifted away. Another group, afloat on a window sash, also hailed the *Ellen,* but they were downwind, so the ship could easily reach them. They were lifted out of the sea, the injured Billy Birch among them.

Eighteen-year-old Henry O'Conner kept afloat, with his tin life preserver and two hatch covers, for seven hours. "Finally he happened to float . . . near the bark *Ellen,* when one of the sailors on board threw him a rope, but he was much too exhausted to hold on with sufficient force to be raised out of the water. While attempting to do so, two men caught hold of the rope, when he requested them to let go, and they did so. (Was politeness ever carried"—*Leslie's* asked in parentheses—"to a more exquisite point?) O'Conner, having the rope to himself, managed to twist it round his body, and by this means was hauled into the ship. When once on board, some sailors helped him into the cabin, when he from exhaustion fell instantly asleep."

Exhausted men, unable to talk: Captain Johnson didn't even know from what ship they had come. But presently he found out, and if you think about it for a moment you'll know how. "At length one of the survivors, who proved to be Captain Badger, hailed the bark at a distance of fifteen or twenty yards, and informed them what all this wreck and ruin meant, stating the name and fate of the steamer lost, and"—taking charge, out there in the darkness—"urging the captain to hasten to the rescue of the scores of living beings, on the point of being swallowed by the angry waves." He was "a stout swimmer, and when taken on board was found much less exhausted than any of the others of those rescued."

The *Ellen* kept at it for hours. "Toward morning," said a man adrift on a raft with four others, "a sea washed off all but one of us, and only two of the four succeeded in recovering the raft—[the others] had become so *chilled* and exhausted that they had no strength to reach it, and were lost." They "perished within a few yards of us, crying for help—which, alas! was far beyond their reach. This left only three of us on the raft out of the six that were on it. . . ." We "saw the bark *Ellen* about five o'clock in the morning, but were so exhausted that we could make no signals of distress as it required all our efforts to maintain our hold." No one on the *Ellen* saw them, but: "In about two hours we had drifted sufficiently near to be observed [and] we were picked up. . . ." They were rescued by one of the *Ellen*'s boats, which the crew had finally been able to launch in the quieting sea, "and taken on board. I do not know the names of the other two saved with me. . . ."

William Osbourn, who had paddled his hatch cover toward a distant light for four hours before losing it, saw it again and paddled for two more hours. This time he reached the *Ellen,* and they lifted him aboard, having already rescued some thirty-five others. "After getting on board, some one asked him if he had seen any one else down that way, when he told them yes, he had seen a very pleasant fellow down to leeward, too, and would like to save him also, as they had floated together some time. 'What's your name?' says Osbourn. 'Stetson,' said he. 'Well, I am Osbourn,' said the other. . . ."

Like Osbourn, John Tice saw the *Ellen*'s lights once again, "this time much nearer him. In a few moments he was able to distinguish the hull of a vessel bearing directly toward him. His hopes were raised, and he was confident that he would soon be discovered and rescued. But when only a quarter mile distant from him, the vessel—the Norwegian bark *Ellen*—altered her course, and kept off, and subsequently her hull and lights disappeared. . . ."

The *Marine* was able to work down toward the place of the wreck that night, Engineer George Ashby said, "but saw no persons in the water, and nothing whatever, except the light of a schooner several miles distant. . . ." And the *El Dorado,* once so close to the *Central America* that ropes could have been thrown from one to the other, searched the ocean until 9:30 Sunday morning, finding not a soul.

But the *Ellen* continued to come upon survivors. John George, who had also watched the *Ellen*'s lights disappear, had finally given himself up for lost. But about five Sunday morning he saw her lights again, and "I slowly drifted toward her . . . till I could make out her hull and one of

259

her masts, and presently I floated close to her, and shouted and was taken up. When I got on the deck I could not stand. I did not know till then how exhausted I was."

Of the two bridegrooms, Easton and McNeil, they found Easton. They rescued Johnny, who ate his sister's grapes. Around seven in the morning they picked up three men afloat on a hatch cover; there had been six, but the others had become exhausted, and slipped off. One of the rescued was the second Casey brother, and the identical twins were reunited. To the south, aboard the *Marine,* the wives and children of some of these rescued men actually saw the distant *Ellen* that morning, not knowing she carried some of their men.

For several more hours the *Ellen* continued to hunt, but no more were found, and now Captain Johnson decided to abandon further search. But Easton, the young bridegroom, urged him to try a little longer, he did, and: "The last person rescued was a Mr. Brown . . . ," a friend of the Birches, afloat with another man on a pair of lashed-together doors; the other man was dead, and they left him.

Of the hundred or so men who'd survived the sinking, Captain Johnson and his *Ellen* saved forty-nine. This is Captain Johnson, his portrait precisely copied from a Fredrick's photograph: "a small, plain unassuming man, with a face beaming with intelligence and hearty good-nature. He is about thirty-four years of age, speaks the English slow, but well. He has been to sea all his life, but says he never encountered anything like the wreck of the *Central America.* He attributes the visit of the bird to the ship to a visitation of Providence. . . ."

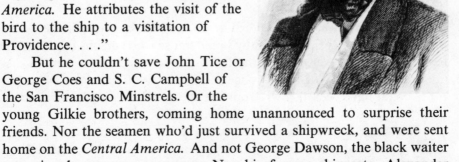

But he couldn't save John Tice or George Coes and S. C. Campbell of the San Francisco Minstrels. Or the young Gilkie brothers, coming home unannounced to surprise their friends. Nor the seamen who'd just survived a shipwreck, and were sent home on the *Central America.* And not George Dawson, the black waiter returning home as a passenger. Nor his former shipmate, Alexander Grant, nor any of the men floating with him on the hurricane-deck raft.

Johnson searched till eleven Sunday morning, "when there being no reasonable hope that any others might be saved, he took the opinion of those rescued and steered for Norfolk. . . ."

5

That morning, far to the east, partway across the Atlantic on her way to Europe, a large ship rigged for cable-laying continued to reel out cable as she had for days. When she had finished, the new transatlantic cable laid and connected, news would cross the ocean instantaneously for the first time in human history.

But now, not quite yet; news still moved between shores as it always had, by ship. And so nowhere in the world did anyone know what had happened to the *Central America.*

Except, of course, those on the *Marine* and *Ellen.* Wet and cold mostly, the rescued sailed slowly toward port, sleeping under wet sails on the *Marine,* women tearing apart sheets to make clothes for their children. And they ate what little food there was, rationed out in cups because there were so few plates: beans, rice, molasses, "Indian gruel," and hard bread. And much the same on the *Ellen.*

Not until five days after the foundering of the *Central America,* on Thursday, September 17, did news of even the storm reach readers of the New York *Times* or any other paper. This news came from ships which had suffered the storm, now putting in at various southern ports along the Atlantic seaboard, their news routinely telegraphed north. All that was known of the *Central America* was that she was overdue and missing. In the absence of any actual news of her, the *Times* story filled in with speculation that she was "making her way, under sail . . . and this is necessarily a very slow process for a large side-wheel steamer, with only a small spread of canvas. . . ."

But that night the *Thomas Swann* steamed into Charleston harbor; she had spoken the *Ellen* on Tuesday last, and Captain Johnson had shouted

HEAVY STORM AT THE SOUTH.

Steamship Central America Missing.

The Southerner at Charleston Almost a Complete Wreck.

The Empire City at Norfolk in Distress.

VESSELS ASHORE.

PARTICULARS OF THE STORM.

The non-arrival of the steamer, and the failure yesterday, to receive any intelligence from her, added somewhat to the public anxiety on her account. The number of her passengers is not known, or who they are; the amount of her treasure-list is said to be over a million of dollars, and those who have cause to expect friends by her, as well as all others interested, manifest much concern for her safety. The steamer *Atalanta,* from Charleston, three and-a-half days, on Monday, the 13th, reports having passed, off his news. Charleston then telegraphed it north, and finally on the morning of Friday, September 18, almost a week after the sinking of the *Central America,* news of it at last reached the world.

But still: in this first *Times* story, only the top line of its multiple heading was accurate concerning the *Central America,* the rest speculation or error, including the name of the Norwegian bark. And the story below the heading shows the *Times*'s frustration. For the news was as big a story, considering the relative sizes of the ships in their times, as the sinking of the *Titanic* would be half a century later. Yet all the *Times* knew for sure was: "The Central America Foundered."

That afternoon, as they later reported, "there was a large and anxious throng at the office of the Company to which the *Central America* belonged, at the corner of Warren and West streets. The visitors . . . had inquiries . . . about a father on board, another a mother, another a brother or sister, and an occasional one sought information of an absent lover. . . . A large portion of the crowd

THE CENTRAL AMERICA FOUNDERED.

Six Hundred and Twenty-Six Persons on Board.

Five Hundred and Sixty-Six Lives Lost.

ONLY SIXTY SAVED.

Forty Picked Up by the Norwegian Bark Eloise.

TWENTY SAVED BY OTHER MEANS.

Correct List of her Officers and Crew.

STEAMERS SENT TO SEARCH FOR HER.

DETAILS OF OTHER DISASTERS.

Statements of the Commanders of the Falcon, Empire City and Atalanta.

The public anxiety in relation to the fate of the *Central America* and her passengers, is at length partially relieved by an announcement that the worst that was feared was nearest to the truth. The *Central America* FOUNDERED ON THE 12th inst., and only SIXTY OF A LIST OF FIVE HUNDRED AND TWENTY-FIVE PASSENGERS, AND HER OFFICERS AND CREW, HAVE BEEN SAVED. We received the melancholy news by telegraph at a late hour last evening. Aside from the general statement of her loss, and the whereabouts of a portion of those who were saved, the dispatch is provokingly devoid of

263

. . . lingered . . . till the hour of closing.

"During the afternoon Commodore Vanderbilt"—who owned a rival ship line—"visited the office to inquire into the particulars of the disaster. . . . He expressed his deep sympathy for the passengers . . . and commiserated the Company for the heavy pecuniary loss."

Finally the *Ellen* herself arrived at Norfolk, Virginia, with the *Marine* not far behind. As the *Marine* entered the bay at Norfolk, Aunt Lucy, the stewardess, who'd been crushed between the lifeboat and the sinking ship's side during her rescue, died; they found the money she'd brought along still tight in her hand.

Since the *Ellen* wasn't going to New York, most of the rescued men transferred to the *Empire City,* which was. Then the *Empire City* headed out of the harbor, hoping to meet the *Marine.*

"Within three miles of Cape Henry," said a local correspondent aboard the *Empire City,* "a vessel was descried ahead in tow of a propellor [ship] bound in. . . . Glasses were leveled at her by anxious groups gathered forward, and as we rapidly closed together, certainty succeeded surmise, and to the joy of all, she proved to be the brig *Marine,* in tow of the *City of Norfolk,* propellor"—who charged $300 for the tow, after demanding $500 and being refused—"her low and confined decks, swarming with wretched-looking objects, many of them women and children, wringing their hands, and weeping and laughing hysterically. Our boats were speedily lowered and Capt. McGowan, in the first, boarded the brig in person, caressed, embraced, and, indeed, half-strangled by the poor women, who threw themselves upon him as he reached the deck.

". . . boat-load after boat-load reached our ship's side and ladder . . . and in a short time the greater portion were comfortably quartered in our cabins. To the bystanders, the recognition and greeting between the [women and children and the rescued men], mother claiming son"—which would have included Henry O'Conner and his mother—"and husband wife"—Virginia and Billy Birch, the newly married Eastons, and others—"the eager scanning of each face in agonizing fear and expectation, the joy or grief manifested as recognition or disappointment awaited the gazer, was touching in the extreme, straining the heart-strings"—nineteenth-century newspaper prose, but I think reality lay underneath it —"and moistening the eyes of many hitherto unused to such manifestation. A portion remained on the brig"—among them Captain Badger and his wife—"preferring to go up to Norfolk, and when all who wished had been taken on board, the *Empire City* again started with her freight of

264

unfortunates for New-York."

But it was a two-day trip, and until she reached New York the papers had to vamp till ready: they had a front-page story without any news.

"In consequence of the reprehensible conduct of the managers of some of the Southern telegraphic lines," the *Times* story actually began on Saturday, "we are unable to present as many particulars of the loss of the *Central America* as we had reason to anticipate. Our agent states that a full report of the disaster was ready for transmission, but those in charge of the lines"—who denied this later—"refused to keep them open, although an arrangement that they should do so had previously been made."

So the *Times* filled in: ". . . In restaurants, counting rooms and offices, nothing was talked of but the loss of the *Central America.*" And quoting someone unnamed, they supplied a candidate, if *The New Yorker* magazine had been there to notice, for Exclamations We Doubt Ever Got Exclaimed: " 'There has been nothing known like it since the sinking of the Arctic,' others exclaimed. 'And in view of the loss of the specie, this is even a worse calamity, occurring as it does during the present pressure on the money market.' "

With a little more feeling of actuality, the *Times* continued: "The newspaper offices were crowded by parties who had relations or friends on board anxious to learn if any additional news had been received. The bulletins on the news offices were besieged by anxious crowds. . . ."

And despite a little snobbery, I think this reporter was describing an actual scene here: "As the day wore on, and the news was more widely circulated, the excitement yet more largely increased, spreading to those classes which usually care little for mere news. The mothers, wives, sisters, daughters, of the crew, hurried in their everyday working apparel, and with no attempt at adornment, to the newspaper offices to learn when later intelligence was expected. 'Was it true that all the crew were lost? If not, who were the rescued? Was this, that or the other man among them?' Until midnight and later, the Times office was visited by those who had relatives on board, their faces blanched with apprehension, utterly unable to repress their tears. . . ."

During that night the *Empire City* arrived off Sandy Hook, sighted the lighthouse there, and swung toward Manhattan. And then finally, as she steamed up toward Quarantine, the *Empire City* was boarded: by the Health Officer and twelve reporters, and the reports from which this story derives were taken down in reporters' shorthand, from the mouths of the actual survivors.

265

This is the scene; the reporters are the men in tall hats. At left center

an anguished woman sits telling her story, and I think it's at least possible that artist Brightly was there, and that this is sketched from life.

Some of the excitement of that day comes through the old print, it seems to me: the *Times* reported that those who "had no friends in the city with whom they could shelter, were conveyed in carriages to the New York Hotel. We are proud to record an act on the part of the hackmen whose carriages were thus employed. *They all refused to receive pay for the hire of their carriages.*"

And: "One man was in so ragged a condition that a stranger, who saw him after he had arrived at Lovejoy's Hotel, went voluntarily and procured for him an entire suit of good clothes."

I think some of the rescued passengers were euphoric. Frank A. Jones, the "rich New-York socialite" friend of Captain Herndon's, was so happy with his appearance in borrowed sailor clothes that he went to the well-known photographer Fredrick's, and had his picture taken against a shipboard background—either sketched in or a studio backdrop.

266

This is the woodcut *Leslie's* made from Jones's portrait.

But other survivors may have felt as Ann Small did: to a *Tribune* reporter she said, at the Astor House where she'd been taken, "I feel as though, if I could only get home, it would be all I could ask. . . ."

And Mrs. Swan, with an infant child, and "having no friends in New-York, was very much affected on the arrival of the *Empire City.* . . . When word was given to the passengers to go ashore, she burst into tears, and wringing her hands said, 'Where shall I go after I go ashore?' And on being asked if she knew no one in the City, she said, 'No, I have no friend in New-York, not in all the world, now that my husband is lost.' She was put into a carriage, and driven to a hotel, with other ladies."

The stories that she, Ann Small, Frank Jones, James Frazer, Virginia Birch, and so many other survivors now told the reporters entirely filled the front pages of the *Times* and other papers for some days, running onto inside pages for column after column; and in the equivalent pages of the *Tribune,* whose actual first pages were advertisements.

But presently all their stories had been published. So had the rumor (a false one: "An Infamous Hoax") that Captain Herndon had been rescued by another ship. So were long lists of the saved and the lost, as well as could be constructed from passengers' memories, since the actual passenger list was in California. And three statements by George Ashby defending himself from charges of desertion. And speculation about whether the *Central America* had been seaworthy, the United States Mail Steamship Company, which owned her, saying yes, others denying it. John Kemble quotes a ballad which went:

"The 'Central America' painted so fine,

Went down like a thousand of brick,

And all the old tubs that are now on the line

Will follow her, two at a lick.

'Twould be very fine were the owners aboard,

And sink where they never would rise;

'Twould any amount of amusement afford,

And cancel a million of lies."

But Captain Badger, who'd sailed in her often, said the *Central America*, in his opinion, had been in excellent condition.

When all of this and everything else the newspaper editors could find or think of had been printed, the story was over. The survivors made their ways home, and by Thursday, September 24, the story of the *Central America* was gone from the papers except for a few last echoes: a statement by Captain Stone of the *El Dorado* explaining convincingly, or so it seems to me, why he could not again approach the sinking ship. And on Monday, October 5, a few more names were added to the list of the lost. And they scaled down the exaggerated quantity of gold lost to the true figure of a million and a half dollars.

But even as people read or skipped over these last remnants of the big story, reporters from every newspaper in New York were hurrying down to Castle Garden. A ship, the *Laura,* had anchored this morning; and from her, by the ship-news reporter who boarded her, came news that brought the sinking of the *Central America* screaming back to the front pages.

Even today, with planes, helicopters, and fast ships, the ocean is hard to search; and when the little *Ellen, Marine,* and *El Dorado* finally gave up on Sunday morning, there were men left behind still afloat and alive. At least two dozen by actual count; and, therefore, almost surely more.

John Tice was one, still hanging to his plank; he alone encountered seven other surviving passengers and crewmen that morning. One was the ship's purser, afloat in a life preserver, I assume. He seemed in good spirits to Tice, predicting that a ship would soon come along. Then he drifted away, never to be heard of again.

And, hanging to his plank, George Dawson was also alive that Sunday morning. Dawson was "a tall, well-built and muscular man, apparently not yet in the prime of life, and one who by nature [had] an iron constitution." So when he saw something floating in the distance, he managed to paddle himself and his plank till he reached it. It was a raft: holding a dozen more men still alive, among them his old shipmate Alexander Grant. There was no room for Dawson, but he stuck with

268

them, hanging to a rope. They'd seen sharks, the others told him, and Dawson may have wished he could climb on and lift his legs out of the water; but at least he was no longer alone.

The day turned hot, the long storm over; and as the sun climbed, glinting and glaring on the subsiding sea, Dawson, Grant, Tice, and everyone else still alive and afloat out here began to suffer from thirst. Some couldn't take it, and began drinking seawater. A coal passer on the raft was one, and he paid the price; by noon he was delirious, slipped off the raft, and drowned as they watched.

That afternoon George Dawson, head higher out of the water than those on the raft, spotted something, watched it drift closer, then saw it was a man sitting on a *Central America* life buoy. Presently they could recognize each other; this was Jacob Gillead, the ship's barber. They all spoke, he was invited to stick with them, but Gillead "felt quite comfortable" on his buoy, he said, wished them a good journey, and drifted away.

More men died and slid off the raft that afternoon, George Dawson

hanging on there at the left in this *Leslie's* artist's notion of how the scene may have looked. Now there was room on the raft for Dawson, and he let go his plank, and pulled himself onto it.

For everyone left still alive out on the Atlantic, there had begun a passive struggle to endure. Most could not: at sunrise next morning only four men still lay alive on the raft. The others, exhausted or delirious from drinking salt water, had slipped off during the night. And when presently the barber's life buoy chanced to drift into sight again, the barber was gone.

A twenty-two-year-old man came riding along on the door to Captain Herndon's room; the men lying on the raft recognized it by a large opening in its upper panel. Sitting on the door with his legs dangling down through the hole, the man paddled over with his hands. Join us, they invited him; plenty of room now. But no, he thanked them pleasantly, saying he preferred his door, and they drifted apart. No one ever saw him again.

Monday ended. On the raft they lay through the night, refusing to drink, surviving. Off in the dark, John Tice "drifted with his plank under his breast. Frequently he fell into a sound sleep that lasted several minutes. But such a sense of desolation came over him on awaking that he preferred to keep awake. Moreover, he was afraid if he got to sleep a sea might dash his plank from him. . . ."

The sun rose again, and suddenly John Tice faced an enormous decision. He saw something floating in the distance and, unspeakably

thirsty, close to exhaustion, still unable to pull off his waterlogged boots, he lay staring, knowing he had to decide whether or not to abandon his plank, and bet his life that he could swim to whatever he saw. He was

young, twenty-seven; a good swimmer. He took the chance and made it.
Tice had found one of the *Central America*'s lifeboats, very likely the one
John Black had
abandoned. But he
couldn't pull himself
into it; had no strength
left; could only hang
on. Then after a while
he did heave and drag
himself up over the side
into the bottom. It was
half full of water, but
he'd made the right
decision: Tice "found

three oars, a pan, a pail . . . four coats and an oilcloth jacket. He made
some changes in his apparel. It was impossible, however, to remove his
boots. . . ." But he bailed out the boat, lashed an oar at the prow, a coat

hanging from it as a
signal, and: "These
things accomplished,
Tice sat down and
surveyed the prospect
before him. Along the
line of the horizon no
sail was to be seen; his
thirst became more and
more intolerable, but he
resisted [drinking
seawater]. Night closed

in . . . he fell asleep exhausted. . . ." But at least, now, he could let himself
sleep.

And so it went; those who could endure, did. Next morning two men
were still alive on the raft: Alexander Grant and George Dawson, survivors before. Small fish could be seen around the raft today, and at first they
couldn't catch any with only their hands. But they kept at it, then finally
Dawson snatched one out, banged its head, and killed it. Grant cut it up,
but the fragments were too tough even to chew. They spread them in the
sun, and that softened them enough so that they could choke down a little.
The rest putrefied, and they threw them away.

Lying in his boat, Tice drifted.

Another night, another sunrise, and then: they found each other. John Tice made out something far across the water, he didn't know what, and found the strength to pick up an oar and try to paddle the big boat, meant to be crewed by several men, toward it.

On the raft, Grant and Dawson watched . . . saw the boat approaching . . . but so slowly they weren't sure anyone was in it. And so, before it could drift away, "Grant resolved . . . to reach it if possible, and accordingly divested himself of his clothing, except his undergarments, and tying a life-preserver around his body, weak and exhausted as he was, committed himself to the sea, and . . . swam towards the boat. How long

he struggled, Grant cannot remember, but he finally neared it, and discovered a man sitting down and trying to scull the boat towards him. On reaching the boat, the man (who proved to be Mr. Tice) helped him in. . . ." Then they rowed back to the raft, and picked up Dawson.

Now the papers had their story: these three men had been saved.

They'd spent four more days out under the sun in that lifeboat; then the captain of a small brig had seen a white speck—Dawson's white shirt—and sailed toward it. He found the three sitting motionless in the boat, no longer "able to move their limbs," but "obliged to sit, sustaining their heads on their knees, waiting silently for succor or death; in this situation they were discovered by the brig. . . ." And nine days after the *Central America* had gone down, her last three survivors—George Dawson, Alexander Grant, and John Tice—were finally lifted from the sea.

Now, two weeks later, they were able to climb from the *Laura*'s boat to the landing at Castle Garden, reporters pressing around them. But for days they'd lain helpless in the rescue ship's bunks, fed by spoon—claret lashed with sugar; gruel; and water—John Tice's boots only then cut from his feet. "We suffered everything but death," he now said to a reporter. "No man could describe what we endured. . . ."

But the reporters tried: this is George Dawson in his white shirt, from a Meade Brothers photograph, taken how long afterward I don't know. But as he and the others stood on the wharf that morning they looked so ghastly that *Leslie's* reporter couldn't stop writing about it: ". . . large sea boils covered [Dawson's] body, the flesh had peeled off his hands, his cheeks were sunken, his limbs emaciated, his powerful frame contrasting with his woe-begone appearance, and showing how much he had suffered."

This is Alexander Grant, who stood with him; his Meade Brothers portrait clearly made later. But now: "The intense sufferings through which he had passed were visible in every lineament of his face. He looked like one, who, having been brought to death's door by a scorching fever, had just passed the crisis of the disease. His large, manly face was white and almost fleshless, showing the bony outlines with ghastly distinctness, and his black, scarred lips looked as though in his agony, he had frequently bitten them through. But the most shocking traces of suffering were in his eyes. Naturally large, they were now preternaturally distended, and wore a fixed, sleepless expression, as though still looking from the frail raft along the dreary horizon for a friendly sail. His voice, too, was hoarse and hollow, and boils had broken out upon his body from prolonged exposure to salt water. . . ."

John Tice—this portrait also from a Meade Brothers photo—appeared to *Leslie's* to have "suffered less than his two companions . . ." but the *Times* man thought "Mr. Tice . . . suffered more. . . ." The interviews at Castle Garden were just about the end of the story. Rescued passengers had talked willingly and at length, but these were seamen and possibly a different breed of cat; except for the bare facts, they didn't have much to say. True, they were "almost suffocated by the crowd which pressed around them," reason enough not to stand around chatting, but it may also be that reporters began asking the wrong questions. "Whether it is true that the two who were saved on the hurricane deck had nothing to eat is not known," the *Times* man wrote (though Grant told the *Harper's* man, at least, that they'd had a few morsels of dogfish). "They say they did not; if they had it must have been that they fed on human flesh. But this Grant stoutly denies while Dawson stubbornly refused to say 'Yes' or 'No,' when [a friend who was there] as delicately as a bluff old sailor could, asked him the question."

Conceivably Dawson may have been simply indignant: I have no idea whether ground for such suspicions existed; maybe the *Times* man just wanted to come back with something titillating. Anyway: "The colored man, Dawson, evidently impatient of the distinguished attention shown him, soon found an opening through the crowd, and limped away."

Grant left for his boardinghouse at 36 Vandam Avenue, preceded by a reporter who raced over to break the news first and get his wife's reaction. She "did not for some time . . . believe it, and was at first quite indignant with the person who informed her . . . thinking that he was trifling with her feelings." And when Grant arrived, he didn't seem to want to be helpful. "It would be useless to expect a graphic account of what occurred to him or anybody else from Mr. Grant, even if he were disposed . . ." the *Times* reporter had to write.

275

John Tice "was conveyed to a carriage by Mr. Ashby, Chief Engineer of the *Central America*. . . . The meeting between Ashby and Tice was quite affecting, and so overpowered Tice that he had to be helped to the carriage." Ashby took him to the Battery Hotel.

And at the home of a friend, Dawson was "at present unable to converse more than a moment at a time, and by the advice of his physician he talks but little on the subject of the wreck."

So at last the story was done; the day after the interviews of the three were published, the *Times*'s front-page headlines were: "The State Temperance Convention" (at Syracuse, New York); and the "Advance of General Havelock upon Lucknow."

Captain Johnson's famous bark *Ellen* was repaired free at the Portsmouth Navy Yard, by order of the Secretary of the Navy. And at the Mechanics' Exchange, in Washington: "A valuable present has . . . been made to Capt. Johnson by James Buchanan, President of the United States, in the shape of a magnificent gold pocket chronometer and chain, which is said to be one of the best the world can produce. Aside from the intrinsic value of the gift [its cost was about $350], the circumstances under which it has been received will add greatly to its value, and will be regarded, in some sense, as a testimonial from the whole people, in the person of their Chief Executive. . . ."

On an inside page of the *Times* some days later, a last word of Mrs. Marvin, the lady who'd volunteered to help pump the foundering *Central America*: "Mrs. Marvin lost her husband and $18,000 on the *Central America*. Having nothing left but the scanty clothing she had on, the citizens of New York supplied her with $250 worth of trunks and clothing, and $50 in money. She started for home, and the cars ran off the track on Tuesday morning, at Corning, New York, completely dashing in pieces her trunks, and very nearly all the contents. The company furnished new trunks, and the passengers went on."

Around noon of the day before Christmas 1882, someone on the trading floor of the New York Stock Exchange released a great gas-inflated balloon in the shape of a jockey. As chins lifted, nearly everyone on the floor watching it rise to the high ceiling, a couple of brokers sneaked through the crowd, each holding one end of a seventy-five-foot rope. When they were on opposite sides of the floor, they began to run, and those of the crowd whose legs weren't yanked out from under them were bound together in a struggling mass, and then dragged around the floor.

When that stopped, someone got hold of an end of the rope, someone else the other, and they began yanking for possession. Each yelled for help, got it, and a huge tug-of-war began. Others rushed to join it, and within seconds there wasn't a handhold left on the rope. So latecomers grabbed the coattails of those near the ends of the line, and as the two sides dragged each other around the floor of the Exchange, coats ripped up the back, and some coattails were torn right off. Hats fell off, too—

THE TUG OF WAR

these were brokers, and wore silk hats—and then most of the rest were knocked off, and all the hats were jumped on. Down at the New Street end of the Exchange a sudden commotion began, and "all eyes were turned toward it," said the *Times*. Then "a howl of delight that deafened the spectators in the galleries went up. Some foragers had captured a hand-organ with its grinder and his wife and baby. One broker took the baby in his arms and . . . triumphantly led the way to the center of the floor. The yelling brokers surrounded the organ whose owner acted as if he thought every moment would be his last." Apparently he didn't speak English, but understood a pantomimed request, and began cranking his organ. "The coin poured in by the handfuls, and in no time the tambourine of the woman was filled to overflowing. When the grinder saw the money coming in he set to work and turned out airs which threw the brokers into a frenzy of joy. They smashed each other's hats, and capered about like

279

madmen. . . ."

A "cotillion was started . . . and those who took the part of ladies entirely disregarded the proprieties of the art terpsichorean and practiced high-kicking." During this everyone "yelled like Comanche Indians, and those who did not dance knocked off hats" and blew tin fish horns.

Pretty soon "brooms and watering cans were brought up from below, and those who looked as though they needed it were sprinkled and swept. . . ." Then "the brokers began kicking a football" around. "A band of Italian harpists was enticed into the salesroom for unlisted securities . . . and there was hilarity without end all day. . . . There was a large pail of hot water on the top of a heater, and this was kept stuffed full of hats. . . ." Men were dragged around the floor by their legs or arms; small-sized brokers were dumped head first into the tall wicker baskets into which used ticker tape ran, and the baskets rolled around the floor.

But if all this surprises you, no one who read the newspaper stories I'm quoting was surprised even a little: this kind of stuff happened every holiday season, and not only at the New York Stock Exchange. At the Produce Exchange on New Year's Eve afternoon of the preceding year, they began whomping each other with inflated bladders tied to strings, splattering one another with hunks of wet dough, and, of course, caving in each other's silk hats. Guests had been invited, each with a reserved-seat ticket, and as they arrived were escorted to the seat. Since all tickets were numbered 401, each was led to the same seat, mounted on a column ten feet high. As each guest stopped to stare up at the inaccessible seat, he was—guess what? —whacked on the head with a stuffed club.

Gilmore's band played, gradually turning white as they were pelted with flour-filled paper sacks that burst on impact. Humorous recitations were given. There were sparring matches, sack races, "an Irish jig by the entire Parnell Brigade," "talking matches," a "laughing match," a walking match. There were wrestling matches on the flour- and dough-covered floor, jumping matches, "dancing matches," there was a fat men's race, and, according to the *Times,* which seemed to be present at all these shenanigans, "singing matches between the flute-voiced members of the Exchange."

FAT MENS RACE

"During the performance," said another paper, "everybody seemed to be happy and the building rang with the laughter of the assemblage. Gilmore's band played almost without ceasing until after dark, and when the members with disarranged neck gear, emerged from the building they expressed the opinion that they had had 'the best day's sport for many a year,' " and I think they were right. I wonder if people didn't have a lot more fun, once, than we do now?

"Mr. W. J. Lewis, of New York City, has invented a flying-machine, which scientific gentlemen pronounce a decided wonder," begins the news story accompanying this illustration in *Leslie's Newspaper* of December 30, 1876. It "is the forerunner of an apparatus," the story continues, "with which he promises to attain a speed through the air of at least one hundred miles an hour."

Then, startlingly, the story provides detailed specifications: ". . . two propellors for lifting, and the shorter part bending downward . . . [with] a propellor at the rear end which is used for driving the machine forward." Its motive power was a huge spring "weighing several pounds," and: "Running through the entire length of the frame is a shaft, connecting with and communicating the power to the different propellors. The shaft of the rear propellor is connected with the main shaft by a universal joint. The propellors are right and left-handed, the flanges or blades, of which there are four to each propellor, are concave-convex in form. Each one is set in motion by four beveled wheels, which are connected with the shafts, and therefore the motion is simultaneous.

"Situated near the center of gravity are a pair of movable planes, slightly convex-concave, one on either side, which are used to guide the machine up or down. In the front is a rudder to give a right or left motion. . . ."

What *about* this? A helicopter flying through the skies of 1876? Well, there's the illustration, which seems to show exactly that; and, the news story continues tantalizingly: "During a formal test, Mr. Lewis directed his machine at various angles, and in all instances it flew"—*"flew"!*— "straight in the direction pointed." And that's all this forgotten story has to say about that.

Is it possible? Could it really have happened? I consulted a designer for Grumman Aerospace Corporation, Joseph Lippert, Jr., who is described by a Grumman official, Robert S. Mullaney, as "one of the most imaginative aerodynamicists and designers since da Vinci. . . ." And in a report headed "The Lewis Flying Machine of 1876," aircraft designer Lippert says: "It is believed that such a device . . . could make short flights since it is indicated to have the necessary lifting forces, and arrangement of forces to provide longitudinal stability, directional and roll control."

So there you have it: the picture and the specifications described in this forgotten story of 1876 apparently make sense to one of Grumman's ace designers. He continues: "From the description and illustration, a 'modern' equivalent may be sketched as follows," and here is designer Lippert's own sketch.

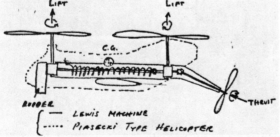

"The counter rotating lifting propellors," he says, "would reduce the overturning torque, but there would be some residual torque. . . . The downward inclination of the rear portion of the fuselage is interesting since this results in a thrust inclination of the rear thrusting propellor which produces a stabilizing influence. This principle is . . . in use today. . . . A minor . . . defect in the design could be the placement of the 'rudder' in the forward position.

283

Some early pioneers did however fly aircraft with forward surfaces. . . . It is concluded that . . . a similar model today . . . could fly and be controllable."

So that's that: a helicopter in the year of the Custer massacre. And which the nineteenth century seems to have forgotten. Maybe so. Because I think the nineteenth century took "Progress" for granted; took stunning inventions in stride. Few soothsayers of the times ever failed to predict that the skies would soon fill with flying machines. So when W. J. Lewis sent a helicopter flying through the air of 1876 I think people weren't a bit surprised. That they'd been expecting it. Probably wondered why it took so long. And then, what with one thing or another, they got busy, the whole thing just slipped the nineteenth century's mind, and they simply forgot to pass the news down to us.

Even Lewis himself soon moved on to more interesting things. He "proposes to construct a boat with pedals," the story concluded, "and by the use of his own strength will attempt a journey to Philadelphia, being quite ready to take any moderate wager that he will reach that city within half an hour from the time of starting," and I certainly wouldn't have bet against him.

In only the year after the Civil War ended, New Yorkers seem to have been considering building an El; to run along Broadway. Since apparently it was meant to have looked like this, it seems too bad that they didn't.

A dramatic news story of February 1882 was the destruction—burned to the ground in thirty minutes—of the old New York *World* building. The most dramatic incident of the spectacular fire was the rescue of this young woman, who stood calmly waiting on a window ledge of the blazing building hoping someone could save her. Someone did, thrilling the entire city, and more than one paper tried to picture the event; *Leslie's* gave their entire front cover to their artist's conception of the rescue.

I came across that drawing some few years ago while preparing to write a novel. Since many of its scenes were to take place in the New York of 1882, I was hunting for material to help me make my fictional scenes as real as I could. The *Leslie's* picture interested me, and I followed where it led: to long published accounts, in several newspapers of the time, of this exciting fire, of which this rescue was the most exciting detail. The young woman, said the news stories—her name was Ida Small—had appeared on a window ledge high on the face of the burning building, black smoke rushing out from behind her, and then stood bravely hoping for rescue. Someone leaned a ladder against the burning building, and although it fell short of where she stood, a stranger raced up it, balanced on the top rung at enormous risk to himself, and managed to get the girl down with him on the ladder. On the ground, the girl rescued, her anonymous and modest savior disappeared into the crowd, telling no one his name.

But I knew who he was. He was the central character of my book. And when I wrote it, he described the great fire in detail as accurate as I could supply from newspapers of the day; it was he who rescued Ida Small; and I included the *Leslie's* cover to prove it.

My fictional account of this actual rescue ended with his reference to "Ida Small . . . [who] still has a life ahead of her." That sentence was meant as a hint: to whoever, reading my book, might know what that life had been after Ida Small disappeared from the old news stories. I wanted to know for my own sake what had happened to Ida Small after she walked away from the burning building into the nineteenth century.

A forlorn hope: I didn't really expect to hear from anyone, but I did. One night a man, retired and living in Florida, sat reading my book. He turned a page, came upon the *Leslie's* woodcut, and sat looking at it in surprise, possibly in astonishment. He had seen the old woodcut innumerable times, for his mother was Ida Small, and she had the same *Leslie's* cover in a scrapbook she had kept of this most enormous event of her life.

But the copy her son had seen so many times in his own long life was different from the one in my book on his lap. On her scrapbook copy his mother had drawn an indignant *X* in purple pencil through the bearded face; because, she told her family, there had been no such person at all.

She hadn't been saved by any anonymous rescuer but by a real person, the fireman just behind the nonexistent bearded man on the ladder, John L. Rooney of Hook and Ladder No. 10, New York City Fire Department; and she was grateful, and remembered him for the rest of her life.

What was the rest of that saved life? Her son, Charles Haight, told me: in a long detailed letter, with which he also sent me photocopies of some of the things in Ida Small's scrapbook. She was twenty-four years old when she was rescued, and she had another twenty-four to live.

In the first of them, ". . . fireman Rooney was given a reception by friends of my mother's, on May 22nd, '83, at which time she presented him with a watch provided by funds" of $300 given by "friends and Ida Small. And friends presented her with a beautiful gold watch and chain for her fortitude. I have the chain now. My brother had the watch."

She married Charles H. Haight a few years later, a widower with two small daughters whom she cared for as though they were her own, and who loved her as their mother. A son of her own was born in 1887, and the following year another, the man who wrote to me.

And then, twelve years after her rescue, Fireman Rooney was killed in a loft fire on Twenty-sixth Street, and Ida Haight wrote this, keeping a copy in her scrapbook. "Yonkers, N.Y. Dec. 29th, 1894," it is dated.

"Dear Friend
"Rev. J. T. Wilds:—

"I have just returned from the home of Mr. John L. Rooney, where his family are in deep sorrow, over the loss of a kind and devoted husband and father.

"To me, he was my Hero!

"In June, 1882 [she remembered wrongly; it was the last day of January], he was the instrument in God's hand of saving me from burning to death. I was alone in the Office on the fourth floor, on the Beekman Street side of the building known as the old 'World Building' 37 Park Row. All escape being cut off except the windows to which the fire was fast approaching, I climbed out, let myself down to the lintel of the window below. Seeing a sign and wire three windows from me, I stepped from one lintel to another over three windows, thinking I might drop to the street in that way, but a gentleman below, warned me to wait for the firemen, which I did.

"It was but a few minutes, when Hook and Ladder No. 10 came bounding past the Post Office. No sooner seen, than Mr. Rooney had a ladder in his hands, and oh how plain I see him now, as he waved his hand to me, and calmly and loudly called, 'keep cool, keep cool!' He was up that ladder in an instant, but alas, the ladder only reached the bottom of the window on which I stood. While we looked at each other in almost hopeless despair, the ladder was suddenly raised by the men below [I hope my hero was at least among them] to almost a perpendicular position bringing him to my feet.

"He stood very near the top round, without anything to hold on to and he directed me in such kind, steady and cheering tones, which gave me such assurance in his ability to help me, that I obeyed.

"He said, 'can you sit down? Hold on to my shoulder, and see if you can put your foot upon the top round.' Then putting his strong hand at my waist, he said: 'Now when I tell you to drop you must do so.' As he took the weight of my body upon him the ladder swayed, slipped, and caught upon the trimming of the windows. Then the people cheered Mr. Rooney, as well they might. My very being was, and ever shall be filled with intense gratitude.

"He tried to say I was the hero, but I can see no heroism in one trying to save their own life; but when a man has a much loved wife and family at home, and risks his life to save another, just because it is a life, I can hear the world exclaim with me, *He was the Hero!*

"Although so brave, he was exceedingly retiring in his nature. When asked to attend a Thanksgiving service held at my church, the 7th Presbyterian, that my friends might have a chance to see and shake hands with my rescuer, he shrank from so much publicity.

"A few months later my friends thought it would be a nice thing to present Mr. Rooney with a watch. Not as a reward for my rescue, for that could not be done, but so that his children might have something to look at as a reminder of his bravery. It was my privilege to present this little testimonial to him in the presence of nearly 2000 people.

"As he stood upon the platform I shall never forget how noble he looked,

PRESENTATION

BY Miss IDA L. SMALL AND HER FRIENDS,
TO

Fireman JOHN L. ROONEY,

Of H. and L. No. 10, New York Fire Department,

In grateful remembrance of his heroism in rescuing her from the "World" Building, burned January 31st, 1882.

TO TAKE PLACE AT THE

7th Presbyterian Church,

COR. BROOME AND RIDGE STS.

On Monday Evening, May 22d,

AT 8 O'CLOCK.

On this occasion, being desirous of expressing their appreciation of the services rendered by the Fire Department, the following distinguished artistes have volunteered their services.

Mlle. MARGUERITE SELVI,
Miss BELL WHITLOCK,
Miss JENNIE DICKERSON,
Mme. ANGELINA COLLETTI HENDERICH.
Miss ANNA LANCASHIRE.
GEO. H. CURTIS, Organist.

Quartette.

Miss ELEANORA McKEE,　　Mr. T. R. S. CONNELL,
Miss SUSIE McILVAINE,　　Mr. J. E. CROSBY.

The Piano used on this occasion is from the warerooms of Weber.
Floral Decorations contributed by Le Moult.

MANNING MERRILL,　　　　　　} *Committee*
S. S. SMITH, JR.,　T. R. S. CONNELL,　} *of*
PETER WEHL,　EDWIN F. CLARK.　} *Arrangements.*

and how his unselfish nature shone out in his reply, which was as follows: 'Ladies and Gentlemen, permit me to mention a couple of facts in connection with the rescue of Miss Small. What I did was strictly in the line of my duty. It is something that is expected and demanded of each and every member of the Fire Department by our superior officers. I am no exception to that rule and I know of no man during my connection of nearly ten years with the Department, who would have shirked under the same circumstances.'

"I have learned that this was only one of the many heroic acts which he performed.

"Later in the summer we all looked upon him with pride, as Mayor Edson pinned the Bennett Medal upon his coat with words of praise.

"Was he not a true Hero? Pray with me that the dear Lord will bless his wife and children and that they may 'Lean Hard' on the widows' God who is always ready to comfort.

"Very sincerely yours,"

Ida Haight, her son told me, was active in church work; died in 1906; and "was a marvelous person and everyone loved her."